Teachers and Football

The 1870 Education Act that opened up elementary education for all children contained no provision for outdoor games. This book explains how teachers, through the elementary-school football associations, introduced boys to organised football as an out-of-school activity. The influence and significance of this work, insofar as it relates to the elementary-school curriculum and the growth of professional and amateur football, are explored in detail including:

- How ideological commitments and contemporary concerns for the physical welfare of children in cities may have led teachers to promote schoolboy football when it was not permitted during school hours.
- The extent to which out-of-school organised football may have led to outdoor games being accepted as part of the school curriculum.
- How elementary-school football in London in the late nineteenth century influenced the development of the amateur game.

This is a fascinating account of the origins of schoolboy football and the factors that influenced its development, and the consequences and benefits that have followed not only for school football but for sport in schools and communities as a whole.

Colm Kerrigan is a retired teacher who has been involved in school football associations for many years. He is also the official historian of the English Schools' Football Association.

Teachers and Football

Schoolboy association football in England, 1885–1915

Colm Kerrigan

RoutledgeFalmer
Taylor & Francis Group

LONDON AND NEW YORK

First published 2005
by RoutledgeFalmer
2 Park Square, Milton Park, Abingdon, Oxon OX14 4RN

Simultaneously published in the USA and Canada
by RoutledgeFalmer
270 Madison Avenue, New York, NY 10016

RoutledgeFalmer is an imprint of the Taylor & Francis Group

© 2005 Colm Kerrigan

Typeset in Garamond by
Integra Software Services Pvt. Ltd, Pondicherry, India
Printed and bound in Great Britain by
TJ International Ltd, Padstow, Cornwall

British Library Cataloguing in Publication Data
A catalogue record for this book is available from the British Library

Library of Congress Cataloging in Publication Data
A catalog record for this book has been requested

ISBN 0–7130–0243–3 (hbk)
ISBN 0–7130–4063–7 (pbk)

Contents

Acknowledgements

In 1967 I took the football team from St Patrick's School, Wapping, for training and matches on the local ochre pitch with goals painted on the endwalls. In 2004, weaker in voice and limb but not in spirit, I still run schoolboy football sides. This exploration in the history of schoolboy football is dedicated to the many teachers I have come into contact with in matches over the intervening 35 years. In addition to offering young people healthy exercise in an educational context they have, from a personal point of view, made a great contribution to my enduring and incurable love of football and its history.

I acknowledge with gratitude the exacting supervision of Professor Richard Aldrich and Dr David Crook over the five years I studied at the University of London Institute of Education to gain the PhD on which this book is largely based. I also wish to thank Professor Roy Lowe and Dr Anne Bloomfield for several helpful suggestions on additional material which has been added to the text. I acknowledge with gratitude the generosity of Terry Richards, at that time Secretary of the South London Schools' Football Association (SFA), and Reg Winters, Secretary of the London Schools' Football Association (LSFA), for making available to me their records, which formed the main sources for this work. I also wish to thank the following people, without whose help I could not have completed the work: Barry Blades, the late Howard Bloch, Bernard Canavan, George Cash, Betty Chambers, James Creasy, Heather Creaton, David Donaldson, Richard Durack, Wayne Gordon, Sarah Harding, Les Jolly, Christopher Lloyd, Ann Morton, the late Fred Newton, the late Horace Panting, Rita Reid, Alan Ronson, the late Poppy Ronson, the late Donald Shearer, the late Arthur Skingley, Richard Smith, Malcolm Tozer, Brian Warren, Brenda Weeden and Fred Wright. In addition, I wish to thank the following members of the East of London Family History Society who responded so generously to my request for information about teachers who took teams in the period under review: J. Adams, Jaqui Ball, Ken Batty, Andrew Beeching, Barbara Carlyon, Frank Graham, Kathy Munson, Joan Renton, T.E. Staines, A.G. Stow, D.S. Turner and Owen Watts.

Abbreviations

ESFA	English Schools' Football Association
FA	Football Association
FC	Football Club
HMI	Her/His Majesty's Inspector
LCC	London Country Council
LFA	London Football Association
LPFS	London Playing Fields Society (Committee until 1899)
LSFA	London Schools' Football Association
NUT	National Union of Teachers
SBL	School Board for London
SFA	Schoolboy Football Association

To avoid repetition, the word 'school' is omitted in identifying schools in the text when it is obvious that the reference is to a school. Thus, for example, Marner Street means 'Marner Street School'. All schools are elementary schools unless otherwise stated, or, as in Chapter 2, where the context makes clear that they are public schools. All elementary schools referred to were in the London area unless another location is given.

The term 'SFA' is used to denote the voluntary body of teachers promoting schoolboy football in all areas even if, as was frequently the case, the organising body was a sub-section of a larger organisation promoting a variety of school sports.

Schoolboy football associations affiliated to the London Schools' Football Association for 1907/08 season. (Source: LSFA, *Handbook 1907/08*)

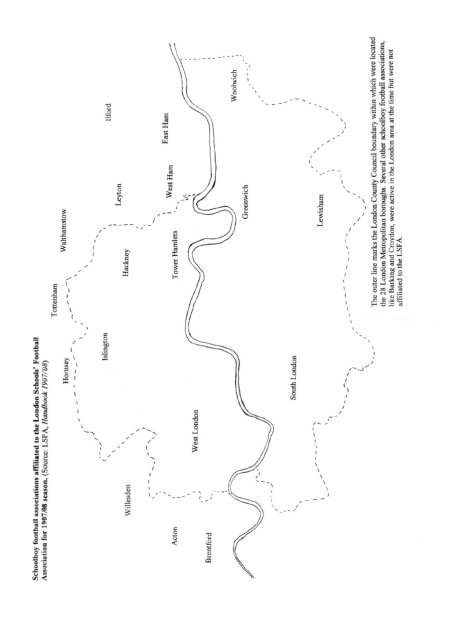

The outer line marks the London County Council boundary within which were located the 28 London Metropolitan boroughs. Several other schoolboy football associations, like Barking and Croydon, were active in the London area at the time but were not affiliated to the LSFA.

Photo 1 Leyton SFA was founded in 1894 and the Harrow Green School team of that year seem to have played in their ordinary school clothes (Borough of Waltham Forest Vestry House Museum).

Photo 2 By 1896, the boys in the Harrow Green School team were all dressed alike (Vestry House Museum).

Photo 3 By 1913, when Harrow Green won the Leyton SFA League, shorts had replaced trousers and the team kit resembled that of adults in the local amateur leagues (Vestry House Museum).

Photo 4 Boys at football training in the playground of Harrow Green School in 1896. This photograph, as well as the three team photographs above, were all taken by the headmaster of the school, Alfred Wire, a well-known local photographer (Vestry House Museum).

1 Introduction

Starting points

Prompted by discussions in the 1990s that led to professional football clubs (FCs) replacing schools as the main agencies responsible for the development of promising young players, this book examines how association football came to be introduced into elementary schools and what significance that might have had for the subsequent development of the game.[1] Following a chapter on other agencies, mostly instigated by ex-public-schoolboys, that preceded the work of teachers in promoting football in working-class areas, the main focus is on the work and influence of elementary-school football associations. It begins with an investigation of how teachers in these associations established and promoted schoolboy football in the London area, and to some extent nationally, in the three decades before the First World War. There is an exploration of the extent to which ideological commitments and contemporary concerns about the physical welfare of children in cities might have influenced teachers to undertake the promotion of schoolboy football at a time when it was not permitted in elementary schools during school time. There is also an examination of the extent to which the work of these teachers might have led to outdoor games eventually being accepted as part of the elementary-school curriculum. It is shown that the football teams in elementary and later higher grade schools helped these schools become an identifiable and prestigious part of the communities of which they were part, as revealed in accounts of honours earned and casualties suffered in the First World War. There is an investigation of the way that elementary-school football in London in the late nineteenth century influenced the development of the amateur game, both through the increased availability of players who had experience of organised football during their schooldays and through the specific contribution of elementary-school 'old boy' FCs. The influence of elementary-school football on the professional clubs in the London area is also examined, in particular the way that some of these clubs substantially decreased their dependence on players from outside the area.

These issues are worth investigating for several reasons. The traditional rural and urban pastime of football was adopted by the public schools in the nineteenth century and transformed into a game with rules that increased in number and sophistication and were co-ordinated and codified by the FA in 1863 and the Rugby Union in 1871. The early teams in association football, besides public-schoolboy teams, consisted mainly of men who had played the game at public schools or at Oxford or Cambridge, the universities attended by ex-public-schoolboys. By the turn of the century, however, the game had been established throughout most of the country and was particularly popular among working men. Various explanations have been offered by historians on how the favourite pastime of the ruling class became, in the course of a few decades, the favourite game of the working classes. Besides the influence of ex-public-schoolboys, these explanations include rapidly increasing urbanisation in the second half of the nineteenth century, increased earnings and free Saturday afternoons for some working men which gave them money and time to attend matches or play the game themselves. Explanations also include improvements in transport to get to and from games, newspaper coverage of matches and, of course, the promotional work of the Football Association (FA) and the Football League. The former introduced the very successful FA Cup competition in 1871 and the latter organised home and away league fixtures for professional clubs in 1888, a form of competition that was soon replicated with the formation of amateur leagues all over the country. Other explanations of the popularity of football in most parts of the country included the intrinsically exciting nature of the game, the relatively few and easily understandable rules that governed play and the fact that an adapted form of the game could be played on any spare piece of ground and on almost any surface.

While the contribution of the public schools to the origins and development of association football has been acknowledged by historians of the game from the late nineteenth century onwards, there has been no equivalent assessment of the contribution of elementary-school football. Although some football historians have taken elementary-school football into account as a contributory factor in the increasing numbers who were playing and watching association football, none has followed it through in any systematic way, either at a local or at a regional level, that might enable conclusions to be drawn about its actual influence on the popularity and growth of the game. This investigation of schoolboy football in London highlights the major role that elementary-school football played in the development of the game from the late 1880s onwards. The study ends in 1915, when professional and much of senior amateur football came to an end, having struggled on through the first full season of the First World War in spite of strenuous attempts to have it terminated earlier. There was no public disapproval of schoolboy football and many districts continued to run competitions during the War, despite a shortage of male teachers in elementary schools. But elementary-school football had by this time been established throughout the country and its influences had already taken root.

The London area was a particularly suitable one in which one could initiate a detailed study of elementary-school football for several reasons. It was an early location for the playing of association football and while elementary schools took no part in the development of the game in the 1860s and 1870s, the emergence of the first schoolboy football associations (SFAs) in London in the 1880s and 1890s, coinciding as it did with the growth of local amateur leagues, offered a fruitful field in which one could explore any connection that might have existed between elementary-school and adult-amateur football. While London was relatively late in its acceptance of the professional game, its adoption in the 1890s by clubs staffed almost exclusively by non-Londoners permitted an examination of any contribution SFAs might have had in changing the profile of London professional clubs in favour of home-grown talent. The records of some public-school missions and university settlements have survived, as have those of some of the organisations they influenced, like the London Playing Fields Society (LPFS). Matches involving public schools and public-school Old Boy clubs were well reported in the local and sporting press from the 1860s and later, when football was introduced into elementary schools, their matches were also given good coverage in many local newspapers. Most important of all, perhaps, a substantial amount of the records of the London Schools' Football Association (LSFA) and the South London SFA have survived, as have the log books of a great number of the schools that took part in schoolboy football competitions in the London area.

Definitions

The *football* that is discussed in this book is 'association football' (often called 'soccer', although this term is not used here except in quotations from other works), unless otherwise indicated. It was one of the two relatively refined versions of the traditional village and urban pastime – the other was rugby – which, in their rule-regulated forms, had become the dominant sport of young men of all classes by the late nineteenth century. The traditional football game of the working classes, in its urban and rural forms alike, had few rules and could degenerate into violence of a degree that could be a danger to life and limb. Such an uninhibited form of recreation was inconsistent with the rigours of employment that came with the Industrial Revolution and the disappearance of many open spaces rendered it more difficult to pursue the pastime. Besides, traditional football's association with disorder, sometimes with a political flavour, was seen by the authorities to have been inconsistent with early nineteenth-century commitments to law enforcement. Moves were undertaken to suppress it, with some success. Any danger of the game disappearing altogether was averted when it was adopted by the public schools, where, in a form that gradually became more refined, it was employed by them as a remedy for the indiscipline of their pupils. In its new role as an agent of public-school reform, James Walvin has written, 'the pre-industrial game was gradually transmuted into a team game which demanded rigid discipline, selflessness, teamwork and physical prowess, and in which the strengths and skills of the individual were subsumed by the greater needs of the team'.[2]

Having been initiated into the refined form of the game at their schools, ex-public-schoolboys have been attributed a leading role in the promotion of football, although the extent of their influence in spreading the game throughout the country has recently been questioned, as has the assumption that football would not have survived if the traditional rural pastime had not been taken up and remoulded by the public schools.[3] While its influence may indeed have been exaggerated, the evidence from the FA's early discussions on the most suitable form of rules to adopt is alone sufficient to indicate that, in the game that has actually come down to us from mid-Victorian times, the public-school influence was considerable.[4] Features of the older football remained, however, down to the period examined in this study, as will be seen in Chapter 2 in relation to the Hackney boys who played street football and had to be taught the refinements of the modern game by the public-school helpers at the Eton Mission to Hackney Wick.

By the beginning of the period examined in this work, football had developed into a game that was clearly distinct from rugby, for, while there had been attempts to accommodate under one code the two main ways of playing the new rule-regulated game that had developed in the public schools during the nineteenth century, these were abandoned with the formation of the Rugby Union in 1871. 'Hacking', which entailed kicking an opponent's shins and which the proponents of what was to become rugby wished to have permitted, was the issue on which agreement could not be reached with the FA, and led to the formation of the Rugby Union. 'Hacking', however, was soon banned in the rugby game also for its obvious danger to life and limb and it was the issue of the players' use of their hands in the two codes that grew into the most distinctive distinguishing feature between football and rugby.

Catching the ball in the air was allowed in the original FA rules of 1863, the player making the catch being awarded a free kick, 'provided he claims it by making his mark with his heel at once'.[5] The offside rule simply required players to keep behind the ball. The players of Richmond FC, having tried out the new rules in a match against Barnes FC in the 1863/64 season, felt the rules were simple and easy to observe and that 'disputes would hardly arise'.[6] Changes in the rules over the next few years led to the abolition of catching (except by the goalkeeper, who could use his hands anywhere in his own half of the field) and to a player being ruled offside if at least three opponents were not between him and the goal when the ball was played forward. Despite the FA's work in standardising and modifying the rules in the mid-1860s to something very close to the present laws of the game, there was still considerable confusion about the rules. This was caused partly by the fact that many clubs did not belong to the FA (clubs had to have been in existence for a year to do so) and that some clubs could not make up their minds which of the two codes they wished to follow. When Grange Court, Chigwell, played Christ's Hospital at the end of 1869, they drew 1–1 but they had the considerable disadvantage, the local newspaper reported, 'of having to play the Christ's Hospital rules, which are mainly those of Rugby'.[7] Many of the men in the team at the Richmond club mentioned above had been educated at Rugby School and wished not only to be allowed to catch the ball but to run with it in their hands as the rules at that public school permitted. Not surprisingly, therefore, the Richmond club was one of those that adopted the code of rules for the game that derived its name from some of their players' old school.[8]

Football spread slowly in the 1860s, with most new clubs, like Clapham and Woodford Wells, both of which were founded in 1869, located in the area around London. The introduction of the FA Cup competition in the 1871/72 season helped to promote the game not only on a wider geographical scale but also to spread a familiarity with and understanding of the rules of football. These rules, even with the refinements and modifications that followed in the two decades after 1863, were still far fewer than those of rugby, something that may have helped football to become a more popular game than rugby in the long term.[9]

Different interpretations of the rules were common as late as the 1880s but by the following decade a football match bore more resemblance to a match in a public park today than to one in 1863. For by 1890 a football team was made up of eleven players, wearing jerseys, knickers and studded boots and the game was played on a pitch where the dimensions and markings conformed with those laid down by the FA. The game was controlled by a referee on the touchline, who was on his way to replacing the umpires, who had usually consisted of an official or extra 'player' from each of the competing clubs. Matches were an hour and a half long and the sides changed ends at half time. A crossbar had replaced tape or string between the posts to mark the spot below which a goal would be registered when the ball passed through. In the original rules a goal was given if the ball passed between the posts at any height.

The play contained most of the features of the modern game. Offside was as explained above, throw-ins were given when the ball was put out of play, goal kicks were taken when the ball was put over the end line by the attacking team and corner kicks when it was put over by the defenders; free kicks were awarded for infringements of the rules, infringements that in most cases could be seen, even to the most casual observer, as likely to give an unfair advantage by the players committing them, whatever their intentions. Team formation had developed from as many as nine forwards in the early matches under the standardised rules to a universally employed 2–3–5 formation, that is to say, a goalkeeper, two full backs, three half backs and five forwards, one on the right side of the pitch, one on the left and three in the middle. One of these three 'inside' men was the centre forward, 'the pivot on which the forward line works', as C.B. Fry put it.[10] Dribbling, that is, taking the ball past opponents by employing clever foot movements, was an essential element in the early game, but dribbling, or rather an over-emphasis on it as the only way to take the ball forward to get in a shot at goal, had in the 1870s given way to passing as football's most conspicuous feature. Both were important, of course, as C.W. Alcock, Secretary of the FA, explained in the 1879 handbook:

> judicious dribbling implies a certain amount of passing on and backing up in the event of a player being likely to lose the ball, as the Scottish team has shown to perfection... Each player represents a compound part of a huge machine, which cannot work to any purpose without the co-operation of every minute particle associated in its composition, and which is thrown into disorder on the first case of negligence, or the most trifling flaw in any portion of the works.[11]

Given the co-operative aspects of the game as set out by Alcock at a time when the first board schools were being built in the major cities, one may wonder why the educational advantages of playing it were not seized upon with more enthusiasm by the bodies responsible for elementary education. This brief survey of football around the year 1890 concludes with two further observations on the game at the time that will be touched upon in Chapters 2 and 7 respectively. The first is that the game had gained such popularity that in some parts of the country large crowds were attending matches as paying spectators, providing sufficient income for many clubs to pay their players, something that had been done unofficially for some time but which had only been recognised by the FA since 1885. The second is that, while the newly formed Football League was an ideal stage on which the professional player could perform (indeed, such an ambitious project could hardly have been contemplated without paid players), there was not a single Football League club in the London area.

Neil Wigglesworth has shown how the idea of *amateurism* developed from those eighteenth-century gentlemen who 'dabbled nonchalantly' in the arts without any thought for mastery or excellence. Those who had a professional interest in the pursuit of the arts and their mastery could not, by definition, be gentlemen. Translated to sport and reinforced by a classical education that lauded the Athenian concept of a class born to rule, reflected in England in the presence of a ruling class based on land ownership, the professional sportsman, like the tradesman, was kept at a distance. The public schools were ideally placed, given their intake and the increasing part sport played in public-school life in the course of the nineteenth century, to reinforce the ideology that playing for diversion was gentlemanly while playing as an occupation was not. The extension of the franchise and the decrease in working hours, allowing working people more time for sport, made it even more imperative that distinctions be maintained. Money alone was not sufficient to maintain the distinctions. Gentlemen, after all, placed bets on horse races and prize fights. Nor was the main concern that working men paid to play would have more time to train and so be able to beat gentlemen in open competition. Rather, Wigglesworth believes, it was 'that social prejudice alone informed the Victorian attitude towards the working man and all his activities'.[12]

This prejudice may indeed have been a significant factor in the attempts to retain the early game of football as the preserve of a public-school educated elite. Some of the more vociferous of the opponents of professionalism like P.N. Jackson, who wanted separate associations for amateur and professional football within the FA and objected to the introduction of the penalty kick because it was a slur on the integrity of a gentleman, seem to have been guided more by snobbery than by considerations for the good of the game. At the same time, however, when the dispute about paying players came to a head, the more conciliatory voices within the FA included those of the Old Etonian Lord Kinnaird and the Old Harrovian C.W. Alcock.[13]

The issue of *professionalism* in football, which had been simmering for some time since the introduction of 'broken time' payments to players who had time off work to play matches, came to a head in 1884 when Upton Park complained to the FA that the Preston North End team that had played them in a Cup tie contained professional players. It was true. 'The Prestonian players posed as amateurs', wrote J.A.H. Catton, who knew many of them, 'but everyone knew they were not'.[14] Rather than deny it, as was usual, Preston admitted that they had brought players to Preston and found them jobs but that other clubs had done the same. Exhaustive enquiries and exhausting discussions by the FA led to the acceptance of regulated professionalism, a decision supported by C.W. Alcock. An extract from one of his speeches on the issue is worth quoting for its positive attitude towards working men:

> Professionals are a necessity to the growth of the game and I object to the idea that they are the utter outcasts some people represent them to be. Furthermore, I object to the argument that it is immoral to work for a living, and I cannot see why men should not, with that object, labour at football as at cricket.[15]

It is this full-time professionalism of players that is being referred to when the term is used in this book and it is interesting to note that throughout the period of this study, and indeed down to our own times, the professional has been invariably seen to 'play' football rather than to 'labour' at it.

While the strands from the various public-school traditions that came together to create the ideology of *athleticism* cannot be considered here, it is necessary to say in general terms what it refers to throughout this work. The increasing concentration on games as opposed to the traditional rural pastimes in which public-schoolboys had traditionally spent their free time in the second half of the nineteenth century led to a great emphasis on the value of outdoor games in the development of character. J.A. Mangan has shown how the resultant ideology of athleticism, which at its most extreme saw prowess at games as more important than academic success, was taken from the public schools to Oxbridge where the next generation of masters were being educated and a cycle of 'schoolboy sportsman, university sportsman and schoolmaster sportsman was created'.[16] Carried into the world outside of school and university, the ideology manifested itself as the public-school spirit, especially evident in the administration of the Empire, in the armed forces and, most pertinent to issues addressed in this book, in religious, social and educational work among the urban working classes.

Closely associated with ideas on sport among the mid-Victorian ruling class in Britain was the concept of *muscular Christianity*. In *Land of Sport and Glory*, Derek Birley described Lord Kinnaird, an outstanding footballer at Eton, a winner of FA Cup medals with Wanderers and chairman of the FA for 50 years, as 'a fervent muscular Christian'.[17] One expression of this was Kinnaird's involvement in voluntary work in the poorer parts of London (an aspect of which is considered in Chapter 2) and the ideology that guided it, based on some of the writings of Charles Kingsley and Thomas Hughes, which laid emphasis on the moral value of sport. While the concept is a wide one, the strand that is of relevance to this book relates to the motivation it provided for young men, often with a background in public-school sport, to work among the urban industrial poor in the late nineteenth century. Aimed initially at stemming the decline in religious practices among the working classes, this missionary work inevitably became involved in schemes to improve the conditions of the urban industrial poor, with particular concern expressed for the inadequate recreational facilities for boys and youths, as is explored in Chapter 2.

Related both to amateurism and to athleticism is the idea of *Corinthianism*, which pertains to the spirit in which the game is played. While the amateur nature of the games that the Ancient Greeks engaged in has been questioned by Manfred Lammer, for example, the attitudes associated with these games in the late nineteenth century were not only those of strict amateurism but of a particular spirit that governed their performance.[18] This Corinthian spirit expressed itself in considerations about *how* the game was played and may be best clarified by citing two instances of its absence. John Major, in reviewing a book on the cricketer W.G. Grace, was clear that the subject of the work, with his gamesmanship and intimidation of umpires, was a man 'playing to the letter but not the spirit of the game'.[19] And Turu Kuroiwa, the author of a Japanese book entitled *The English Way of Life*, said recently in an interview that the installation of video cameras at golf links, to prevent false claims of a hole-in-one, was a sad indication that some players 'had failed to grasp the spirit of the game'.[20] Besides a refusal to accept money for athletic performances, the emphasis was on the values of fair play, self discipline, the acceptance of defeat with dignity and something very close to, but not quite, playing for fun. The original Corinthians FC was founded by F.N. Jackson in 1882 and still survives today as Corinthian Casuals, playing in the Ryman (Isthmian) League. In a recent interview, the manager explained that while the club's many teams in all age groups try as hard as any other team to win matches, the result of matches was thought less important than the manner in which the game was played.[21] This, of course, would not distinguish the club from thousands of others that field teams, especially those that feature young players.

Definitions of three more explicitly educational terms that are frequently referred to in this book, remain to be examined. The first is that of the *elementary school*. It was in elementary schools that the teachers who founded the first SFAs worked and it was for their pupils that they organised inter-school football matches. These schools had been increasing in number throughout the nineteenth century but there were still many children who could not or would not attend them. The Education Act of 1870 was aimed, first, at increasing elementary-school provision so that every child of school age would have a place, and second, at trying to get parents to send their children to school. By the time the LSFA began its work (1892), school attendance was compulsory and school boards had been set up in those areas where elementary-school provision was needed. The School Board for London (SBL) was the largest of these and covered an area of 114 square miles, divided into ten electoral districts. This body had power to raise a rate, adapt buildings for school use or build new ones where necessary, appoint teachers and support staff, including school-keepers and attendance officers and generally oversee the progress of elementary education in what later became known as the 'inner London' area. Other districts within the London area, and in which the LSFA was to become active, like West Ham, had their own school boards. In board schools, as indeed in the voluntary schools provided by the churches in urban areas in the period under review, those attending mostly consisted of working-class children, although in some such schools there were substantial numbers of children of lower middle-class parents.

The standards of achievement of elementary-school pupils increased considerably during the school board period so that when the control of education passed to the London County Council (LCC) (which had taken over the education work of the SBL) and the 'outer' London boroughs (which had taken over their local school boards) early in the new century, there were many pupils in *Higher Grade Schools*. These were schools where the school boards concentrated resources by providing one school among a group of schools where the higher Standards were taught more effectively and where a limited number of new subjects could be introduced.[22] This meant that some schools eventually had a much larger number of pupils in the older age group and the implications of this for the LSFA's competitions will be discussed in Chapter 4.

The term *extra-curricular* needs little explanation except to note that it was not used during the period under review and is used here as a convenient way of identifying those activities engaged in jointly by teachers and pupils over and above those that could be considered to constitute part of the school day. For most of the period under review, schoolboy football was played by boys outside school hours and supervised by teachers, not as part of their teaching load, but additional to it, and without expectation of additional remuneration. After 1906, when outdoor games became an acceptable part of the elementary-school curriculum, some football practice took place during school hours, but the vast majority of matches continued to be played outside school hours, as they are to this day.

Schoolboy football and histories of football

Underlying this review of secondary literature is an awareness that while there is an abundance of works on the origins and influence of public-school football, the origins and influence of elementary-school football have not been sufficiently acknowledged either in histories of football or in histories of physical education. The vast literature relating to public-school games will be considered here only insofar as it touches on issues that later became relevant to the introduction of football in elementary schools. Besides the public-school missions to working-class areas, these include issues like the value of games for good health, character building and *esprit de corps*, issues which surfaced again when teachers, influenced by these ideas at training colleges, later tried to transmit them to their elementary-school pupils. Works on the history of childhood, of physical education in London elementary schools and the teaching profession will be examined for evidence of the extent that the voluntary work of teachers involved in the promotion of football as an extra-curricular activity was acknowledged. Finally, literature on the history of football, including that of SFAs, will be reviewed to determine the extent that elementary-school football has been taken into account as a factor in the diffusion of the game.

Public-school football

In his detailed study of the influence of public schools, Mack exonerated Thomas Arnold, the reforming headmaster of Rugby, from direct responsibility for many subsequent developments in education that could have been traced to his influence and suggested that he would have heartily disliked many of them, including athleticism, defined above.[23] This is almost certainly true, as the only mention Arnold's biographer makes of sports in the chapter on his work at Rugby is to refer to them as an antidote to intellectual exertion.[24] However, by discouraging traditional pursuits like hunting, birding and fishing, Arnold indirectly guided boys into playing more games. Honey has shown how the concentration on games at Marlborough under J.E.G. Cotton strengthened control of school authorities over the boys and engendered *esprit de corps* through loyalty to house and school teams.[25] Edward Bowen, a master at Harrow for the last four decades of the nineteenth century, saw games as being 'of indescribable value', especially in the subordination of a boy's will to the needs of the many.[26] Ollard, in his history of Eton, has identified how a school could rely too heavily on the efficacy of games and that once they had been established as a regular part of the life and discipline of the school, they could dominate it.[27] Mangan's study of the development of athleticism at six public schools has shown how headmasters in five of them had, either from ideological commitment, from expediency or in imitation of others for the sake of survival, succeeded in establishing organised games in place of the boys' countryside pursuits, with masters and prefects playing a greater or lesser role in the various schools' transformation of the way boys spent their time outside lessons. By the middle of the 1870s, however much boys might have hankered after their traditional access to the countryside, leisure pursuits in the five schools were being confined to the playing fields 'and a passion which grew into an obsession was being assiduously cultivated by the zealous'.[28]

In *Godliness and Good Learning* Newsome acknowledged Bowen's qualities as an educator but felt that it was Edward Thring, headmaster of Uppingham, 'who most determined the shape of things to come'.[29] Like Bowen, Thring was an outstanding games player in his youth and Tozer's work has shown how he extended greatly the playing fields of the school, had a gymnasium built and employed the first gymnastics instructor in England. Thring encouraged games in many other ways, including taking part in them himself and offering prizes in athletic activities, not as rewards for achievement but as incentives to work harder at the tasks. He believed that games offered the poorer scholars an opportunity to earn praise, provided a healthy setting for competition and helped train character.[30] Thring was reflective enough about the value of playing games to question it later in life.[31] His attitude towards them, however, did reflect many of the best aspects of the public-school games that were later taken up by elementary-school teachers.

These playing fields of the public schools were the cradles of modern football. 'Since it was a vehicle through which "manly" virtues could be expressed', wrote Dunning and Sheard, 'football was an activity common to all public schools.'[32] The original rules agreed by the FA at the end of 1863 were based on those of Cambridge University, rules that had been framed earlier by young men who had attended Eton, Harrow, Rugby, Shrewsbury and Winchester public schools and who, at university, wished to play football without the inconvenient variations in rules that had prevailed in their various schools. J.G. Thring, a past pupil of Shrewsbury and at this time a master at Uppingham, where his brother Edward was headmaster, made a specific contribution to the discussion of rules for football as they were being formulated and enrolled his school as an early member of the FA.[33] The role of ex-public-schoolboys in the diffusion of the game was also considerable, although the extent of this, as noted earlier, has been questioned. Evidence for public-school influence in the early development of the game might include the predominance of FA administrators with a public-school background and the success of public-school 'old boy' teams in the early years of the FA Cup competition, an event adapted by C.W. Alcock from the inter-house knock-out matches he had witnessed as a boy at Harrow.[34] Dunning has drawn attention to the way in which the public-school 'old boy' associations were active in the formative stages of both football and rugby, placing public-school attitudes to games in a position to influence late nineteenth-century attitudes to sport so that sports fields became the locations for the learning and display of gentlemanly ideals: 'character', 'style', 'good form', 'fair play', 'group loyalty' and 'self-control' amongst others.[35]

As its title suggests, Money's recent book, *Manly and Muscular Diversions: Public Schools and the Nineteenth Century Sporting Revival*, traces the contribution of the public schools in promoting and formulating rules for many of the games that later became popular with a wider section of society.[36] It does not, however, address the issue of how the games took root throughout the country or how the public-school missions might have contributed to this. Tozer has written on the first public-school mission, that of Uppingham to North Woolwich, but no sporting dimension to the mission has been traced.[37] Eager identified the significance of games in the youth clubs associated with the public-school missions and recognised that the ideas on sportsmanship they were trying to inculcate were later taken up by games advocates in elementary schools.[38] Chapter 3 of Parker's *The Old Lie: The Great War and the Public School Ethos* is entitled 'Spreading the Word' and traces the diffusion of the public-school ethos beyond the walls of the schools *via* fiction, boys' magazines, stirring patriotic poetry and the public-school missions.[39] Parker sees the latter, along with the uniformed brigades, as 'intended to bring the benefits of a public-school education to the working classes'.[40] The Eton Mission to Hackney Wick is the principal mission examined and the role of sport in its work is acknowledged, as is that of the Federation of Boys' Clubs in promoting *esprit de corps*. As it is outside the scope of his book, however, Parker does not comment on any permanent value the sports dimension of the mission's work may have had for the Hackney area, an issue that is addressed in Chapter 2 of this book. Attention was directed to the sporting dimensions of many public-school missions in a series of articles published in the *Boy's Own Annual* during the First World War.[41] Although brief, they are informative on the missioners' attempts to pass on the sporting attitudes associated with the public schools to working-class boys and, in some instances, show how sporting prowess was of benefit to the missioners in making contact with the communities they came to serve.

Assessments of Canon Barnett's work at the University Settlement in Whitechapel have not explored the contribution the youth clubs sponsored by the Settlement might have made to the development of sport in the area.[42] On the other hand, the games aspects of the uniformed movements have been explored in several publications. The promotion of 'true Christian manliness' in members of the Boys' Brigade has been seen as reflecting a debt to the public-schools' games ethos, as has the extension of public-school *esprit de corps* to working-class and middle-class youths in the Brigade's sporting events.[43] Similarly, the Cadet Corps offered to working-class lads the advantages of a public-school training, 'which has so great an effect on moulding the character of the upper and middle classes' and in the sanctions of the Scout Law, Rosenthal has seen Baden-Powell's attempt 'to create from scratch the values and assumptions that were developed over time in the public school'.[44] All the uniformed movements had a football dimension, and Springhall has noted that the highly organised structure of the Boys' Brigade football leagues permitted some boys to progress to the top level of the game.[45] No account is taken in any of the histories of these movements, however, of the football the boys belonging to them are likely to have played in their elementary schools before wearing the movements' uniforms.

Elementary-school football

Even before the 1870 Elementary Education Act the implications of games in education beyond the boundaries of public schools had been considered by Herbert Spencer, who felt that 'our present methods of bringing up children do not sufficiently regard the welfare of the body'[46]. He was particularly concerned about the absence of physical exercises from the timetables of men's training colleges.[47] McIntosh has drawn attention to 'one small concession on physical education' in the Act that permitted the SBL to introduce drill for boys as one of the subjects in their elementary schools for which Government grant could be claimed.[48] In his recent book, Penn shows how, with the influential advocacy of the Society of Arts, this military drill was established and retained in the elementary schools for its widely acknowledged benefits to discipline.[49] He also explains how drill gave way in time to exercises of a non-military character like gymnastics and how the Education Department, in revisions to the Code communicated to Her Majesty's Inspector (HMI) in 1896, acknowledged that the best form these exercises might take would be that of 'healthy games', although conditions in most urban areas made provision for the latter impossible.[50] Philpott's generally uncritical appraisal of the work of the SBL, published in 1904, recorded how swimming in the elementary schools had its origins in the energies of the London Schools' Swimming Association which, as a voluntary body of teachers that awarded certificates of proficiency and arranged galas, could be seen as bearing many resemblances to the early SFAs.[51] Philpott also noted that cricket and football were being encouraged in London schools and that many teachers were 'spending much time in arranging matches and competitions, coaching the young captains and umpiring at matches' and at times had to put their hands in their own pockets to meet expenses. The benefits of football were particularly noted: 'It may almost be said that football has been the moral salvation of some of the rougher lads, who have been won by the teachers' sympathetic interest in their sports to an allegiance scarcely anything else would have inspired.'[52]

Given concerns about the unhealthy conditions of the urban poor in the late nineteenth century, especially insofar as they related to children's need for clean air and healthy exercise, it is surprising that so little reference was made by contemporaries to the introduction of football into so many elementary schools, which, as a headmaster of a school in the overcrowded East London district of Bromley-by-Bow put it in 1895, could offer the boys the opportunity to 'spend a day in good country air'.[53] Nor have historians been any more generous. Maclure's history of education in London does not mention schoolboy football at all and even a specialist work on the history of physical education like that of McIntosh, while referring briefly to the work of the South London SFA and the spread of elementary-school football in the 10 years after its foundation, makes no attempt to examine either the pioneering nature of its achievements or the obstacles it encountered.[54] He does, however, identify teachers' own interest in team games as a motivating factor in their promoting inter-school competition among their pupils, something that is broadly confirmed in Chapter 5 of this book.[55] May's thesis on the development of physical education under the SBL might have been expected to focus more closely to the work of SFAs, but it did no more than briefly acknowledge that the voluntary work of teachers represented a 'real advance' towards the provision of outdoor games in elementary schools at the time.[56] Sexby's book on London's public parks was written at the time when the SFAs were continually preoccupied with the need to find suitable pitches within easy access to schools.[57] He makes no mention of schoolboy footballers in his book, however, and the centenary history of the LPFS, published in 1990, makes no reference to SFAs, despite the fact that teachers representing these associations were among the Society's earliest active supporters and schoolboy players were among the first to benefit from the increased availability of playing fields that came about as a result of the Society's work.[58] Histories of childhood at least acknowledge football's existence, if only briefly. In *The Lore and Language of Schoolchildren* the Opies mentioned elementary-school football in their discussion of lucky charms and in quoting the victory chant that begins 'Rolling down the Old Kent Road'.[59] Walvin's brief section on physical fitness in the elementary schools in his history of childhood drew attention to the cheapness and adaptability of football, factors that made it suitable for the cramped playgrounds of schools in working-class areas.[60] While acknowledging the increasing acceptance of games in elementary schools in the last decades of the nineteenth century, he did not make any reference to the role of teachers' voluntary organisations in bringing this about.

In *Defining Physical Education*, Kirk drew attention to Mangan's suggestion that state officials denied games to elementary schools before 1900 and did not greatly encourage them after that date. But the picture is much more complicated than that, as this book will illustrate. Kirk also noted that there had been 'advocacies for children who attended state-run elementary schools to play games from before the turn of the century', but does not elaborate on the degree of success that teachers achieved or the factors that may have limited their progress.[61] In his next book, Kirk explored the role of physical education in the construction of the modern body in the Foucauldian sense.[62] More recently, in *Schooling Bodies*, he has identified physical exercises, medical inspections and sport as three of the sets of practices that emerged in the late nineteenth century 'that had a specific and specialised relationship to schooling bodies'.[63] The reference is to the regulative aspects of games, 'in which the rules of games require bodies to perform within strictly defined parameters'.[64] Hargreaves, a writer frequently cited by Kirk, drew specific attention to the work of SFAs in his analysis of sport, power and culture, although his interpretation of what they were setting out to achieve will be shown in Chapter 3 to be rather at variance with what is known about their declared intentions.[65] Mangan and Hickey's recent article examined games promoted by the headmasters of two elementary schools prominent in South London school sport, one of whom was W.J. Wilson, the founder of the South London SFA, and saw them as spearheading an ideology of athleticism, appropriately adapted to conditions in elementary schools.[66] While acknowledging an athleticist element in the motivation of some teachers in the promotion of football in Victorian and Edwardian elementary schools, this book identifies other factors like a concern for the physical welfare of children, that may have been equally influential.

Whatever the motivation of the teachers who introduced football to elementary-school pupils at a time when outdoor games did not form part of the curriculum, their pioneering work is shown in this book to have been a major contributory factor in having outdoor games accepted as part of the elementary-school curriculum. Yet it has received no mention in the major works that trace the history of the curriculum or the development of the teaching profession during that period.[67]

Histories of football

If the work of SFAs and the teachers who founded and ran them have merited little more than a passing mention in studies of youth and physical education, it has fared little better in histories of football. Alcock makes no mention of elementary-school football in his book, *Association Football* (1906), despite the fact that he actually refereed one of the matches between South London SFA and Sheffield SFA at the Oval, Kennington.[68] In Gibson and Pickford's *Association Football and the Men Who Made It* (1905/06), the profile of W.J. Wilson, at that time a member of the FA Council, contained a brief tribute to his pioneering work for schoolboy football and, in a section on football in the Metropolis, London teachers are complimented for their 'splendid enthusiasm' in promoting the game.[69] *The Book of Football*, which was published in 1905, carried what is perhaps a more informative account of the origin of schoolboy football than any that has appeared in histories of the game in the following nine decades. Written by H.J.W. Offord, a teacher in Stroud Green in north London and a member of the Council of the LSFA, it begins with the aphorism that the boy is father to the man and that therefore:

> it is a matter for congratulation that the lads of the elementary schools of Great Britain are being trained to thoroughly good football. From the youngsters of today we shall obtain our great players of the future. That the supply will not be deficient is patent to those who have watched the skilful schoolboy teams at work.[70]

Of the many issues raised in Offord's short article, two in particular are examined in detail in this book, namely, the identity of the first SFA (an issue that is explored in Chapter 3) and his contention that the aim of school-boy football was to provide healthy exercise and 'instil self-command' in the boys rather than 'the manufacture' of future professional players, which is considered in Chapter 7.[71]

In the years after the Second World War several histories of football appeared in which attempts were made to account for the popularity of the game. In *The Official History of the Football Association* (1953), it is recorded how the FA Council passed a resolution expressing satisfaction at the progress of schoolboy football as early as 1901 but for the next 25 years took no active part in promoting either schoolboy or youth football.[72] In an excel-lent chapter entitled 'The popularisation of football' in *A History of Football*, Marples omits any mention of elementary-school football, but the main focus of his book is in fact on the period before football was organised for these schools.[73] In Fabian and Green's four-volume *Association Football*, the 25-page entry on schoolboy football was written by Ward, an English Schools' Foot-ball Association (ESFA) Council member, and is mainly concerned with the development of the national association. Young's *A History of British Football* is of particular interest in that, in tracing the spread of association football after Forster's Act of 1870, the author noticed an emerging 'triangular pat-tern of church, education and organised football' taking shape, and relates the case of Wolverhampton Wanderers, which had its origin in St Luke's School, Blackenhall, Wolverhampton, and the promotion of the game there by the headmaster and some of his staff.[74] When Wolverhampton Wanderers won the FA Cup in 1893 it was, perhaps, significant that the team was entirely composed of Englishmen and nearly all had grown up in Wolverhampton.[75] This locality-based composition of the team contrasts sharply with that of Tottenham Hotspur when it won the FA Cup in 1901, an issue that is explored in Chapter 7.

In *The People's Game*, Walvin was the first modern football historian to give a full acknowledgement to the part played by elementary-school football in the promotion of the game. First tracing the gradual recognition of the value of physical culture and outdoor activities in elementary schools, he lists several well-known football clubs, including Queen's Park Rangers in west London, that had their origin in elementary schools and gives his view that inter-school and inter-district competitions 'became of crucial importance in generating and maintaining the youthful commitment to football, particularly among working-class boys whose occupational opportunities were limited'. For Walvin, this new emphasis on football in state schools was, by the turn of the century, 'perhaps the most important factor in guaranteeing the future of football as a mass game and was undoubtedly a determining factor in making football the national game'.[76] As in his history of childhood reviewed above, Walvin did not acknowledge either the SFAs or the teachers who were instrumental in achieving what he has confirmed was a crucial contribution to football. His view on the influence of football in state schools, nonetheless, is one that is largely substantiated in this book.

In his review of football in elementary schools in *Association Football and English Society*, Mason drew attention to the great number of SFAs that were in existence throughout the country from the 1880s onwards. He referred to the increasing number of male teachers in elementary schools in the decades that followed the 1870 Education Act and the importance of teacher training as likely influences in the promotion of the game. He precedes his considera-tion of schoolboy football in Birmingham with a discussion on the strength of the game in St Peter's College, Saltley, where many of the teachers in ele-mentary schools in the Birmingham area were trained. While acknowledging the 'grass roots activity' of SFAs, he does not refer to the records of any of the many such associations in the Birmingham area or elsewhere that might explain what form their competitions took, what the teachers were trying to achieve in their pioneering work, what ideology if any might have motivated them and what the outcomes of their efforts were other than that more boys learned to play the game at school.[77]

In the first chapter of his recent book, *Football and the English*, Russell couples state education with the popular press as contributory factors in the victory of association football over rugby as the main winter game in the late nineteenth century. He returns to the theme in the following chapter and in the short space devoted to schoolboy football draws attention to the fact that association was preferred to rugby at that time because it was safer to play on the hard surfaces of school playgrounds and 'was suitable and comparatively safe for the physically underdeveloped and undernourished youngsters that schools so often had to cater for'.[78]

While the histories of several SFAs have been written, usually in connection with a fiftieth, sixtieth, seventyfifth anniversary or centenary celebration, these tend to focus on local inter-school competitions, the achievements of the dis-trict team in national competitions and prominent teachers and players in the course of the association's life.[79] Few consider the work of the association either in the context of the development of football in their area or in relation to the development of football regionally or nationally, and issues like the motivation of the teachers and any ideology that might have accompanied the transmission of the game from teacher to pupil are not considered. They do, however, especially in their summaries of competitions organised and matches played, testify to the enormous amount of energy employed by teachers in the promotion of the game in the days before most schools had a telephone.[80]

Of the books written by international footballers who as boys had played in competitions organised by the LSFA or associations affiliated to it, that by Dimmock is largely instructional and in the brief autobiographical section the author does not mention playing for Edmonton SFA in the 1913/14 sea-son.[81] On the other hand, in what is perhaps the most interesting and informative book about football written by a player from that era, Buchan, whose football career will be examined in Chapter 4, recalls learning to head the ball at Bloomfield Road, Woolwich, with whose team he won his first medal in the final of the local inter-schools shield.[82]

None of the published histories of amateur clubs referred to in Chapter 6 provides the detailed background information on players, including their schools, that would have been helpful in tracing the links between schoolboy and amateur football explored in that chapter.[83] Of the histories, statistical works and biographical ('Who's Who?') publications that give information on the background of players in the professional clubs discussed in Chapter 7, those of Campbell on Charlton Athletic and Hogg and McDonald on West Ham United have been most useful in providing details of players' schoolboy football careers, followed by Goodwin's book on Tottenham Hotspur, Ollier's on Arsenal and Turner and White's on Fulham.[84] While the achievements of individual elementary-school players have been acknowledged in these and other works, the contribution of elementary-school football to the development of the amateur and professional game, as examined in Chapters 6 and 7 of this book, has not previously been explored, either in the context of London or of any other area.

Review of primary sources

The principal sources examined have been the records of the LSFA (1892–1919), the South London SFA (1885–1919) and the ESFA (1904–25). For the period under review, all three sets of records include minute books of committee meetings and annual general meetings (but with some gaps for the LSFA and the South London SFA), handbooks, photographs and a small number of match programmes and team lists. While these have been sufficiently comprehensive to examine the structure of the work of teachers in promoting football at the time, an indispensable source in discovering how their work revealed itself in practice and was seen by parties outside schools was found in a specialist football newspaper, the *Football 'Sun'* (incomplete runs only between 1896 and 1904 have been found) and local newspapers. Local newspapers for most districts in London that had SFAs affiliated to the LSFA in the period under review have been consulted for some part of the period at least, and the following four have been read for most of the period: *Stratford Express*, *Tottenham and Edmonton Weekly Herald*, *South London Press* and *East End News*. The log books of forty-three schools that had football teams at the time have been read, and while many contained nothing directly related to outdoor games at the school, some had entries which helped form a picture of how head teachers regarded such games as curricular and extra-curricular activities. The records of the training colleges of Borough Road, St John and St Mark were useful in tracing the background of some of the teachers involved in promoting schoolboy football. Reports from the Education Department and the Board of Education on the progress of elementary education from 1888 to 1909, including inspectors' reports, have been valuable in tracing what is one of the main arguments of this book, namely, that the voluntary efforts of teachers in promoting football in elementary schools as an extra-curricular activity played a significant role in having outdoor games eventually accepted as part of the elementary-school curriculum.

Records of football at Eton, Brentwood, Felsted and Forest public schools have been consulted, in addition to the various published public-school lists of old boys, in tracing the public-school origins of players at Upton Park FC and as leaders at the boys' clubs associated with the university settlement and public-school mission movements. The records of the Eton Manor Clubs, who continued the youth work of the Eton Mission from 1913, were valuable, as were those of the Broad Street Clubs and the clubs associated with Toynbee Hall, Oxford House and the Mansfield Settlements.

The records of the LPFS were useful in identifying many of the ex-public-schoolboys who had been associated with the university settlements and public-school missions and who were also involved in promoting better opportunities for play for Londoners. They were often assisted in this by elementary-school teachers. Many of both groups, ex-public-schoolboys and elementary-school teachers, were also prominent in the London Football Association (LFA), the records of which have been consulted.

The shape of the book

At an early stage of investigating the origins of schoolboy football, it became clear that such an enterprise could only be fruitful if it were preceded by an examination of other agencies that were involved in promoting the game among working-class boys and youths in London in the period immediately before the introduction of elementary-school football. Chapter 2, therefore, is an exploration of how association football was promoted in working-class areas of London in the last four decades of the nineteenth century: by philanthropic rescue work among the poor, by the location of public-school 'old boy' clubs in a working-class area and by the university settlement and public-school movements. Chapters 3 and 4 trace the origins and development of SFAs in the London area from the 1880s, their affiliation to the LSFA, the latter's work in promoting football in London schools and its influence on schoolboy football nationally up to the First World War. Chapter 4 also studies four players who had been prominent in London schoolboy football and whose subsequent careers in football are known, with a view to establishing what their attitudes to the game might have been. Chapter 5 explores the background, education and professional training of a number of teachers who were active in promoting schoolboy football in the London area at the time with a view to establishing something about their reasons for promoting football in their schools. Chapter 6 examines the influence of elementary-school football on the growth of the amateur game in working-class and lower middle-class areas in London in the late nineteenth and early twentieth centuries. Chapter 7 explores the view that, however much its founders may have been guided by the spirit of amateurism, the work of the LSFA and its affiliated associations was instrumental in changing the profile of the playing staff of London professional clubs from that of domination by players from Scotland, the North and the Midlands to one where Londoners were numerically well represented. Chapter 8 draws together conclusions of previous chapters in a manner that indicates the significant contribution of the LSFA and its affiliated associations as they affected, in turn, the changing policy towards outdoor games in elementary schools, the elementary-school teachers themselves and their pupils and the development of amateur and professional football in London.

Notes

1 The new regulations were formulated by Howard Wilkinson in 1997. FA, *Football Education for Young Players: 'A Charter for Quality'* (London: FA, 1997).

2 J. Walvin, *The People's Game: A Social History of British Football* (Newton Abbot: Allen Lane, 1975), p. 29.

3 A. Harvey, 'Football's missing link: The real story of the evolution of modern football', *The European Sports History Review*, 1 (1999), pp. 92–116; A. Harvey, ' "An epoch in the annals of national sport": Football in Sheffield and the creation of modern soccer and rugby', *The International Journal of the History of Sport*, 18, 4 (2001), pp. 53–87; J. Goulstone, 'The working-class origins of modern football', *International Journal of the History of Sport* 17, 1 (2000), pp. 135–43; J. Goulstone, *Football's Secret History* (Upminster: 3–2 Books, 2001); E. Dunning, 'Something of a curate's egg: Comments on Adrian Harvey's "An epoch in the annals of national sport" ', *The International Journal of the History of Sport*, 18, 4 (2001), pp. 88–94; A. Harvey, 'The curate's egg put back together: Comments on Eric Dunning's response to "An epoch in the annals of national sport" ', *International Journal of the History of Sport*, 19, 4 (2002), pp. 192–9; E. Dunning and G. Curry, 'The curate's egg scrambled again: Comments on "The curate's egg put back together" ', *International Journal of the History of Sport*, 19, 4 (2002), pp. 200–4.

4 A measure of public-school influence on the early modification of rules may be inferred from the fact that in 1867 the FA was persuaded by Charterhouse and Westminster to modify its offside rule to accommodate the cramped conditions under which the game was played at these schools. R. Airy, *Westminster* (London: G. Bell & Sons, 1902), pp. 134–5.

5 G. Green, *The History of the Football Association* (London: Naldrett Press, 1953), p. 35. For a detailed account of the early development of the laws of the game see G. Williams, *The Code War: English Football Under the Historical Spotlight* (Harefield: Yore Publications, 1994), pp. 6–21.

6 E.J. Ereault, *Richmond Football Club: From 1861 to 1925* (London: Howlett and Sons, 1925), p. 10.

7 *Stratford Express*, 18 December 1869. During the 1880s at Christ's Hospital, football was still 'a hybrid game, half rugby, half Association'. N.J. Humble, 'Leaving London: A Study of Two Public Schools', *History of Education*, 17, 2 (1988), p. 152.

8 Ereault, *Richmond FC*, p. 11.

9 D. Russell, *Football and the English: A Social History of Association Football, 1863–1995* (Preston: Carnegie Publishing, 1997), p. 20.

10 C.B. Fry, 'Association football' in A. Budd, C.B. Fry, T.A. Cook and B.F. Robinson (eds), *Football* (London: Lawrence and Bullen, 1897), p. 63.

11 C.W. Alcock (ed.), *The Football Annual* (London: FA, 1879), p. 10. For an assessment of Alcock as a player, see Keith Booth, *The Father of Modern Sport: The Life and Times of Charles W. Alcock* (Manchester: Parrs Wood Press, 2002), pp. 39–43.

12 N. Wigglesworth, *The Evolution of English Sport* (London: Frank Cass, 1996), p. 89.

13 For Jackson see D. Birley, *Land of Sport and Glory: Sport and British Society 1887–1910* (Manchester: Manchester University Press, 1995), p. 36.

14 J.A.H. Catton, *Wickets and Goals: Stories of Play* (London: Chapman & Hall, 1926), p. 139.

15 Alcock is quoted in (Green), *Association Football*, p. 105.

16 J.A. Mangan, *Athleticism in the Victorian and Edwardian Public School: The Emergence and Consolidation of an Educational Ideology* (Cambridge: Cambridge University Press, 1981), p. 126.

17 Birley, *Land of Sport and Glory*, p. 33.

18 M. Lammer, 'The Concept of play and the legacy of Ancient Greece' in *La place de jeu dans l'education: Historie et Pedagogie* (Paris: Federation Francaise d'education Physique et de Gymnastique Volontaire, 1989), pp. 75–80.

19 *Sunday Times*, 14 June 1998. The book under review was S. Rae, *W.G. Grace: A Life* (London: Faber & Faber, 1998).

20 *Sunday Times*, 16 November 1997.

21 *The Non-League Paper*, 11 March 2001.

22 S. Maclure, *A History of Education in London 1870–1990* (London: Allen Lane, 1990), pp. 51–2.

23 E.C. Mack, *Public Schools and British Opinion 1780 to 1860* (New York: Columbia University Press, 1938), p. 276. Mack was responding to Strachey's comments on the 'strange after-histories' of teachers and prophets, where Arnold, striving to make Christian gentlemen of boys by employing principles based on the Old Testament, 'proved to be the founder of the worship of athletics and the worship of good form'. L. Strachey, 'Dr Arnold' in *Eminent Victorians* (London: Chatto and Windus, 1938 edn), p. 207.

24 A.P. Stanley, *The Life and Correspondence of Thomas Arnold, D.D.* (London: B. Fellows, 1882 edn), p. 102.

25 J.R. de S. Honey, *Tom Brown's Universe: The Development of the Victorian Public School* (London: Millington, 1977), p. 107.

26 W.E. Bowen, *Edward Bowen: A Memoir* (London: Longman, Green and Co., 1902), pp. 299–300.

27 R. Ollard, *An English Education: A Perspective of Eton* (London: Collins, 1982), p. 84. Neither this work nor T. Card, *Eton Renewed: A History of Eton from 1860 to the Present Day* (London: John Murray, 1994), where an over-emphasis on games is also mentioned (p. 101), provide any sustained criticism of the games cult at the school.

28 Mangan, *Athleticism*, p. 88.

29 D. Newsome, *Godliness and Good Learning: Four Studies on a Victorian Ideal* (London: John Murray, 1961), p. 220. Newsome's emphasis on Thring's significance has been questioned. J.A. Mangan, 'Muscular, Militaristic and Manly' in *International Journal of the History of Sport*, 13, 1 (1996), pp. 32–6.

30 M. Tozer, *Physical Education at Thring's Uppingham* (Uppingham: Uppingham School, 1976), pp. 84–5.

31 P. McIntosh, *Physical Education in England since 1800* (London: Bell and Hyman, 1968 edn), p. 63.

32 E. Dunning and K. Sheard, *Barbarians, Gentlemen and Players: A Sociological Study of the Development of Rugby Football* (Oxford: Martin Robertson, 1979), p. 66.

33 Green, *Football Association*, pp. 24, 32.

34 Ibid., p. 49.

35 E. Dunning, 'The origins of modern football and the public school ethos' in B. Simon and I. Bradley (eds), *The Victorian Public School: Studies in the Development of an Educational Institution* (Dublin: Gill and Macmillan, 1975), p. 176.

36 T. Money, *Manly and Muscular Diversions: Public Schools and the Nineteenth Century Sporting Revival* (London: Duckworth, 1997).

37 M. Tozer, ' "The readiest hand and the most open heart": Uppingham's first mission to the poor', *History of Education*, 17, 4 (1989), pp. 323–32.

38 W.McG. Eager, *Making Men: The History of Boys' Clubs and Related Movements in Great Britain* (London: University of London Press, 1953), pp. 209–10.

39 P. Parker, *The Old Lie: The Great War and the Public School Ethos* (London: Constable, 1987), pp. 140–7.

40 Ibid., p. 145.

41 A.B. Cooper, 'Public School Missions'. This was a series of articles in *Boy's Own Annual*, 38 (1915–16) and 39 (1916–17).

42 A. Briggs and A. Macartney, *Toynbee Hall: The First Hundred Years* (London: Routledge & Kegan Paul, 1984); S. Meacham, *Toynbee Hall and Social Reform 1880–1914: The Search for Community* (New Haven: Yale University Press, 1987).

43 J. Springhall, B. Frazer and M. Hoare, *Sure and Steadfast: A History of the Boys' Brigade 1883 to 1983* (Glasgow: Collins, 1983), p. 39; J. Springhall, 'Building character in the British boy: the attempt to extend Christian manliness to working-class adolescents 1880–1914' in J.A. Mangan and J. Walvin (eds), *Manliness and Morality: Middle-Class Masculinity in Britain and America 1800–1940* (Manchester: Manchester University Press, 1987), p. 57.

44 The quotation on the Cadet Corps is from Col. Beresford, in J. Springhall, *Youth, Empire and Society: British Youth Movements 1883–1940* (London: Croom Helm, 1977), p. 77. M. Rosenthal, *The Character Factory: Baden-Powell and the Origins of the Boy Scout Movement* (London: Collins, 1986), p. 106.

45 Springhall, 'Building character', p. 57.

46 H. Spencer, *Education: Intellectual, Moral and Physical* (London: Watts, 1929 edn), p. 160.

47 McIntosh, *Physical Education*, pp. 103–4.

48 Ibid., pp. 108–9.

49 A. Penn, *Targeting Schools: Drill, Militarism and Imperialism* (London: Woburn Press, 1999), pp. 43–66.

50 Penn, *Targeting Schools*, pp. 38–9.

51 H.B. Philpott, *London at School: The Story of the School Board for London 1870–1904* (London: T. Fisher Unwin, 1904), pp. 115–16, 122.

52 Ibid., pp. 126–7.

53 Marner School (Boys) Log Book, September 1895. The date of the month is not entered. I am grateful to Mrs O'Keefe, head teacher of Marner Primary School when she allowed me to consult the school log books. Although only a mile from the school, Wanstead Flats, where the matches referred to were played, was (and still is) part of Epping Forest and administered by the City of London Corporation.

54 McIntosh, *Physical Education*, pp. 121–2. The South London SFA is again acknowledged, as is the self-sacrifice of teachers promoting games and the benefits to the boys, in D.W. Smith (ed.), *Stretching their Bodies: The History of Physical Education* (Newton Abbot: David and Charles, 1974), pp. 99–100.

55 McIntosh, *Physical Education*, p. 121.

56 J. May, 'Curriculum Development under the School Board for London: Physical Education', PhD (University of Leicester, 1971), p. 236.

57 J.J. Sexby, *The Municipal Parks, Gardens and Open Spaces of London: Their History and Associations* (London: Elliot Stock, 1905).

58 H.W. de B. Peters, *The London Playing Fields Society Centenary History 1890–1990* (London: LPFS, 1990).

59 I. and P. Opie, *The Lore and Language of Schoolchildren* (Oxford: Oxford University Press, 1967 edn), pp. 229–30, 353.

60 J. Walvin, *A Child's World: A Social History of English Childhood 1800–1914* (Harmansworth: Allen Lane, 1984 edn), p. 85.

61 D. Kirk, *Defining Physical Education: The Social Construction of a School Subject in Postwar Britain* (London: Falmer Press, 1992).

62 D. Kirk, *The Body, Schooling and Culture* (Victoria: Deakin University Press, 1993), p. 39.

63 D. Kirk, *Schooling Bodies: School Practice and Public Discourse 1880–1950* (London: Leicester University Press, 1998), p. 14.

64 Ibid., p. 15.

65 J. Hargreaves, *Sport, Power and Culture: A Social and Historical Analysis of Popular Sports in Britain* (Cambridge: Polity Press, 1995 edn), p. 62.

66 J.A. Mangan and C. Hickey, 'English elementary education revisited and revised: Drill and athleticism in tandem', *The European Sports History Review*, 1 (1999), pp. 63–91. 'Adapted athleticism' is reaffirmed as the driving force behind elementary-school games in J.A. Mangan and Hamad S. Ndee, 'Military drill – rather more than "brief and basic": English elementary schools and English militarism', *The European Sports History Review*, 5 (2003), pp. 86–7.

67 A. Tropp, *The School Teachers: The Growth of the Teaching Profession in England and Wales from 1800 to the Present Day* (London: Heinemann, 1959 edn); P.H.J.H. Gosden, *The Evolution of a Profession: A Study of the Contribution of Teachers Associations to the Development of School Teaching as a Professional Occupation* (Oxford: Basil Blackwell, 1972); M. Lawn, *Servants of the State: The Contested Control of Teaching 1900–1930* (Lewes: Falmer Press, 1987); T.R. Phillips, 'The National Union of Elementary Teachers, 1870 to 1890', MPhil Thesis (University of London, 1990).

68 C.W. Alcock, *Association Football* (London: George Bell and Sons, 1906). Alcock recalls officiating at the match in a letter to the ESFA, 12 February 1906, attached to Min ESFA (Council), 30 June 1906.

69 A. Gibson and W. Pickford, *Association Football and the Men Who Made It* (London: Caxton, 1905–06), 3, p. 53.

70 H.J.W. Offord, 'Schoolboy football', in *The Book of Football* (Westcliffe-on-Sea: Desert Island Books, 1997 edn), p. 151.

71 Ibid., p. 152.

72 Green, *Football Association*, pp. 131–2. A later official history makes no mention at all of the FA's attitude to schoolboy football until the establishment of the Lilleshall National School in the 1980s. B. Butler, *The Official History of the Football Association* (London: Queen Anne Press, 1991), pp. 225–6.

73 M. Marples, *A History of Football* (London: Secker and Warburgh, 1954).

74 P.M. Young, *A History of British Football* (London: Arrow, 1973 edn), p. 162. See also P.M. Young, *The Wolves: The First Eighty Years* (London: Stanley Paul, 1959), pp. 23–6. The same author's *Football in Sheffield* (London: Stanley Paul, 1962), takes no account of elementary-school football in Sheffield, which had one of the earliest and strongest school-boy football associations in the country.

75 M. Tyler, *The Story of Football* (London: Cavendish, 1976), p. 52.

76 Walvin, *The People's Game*, p. 59.

77 T. Mason, *Association Football and English Society 1863–1915* (Brighton: Harvester Press, 1981 edn), pp. 83–7. There is an account of football at the college in J. Osborne, *Saltley College Centenary 1850–1950* (Birmingham: Saltley College, 1950), pp. 135–40.

78 Russell, *Football and the English*, pp. 19, 36.

79 Those relating to London are listed in Section 3 (c) of the Bibliography.

80 In 1912, when Park's C. Beal, whose career is examined in Chapter 5, had to arrange a Dewar Trophy (LSFA individual schools' championship) match for his school against Westbury, Barking, about four miles away, he had to make the journey there beforehand to discuss the details. Five years later, when parents came up to the school asking to collect their children because they were expecting an air raid, the headmaster, presumably not having a telephone, had to send a teacher around to the police station in person for information. 'He returned with the news that it was a false report'. Park (Boys) Log Book, 13 March 1912, 14 June 1917.

81 J. Dimmock, *Association Football* (London: C. Arthur Pearson, 1927).

82 C. Buchan, *A Lifetime in Football* (London: Phoenix House, 1955), p. 10.

83 Anon., *The History of Dulwich Hamlet Football Club* (London: Dulwich Hamlet FC, 1968); Anon., *Nunhead Football Club 1888 to 1938: A Souvenir* (London: Nunhead FC, 1938); M. Blakeman, *Nunhead Football Club 1888–1949* (Harefield: Yore Publications, 2000).

The latter work contains a list of all Nunhead's known players (pp. 74–8), some of whom can be linked to their elementary schools, as shown in Chapter 6.

84 C. Cameron, *The Valiant 500: Biographies of Charlton Athletic Players Past and Present* (Sidcup: The Author, 1991); T. Hogg and T. McDonald, *Who's Who of West Ham United* (London: Independent Sports Publications, 1994); B. Goodwin, *The Spurs Alphabet: A Complete Who's Who of Tottenham Hotspur FC* (Leicester: ACL and Polar, 1992); F. Ollier, *Arsenal: A Complete Record 1886–1992* (Derby: Breedon, 1992); D. Turner and A. White, *Fulham: A Complete Record 1879–1987* (Derby: Breedon, 1987).

2 Public-school games and working-class football

Introduction

This chapter examines some of the agencies that preceded elementary-school football associations in promoting football among boys and youths in London in the last four decades of the nineteenth century. Each of the three sections into which the chapter is divided is concerned with the activities of ex-public-schoolboys in parts of London that were, or were to become, predominantly working-class districts. In the sections "Quintin Hogg and Muscular Christians in Central London" and "Upton Park FC (1866–1887) and the Promotion of Football" which consider the contributions of Quintin Hogg and of Upton Park FC respectively, the transmission of the game and the attitudes that went with it are shown in a context where the game was promoted, as it were, by example, rather than as part of any considered programme related to the benefits of football for those who played it. The section "University Settlements and Public-School Missions" which focuses on the football dimensions of the university settlements and public-school missions, examines, first in general and then by means of a particular example, the part football played in these movements and their contribution to the elementary-school football that followed, and in some cases developed alongside, their endeavours.

Quintin Hogg and muscular Christians in central London

The biography of Quintin Hogg, written by his daughter and published the year after his death, makes it clear that three of the guiding passions of his life, football, religion and education, were evident at an early age. Quintin, the fourteenth child of a successful Irish barrister, took up football at his first school in Berkshire at the age of eight or nine, combined it with cricket at his next school in Brighton, and at Eton added fives and boating to his sporting repertoire.[1] Although accomplished in all these sports, it was at football that he excelled. At Eton in the 1860s, when the games cult was gaining momentum, he was in the Football XI for 1863 and continued to play at a high level for many years.[2] His achievements in the game as an adult included an appearance with Old Etonians in the 1876 FA Cup final and a place in the Scotland team for the first international match against England in 1870, the latter an honour for which he was, presumably, considered qualified by virtue of his remote Scottish ancestors.

The high status that went with being a football player at Eton helped him to promote his second enthusiasm, that for religion, of an evangelical but unsectarian description, where the emphasis was on the Christian's direct contact with the Redeemer, deepened by his interpretation of the Scriptures.[3] A group known as the 'Synagogue' met in Hogg's room at Eton to study the Bible and had the future Lord Kinnaird among its members. That the Christianity espoused was muscular in tone may be inferred from the fact that an unsympathetic atheist was once confronted with the threat that he would be 'taken on at football'![4]

Hogg's third passion was education. Although he had no training in teaching of any kind, he seems to have had an instant rapport with pupils and, several years before Forster's Act, became aware that improvements for the working poor were dependent on some form of elementary education. Later, when his work moved more towards meeting the needs and aspirations of higher working-class and lower middle-class youths, he saw the importance of technical education, and set about providing it, again, several years before national and local authorities were to do so.

On leaving Eton, Hogg pursued a career in the tea trade in the City while devoting his evenings to rescue, educational and evangelical work. Seeing the conditions of life endured by working boys and inspired by the sense of duty refined by his Bible study, his first attempt at rescue work was in trying to teach a couple of crossings' sweepers to read. In order to understand better their way of life and to enable himself to make more fruitful contact with them, he actually went out at night shoe-blacking among the boys he intended to rescue. With Lord Kinnaird from his Bible study group at Eton, he hired a room in Of Alley, situated on the site of the old palace of the Duke of Buckingham, and opened a ragged school.[5] Those invited to the opening included Tom Pelham, who had been a prominent cricketer at Eton as well as a member of Hogg's Bible study group, and who later, with Kinnaird, founded the Homes for Working Boys.[6]

Ragged schools had been in existence since 1840 or before, but the movement to provide an elementary education for the most destitute sections of the population gained momentum with the involvement of Lord Shaftesbury and the formation of the Ragged School Union in 1844. There had been a decline in the number of ragged schools in London in the 1860s mainly due, according to the movement's historian, to the effects of epidemics on children and to some extent on their teachers, most of whom were volunteers and whose parents would have been likely to 'overrule the will of a daughter teaching in a plague-stricken district'.[7] A teacher from the City of London Mission was put in charge of the school, where, when an evening department was started for older boys and youths, Hogg himself agreed to do some teaching after his day's work, something he was to continue for several years. From his own testimony and that of others, it is clear that Hogg had a natural talent for keeping boys interested in learning, and was even able, as Pelham acknowledged, to bring to heel those who had got out of control while being taught by others.[8]

While there is evidence that Hogg and Kinnaird continued to play football during the years they were engaged in the rescue, evangelical and ragged school work, there is little direct evidence of them either promoting games among the boys they worked with or using their status as outstanding footballers to impress their charges. Lacking facilities to play football in the crowded rookeries, they may, like many education authorities after them, have decided not to try to organise games, despite appreciating their value. Once away from the crowded streets and tenements, however, things were different: at a trip to Southend for shoeblacks, organised and supervised by Hogg and Kinnaird, the pleasure of bathing 'was varied by football, cricket, rounders and donkeys'.[9]

With improvement in the behaviour, appearance and disposition of the boys and youths due to the influence of the Ragged School's day and evening classes, many of them were able to get apprenticeships. These youths in turn brought their friends along to the classes. By the time the enterprise moved to new premises in 1871 the name was changed to the Hanover Institute and the kind of youth availing himself of the facilities was considerably higher up the social scale than those with whom Hogg had begun his work at Of Alley. As Hogg himself put it many years later, 'the success of a ragged school rings the knell of the ragged character'.[10] Seven years later, with a membership of 500 and a long waiting list, another move was required, this time to Long Acre. Trade classes were introduced by Hogg and Robert Mitchell, who had been Honorary Secretary of the Institute since 1871. In 1879 Hogg purchased 24 acres of land at Mortlake for playing fields for the Institute. From the record he has left of his thoughts at that time about the kind of educational institution most suitable to meet the needs of the young men under his care, it is clear that he saw the provision of religion and facilities for games as of particular importance. What the Institute was trying to develop, he said, 'was a place which should recognise that God had given man more than one side to his character, and where we would gratify any reasonable taste, whether athletic, intellectual, spiritual or social'.[11]

When the Polytechnic building in Regent Street became available – it had most recently been used as a science exhibition centre – and with funding obtained from a body set up to administer City of London parochial charities, Hogg was able to realise his ambition to open a technical institute that paid due regard to the young men's religious and athletic development as well as their technical and general education. The name 'Polytechnic' was retained when the Institute moved into the Regent Street premises in 1881, with Hogg as president. Helped by the City and Guilds, a programme of evening classes was organised, which aimed at providing, in what Hogg saw primarily as a Christian Institute, 'some training for the hand, the head, and the heart'.[12]

In 1886, full-time secondary education was introduced in the Regent Street building. 'Springing as it did from the muscular brand of Christianity practised by Q.H. and his disciples', wrote the school's historian, 'and living within the ambience of the Poly which was so much a power in amateur sport, the School naturally attached much importance to games.'[13] It still exists as Quintin Kynaston School in St Marylebone, the second half of the name deriving from an amalgamation with the Kynaston School.

J.E. Kynaston Studd, after whom the Kynaston School was named, first became involved in the work of the Polytechnic in 1885. A member of the famous cricketing family, he had, like Hogg, been outstanding at games at Eton, and like him had also worked for a tea company and was influenced by the evangelical preaching of Moody and Sankey. They had actually met at one of the American preachers' missions in London. Secretary of the Polytechnic from 1885, Studd played cricket with the Poly team and helped with coaching. He was clearly in the same mould of muscular Christian as Hogg, whom he was to succeed as president later.

Studd had been a good footballer until he damaged a knee, and initially made some appearances for the Polytechnic side.[14] The Poly team had been founded in 1875 by Hogg, aided by Kinnaird and Pelham, and was originally known as Hanover United. The team's matches were reported in detail in the Hanover Institute's monthly magazine, and it is clear from the teams listed that, just as public-schoolboy teams at the time included masters, staff at the Institute were among those who appeared regularly for Hanover United. It is also clear that from its earliest matches the team was expected to embody the highest sporting ideals associated with the public schools. When the team played Excelsior at London Fields in 1879, for example, the Hanover players, who included Kinnaird but not Hogg on this occasion, waited so long for their opponents' captain to arrive that the game ended in darkness. Waiting around in the cold, however, had not blunted the spirit of fair play. The match report concluded that the game had been played 'in a most fair spirit throughout, and when an infringement of the rules occurred, the appeal was allowed without dispute from either side, a practice we should like to see more universal'.[15]

The Hanover United club had an important role in the early development of the game in London. In an interview in 1895, Hogg was asked about the social and athletics element in the Polytechnic's work. Hogg, who still played football regularly at the time, answered that he was a strong advocate of the practice of athletics, adding that playing games kept young men out of trouble.[16] This belief in the practical value of games, as well as the commitment to the public-school games ethos so often enunciated and exemplified by himself, Kinnaird, Pelham and Studd, ensured that the team transmitted the essential elements of association football and its accompanying ideology from the public school to a section of lower middle-class and working-class youths of London.

In 1875 the Hanover Institute team was involved in probably the first attempt to make football part of the regular programme of youth club events, when it organised a fixture with the working lads of St Andrew's Home for Boys, a Soho youth club. The youth club's manager, George Biddulph, had great difficulty getting matches for his team during the decade that followed that game, from which it may be assumed that in the 1870s and early 1880s few teams existed in London that made provision for young players.[17] This may be seen as evidence not only of the pioneering work of Hanover United and the small number of other youth clubs promoting the game among the young, but of the importance of the work of SFAs that followed them in promoting the game from a much broader base than was possible in boys' clubs.

The younger players at the club could hardly have had a better example of the strenuous aspects of the game than Kinnaird, the man assigned to them for their guidance at the Junior Hanover Club, while Hogg concentrated on the senior team.[18] Kinnaird's later reputation as a conciliatory figure, when as Chairman of the FA he helped steer a middle course between the demands of the largely working-class proponents of professional football and the predominantly public-school advocates of a strict amateurism, has already been mentioned in Chapter 1. His attitudes were no doubt due in some measure to the insights into a way of life different from his own that he came into contact with in the course of his rescue, educational and sporting work in association with Quintin Hogg.

Upton Park FC (1866–87) and the promotion of football

Two factors determined the choice of Upton Park as a club likely to shed light on the connection between the football played in public-school 'old boy' clubs and the growth of the game in working-class areas of London. The first was that the Club's early players included several who were associated with the public-school games ethos and were influential in the early development of the Football Association. The second was that the area of West Ham, in which the Club was located, was one of the leading districts in the country in schoolboy football during the 30 years immediately following the demise of Upton Park FC.

The players included C.W. Alcock, who, in addition to his renown as a player, was also prominent as an early administrator of the game.[19] Having first served on the FA Committee in 1865, he was later its secretary, first in an honorary capacity and, from 1886, with a salary. But it was through his editorship of the semi-official *FA Annual* that he had perhaps the greatest influence on the early development of the game.[20] This provided players and supporters with detailed information on changes to FA rules, matches played in one season and arranged for the next, lists of prominent players and representative sides, as well as information on all clubs that belonged to either the FA or the Rugby Union, with details of the number of members, the location of grounds and the addresses of secretaries. Two other Upton Park players may be briefly mentioned. One was N.L. Jackson, champion of amateurism and the Corinthian spirit in football, founder of the Corinthian FC for the best fifty amateur footballers in the country and to which several Upton Park players later gained admittance.[21] The other was A. Stair, an early treasurer and secretary of the FA and referee in the first three FA Cup finals.

Upton Park FC was founded in 1866. No records of the Club have been located, but its matches and annual sports days were reported in the *Stratford Express* with reasonable consistency from 1868. Surprisingly, none of these reports makes any reference to the club's origin. The report on the 1868 sports day notes that the president was H.A. Alexander. He had hitherto been an active member of the Upton United Cricket Club. But as none of the other players, officials or donors of prizes in the early days of the football club seems to have played for the cricket club, it would be rash to speculate on it being any more than a possibility that the former might have had its origin in the latter.

The 700 'ladies and gentlemen' who came to enjoy the club's 1868 sports day were enabled to do so, the *Express* reported, because of the fine weather and 'owing to the rough element being excluded'.[22] No details were given of the tactics used to keep out the unwanted guests, but considerable manpower must have been employed, as the track used was no more than an unenclosed section of the north-east corner of John Gurney's spacious grounds, then called Upton Park but shortly to be acquired as a public amenity and given its present name of West Ham Park. Nor did the report say what threat the 'rough element' posed. Did they wish to disrupt an event organised with great attention to detail by their 'social superiors' or did they merely want to run in the races? If they simply wanted to take part, their resentment was perhaps understandable, as traditional athletic and football events, normally held in conjunction with festivals, were usually open to anyone who wanted to take part.

Who were the members of this Club, who so clearly distanced themselves from 'the rough element' in an area that was rapidly increasing in the size of its largely working-class population?[23] With the help of Alcock's *Annuals*, the Minutes of FA Committee meetings, football histories, local directories and lists of public-schoolboys, university students and clergymen, it has been possible to establish something about the club members whose names appeared in reports. For the purposes of this part of the study of the club, its members will be divided into those whose names appeared in the period before 1870, those in the 1870s and finally those in the 1880s. While there will be some overlapping, players will normally be considered under the period in which their names first appeared.

Club members before 1870

At the 1868 sports day referred to above, prizes were donated by Alexander, A.J. Jutsum, J.F. Bringes and G. Pagenstecher. Alexander was an architect and surveyor and sat on the controversial West Ham Board of Health. Jutsum, whose son was a prominent player in the team up until the mid-1870s, was a partner in Denton and Jutsum, oil merchants and petroleum refiners at Bow Common Lane. Bringes had an engineering firm in Stepney and Pagenstecher was agent for the Gurney family, owners of Upton Park, and a key figure in having the property acquired as a public open space a few years later.[24]

Besides Alcock, several players from this period can be identified as having attended public schools. H. and F. Wilton both went to Brentwood, the latter appearing in a team photograph that is still preserved at the school.[25] C.E. Wilson, who in later life became clerk to the East Ham Local Board, and who played alongside the Wilton brothers in the Upton Park formation of six forwards that beat Civil Service at the end of 1868, went to Felsted.[26] The S. Curwen who was third in the mile at the 1868 sports was almost certainly one of the sons of John Curwen, the Plaistow minister and publisher, both of whom had the initial 'S' in their names and one of whom went to the City of London School.[27] J.H. Capper who won a prize at the same sports was the boy who, 9 years earlier, had been admitted to St Paul's School as the son of Charles Capper, manager of the Victoria Docks and a resident of The Grove, Stratford.[28]

The school attended by F. Barnett, one of the full backs in the Civil Service match, has not been traced, but he is recorded in the 1881 Census as a stockbroker, the same profession as that of H.R. Barnett, possibly his brother, who went to Felsted and later played for Upton Park.[29] F. Barnett, who was later to become secretary of the Club and to serve on the FA Committee, was complimented by N.L. Jackson as 'a splendid organiser' and Gibson and Pickford referred to him as 'an apostle of amateurism' in their historical survey of football in the London region up to 1905.[30]

Of the remaining three players from this period about whom information could be found, one was the son of a man who had a clothing contract with the Army, another was later a hay salesman resident in Walthamstow and the last was described as an 'agent to Lloyds'.[31] While not enough players were traced in this period to permit any but the most tentative conclusions, there seemed to be grounds for believing that in the early days of the club a great number of the members were either expensively educated or held important positions in the commercial world.

Club members in the 1870s

In the first 10 years of the Club's existence the team's fixtures were almost entirely friendly matches against other clubs in the London area and against those Essex public schools that played association football at the time – Brentwood, Chigwell, Felsted and Forest. For even though the Club took part in the FA Cup, the team was knocked out in the early rounds each season up to 1876/77, when Upton Park came to national attention in sporting circles by reaching the last six of the competition, and narrowly failed to reach the final. This was followed by an equally impressive run in 1877/78, when the team won through to the fourth round before going out to Old Harrovians.[32]

Insofar as can be judged from the evidence available, it would seem that Upton Park had raised the level of its team to one of the strongest in the country by retaining many of the good players from the early years of the Club and by judicious recruitment from past pupils of Essex public schools and, to a lesser extent, from local clubs. One player who did not quite fit into either category was England's goalkeeper Conrad Warner, who had attended a Quaker school in Tottenham and whose achievements at Upton Park had earned him an England cap.[33] Some of the ex-public-schoolboys came from Forest in Snaresbrook, but as that school had a successful 'old boy' team, their number was small and none at all seems to have come from Chigwell, a school almost as local as Forest and with an equally high reputation for producing players of outstanding ability.[34] Most of Upton Park's ex-public-schoolboy recruits in the 1870s in fact came from Brentwood and Felsted.

Brentwood and Felsted were two of the public schools which, during the second half of the nineteenth century, improved their sports facilities in line with the views fashionable on the value of games at the time.[35] Brentwood had fixtures with other schools and clubs, including Upton Park, from the 1860s and although Felsted did not begin to play other schools until 1875 when it adopted the FA's rules, both schools were playing the game at a high level before 1880.[36] Several 'old boys' from both schools came to Upton Park, two of whom became international players. R.A. Ogilvie spent three seasons with Upton Park after he left Brentwood and before he transferred to Clapham Rovers, with whom he played in the 1878/79 FA Cup final and gained an international cap against Scotland.[37] C. Mitchell left Felsted, where he had been football captain, in 1879, played in many of Upton Park's great matches in the 1880s and earned five England caps while with the Club.[38]

The number of players from other clubs in the area who transferred to Upton Park was small. Of the six who have been identified as having come from the nearby clubs of Leyton and Trojans in the 1870s, details of one could not be traced, one was listed in the 1881 Census as a merchant's clerk, another was a clerk in the London Docks, two were schoolmasters and the sixth was a solicitor. This last was S.R. Bastard, one of Upton Park's greatest players, who gained one England cap while at the Club and had the honour of refereeing the 1877/78 FA Cup final.[39] The fact that all five of the players traced were born in the East London area gave grounds for an hypothesis that the Club's continued recruitment of talented players locally would lead inevitably to working-class men from the surrounding area gaining places in the team. The hypothesis proved false.

Club members in the 1880s

Upton Park established itself as the top club in London in the early 1880s by winning the London Cup in 1882–83, the first season it was contested, retaining the trophy the following season and enjoying several FA Cup runs that compared favourably with those of the previous decade.[40] Of the team that beat Quintin Hogg's Hanover United in the second round of the FA Cup at the end of 1881, the schools of eight of the eleven players have been traced, and show that four had been to Felsted (C. Mitchell, H.P. Ward, H.R. Barnett and H.M. Joselyne), and that one had attended each of the following: Repton (H. Lafone), City of London (S.R. Bastard), Aldenham (J.J. Barnard) and Grove House Quaker School (C. Warner).[41] Of the seven occupations known to have been engaged in by the players at that time or in their future lives, three were solicitors, two were doctors, one was later a clergyman, one a ship-broker and one was in business with a firm of stationers. Significantly, none of the eleven players appears on the alphabetical list of names for the county of Essex, compiled by the University of Utah Genealogical Project from the 1881 Census returns.

The teams that played for the remainder of the decade until the Club was disbanded in 1887 were noteworthy not for any decline in the presence of ex-public-schoolboys but for a decrease in those who had been to Felsted and an increase in those who had been to Aldenham. Twenty-one ex-public-schoolboys have been identified as playing for the Club in the last four years of its existence (1883–87), excluding those listed in the previous paragraph who continued to appear in the team after 1883. Of the twenty-one, nine had been to Aldenham, four to Charterhouse, three to Repton, two to Felsted and one to each of Brighton, Eton and Lancing.[42]

G.M. Lambrick (Repton) was curate of St Phillip's, Stepney and H.C. Duthoit (Charterhouse) was curate of St Andrew's, Plaistow, at the time they were playing for Upton Park and ex-Felsted Football XI captain R. Stuart King, who had gained an England cap before joining the Club, was ordained in 1887 and was later Rector of Leigh-on-Sea.[43] J.J. Barnard, who first played for the Club in 1879, qualified as a solicitor in 1883, was ordained in 1889 and later became Vicar of Rochford in Essex. As the first of the ex-Aldenham players to come to Upton Park, he might be thought to have been respon-sible in some way for the others joining the Club, although the late Donald Shearer, the school's greatest player and the historian of the Old Aldenhamians, made the point that E.H. Marriette, a later arrival, was known to have been an influential figure among Aldenhamians. He also drew attention to the importance of distance in those days before the motor car and the relevance of the fact that no less than seven of the ex-Aldenham players at Upton Park actually came from the London area.[44] Marriette, who had the unusual dis-tinction of being captain of the school XI for two seasons, later returned there as house master. Of the other Old Aldenhamians, two were later farmers in Australia and New Zealand, one became a corn merchant and maltster and another a brewer, while others pursued careers in medicine, surveying, the law and business. One, E.R. Ross, was general manager of the Natal Govern-ment Railways before his appointment to a similar position with Rhodesian Railways in 1911.

Of the small number of players from this period who have been identified as living locally or of local origin, only four, besides the two curates, could be traced. The Hewett brothers, who had both been to Charterhouse, were the sons of a smack owner engaged in the Barking fishing industry, another was a railway clerk living in West Ham and the fourth, P.M. Evans, who took over in goal for a match when the regular goalkeeper was unavailable, was an Oxford graduate in law and the son of John Evans, 'gent.' of Stratford.

Writing 50 years afterwards, N.L. Jackson recalled how much he had enjoyed his football at Upton Park in the 1870s. He regretted, however, that in 1887 the Club 'was compelled to disband because younger and more energetic rivals had encroached upon their recruiting ground'.[45] This is highly questionable. It is true that several other clubs like Barking, Dreadnought, Ivanhoe and Romford were established locally in the 1870s and 1880s and that most players in their teams came from the East London and South-West Essex areas. The occupations of the players in those teams that could be traced indicate that while the majority were clerks, a substantial minority were tradesmen or unskilled workers. The Dreadnought players included a brass turner, a blacksmith and a labourer and Romford, although heavily dominated by clerks, many of them employed in the local brewery, also had a brickmaker, a painter and two carpenters among the players.[46] There is no indication that Upton Park ever made any effort at recruitment among the local lower-middle or working-class population that surrounded the Club in increasing numbers as the century progressed. Instead, there seems to have been a preference for recruitment from among players who had established their reputations at their public schools or at Oxford and Cambridge.

In the short term, of course, recruiting ex-public-schoolboys paid most dividends, as may be judged by the Club's continued success on the field against some of the best teams in the country, including some who were professional in everything but name. But the future of football at the highest level in East London and South-West Essex, as elsewhere, lay among the working-class boys kicking footballs (or bound-up rags or paper) around the streets, courts and alleyways and on the hard-surfaced playgrounds of the elementary schools. It is to the credit of teachers in some of these schools that they saw a potential in those boys that was not recognised by the officers of Upton Park and that within 5 years of the disappearance of the Club, the West Ham Schools' Football Association had been founded, an inter-school competition was in existence and a schools' district team was being selected for a match against the schoolboys of Tower Hamlets, West Ham's neighbour on the opposite side of the River Lea.

Even if the Upton Park officials had recognised the football potential of local working-class boys, there is no certainty that they would have wished to harness it. The Club's known commitment to amateurism and the Corinthian idea of sportsmanship, imbibed at the public schools, carried with it an underside of exclusivism and the snobbery identified by Wigglesworth to which reference was made in Chapter 1. Gentlemen wanted to play with and against gentlemen.[47] The story of Upton Park's objection to Preston North End in the 1883–84 FA Cup on the grounds that players were being paid, which led directly to the expulsion of the Lancashire club from the competition and indirectly to the acceptance of a strictly controlled professionalism by the FA, has often been told, most recently by Dave Russell.[48] The fact that so few of the Upton Park players lived anywhere in the East London or South-West Essex area but seem to have been recruited from far and wide through the 'old boy network' with the object of winning matches at the highest level of football would suggest a recruitment policy not dissimilar to that of Preston, the main difference being that the Northern (and Scottish) players who represented the latter club could not afford to take part in such complicated and expensive recruitment and playing arrangements without financial compensation.[49]

If Upton Park made little direct contribution to promoting the playing skills of local youths, it might have made a considerable indirect contribution to two aspects of local football. Large crowds went to see the FA Cup matches in West Ham Park against some of the strongest sides in the country. This exposure to the skills of the leading players of the time might have been influential in motivating West Ham youngsters to attempt to attain that level themselves. It is possible that the spectacle of top-class football that was witnessed regularly by spectators of all ages might have given the local population a taste for the finer points of the game that was to be satisfied later by Clapton FC in the FA Amateur Cup, by West Ham United in the Southern League and to a lesser extent, because their major fixtures were understandably less frequent, by the West Ham Schools' Football Association's campaigns in London, Essex and national schoolboy championships.[50] This is difficult to prove, of course, and all we really know with any degree of certainty about the crowds that attended Upton Park's matches is that they were enthusiastic. So enthusiastic, in fact, that at the end of 1884 there were reports that because of encroachments on the pitch 'the Upton Park Committee are considering whether it is not advisable to play as many matches as possible on other grounds than their own'.[51] Despite a suggestion in the local newspaper that the Club should consider roping off the pitch in West Ham Park before taking the extreme step of leaving, the move went ahead and the Club played its home matches in Wanstead for the remaining 2 years of its existence.[52]

University settlements and public-school missions

Settlements and boys' clubs

The Whittington Club, founded in Leman Street, Whitechapel, in 1884, was one of the first projects undertaken by the residents of Toynbee Hall. The Club aimed:

> to provide the means of recreation for some of the working lads in the neighbourhood...classes are held, lectures given, cricket, football and

athletics in the seasons, country rambles, etc.... The internal organisation of the club is left as far as possible to a committee of the members, elected half yearly by the club, and special efforts are made to teach the members to do things for themselves... Cadet Corps (is trained there), which by teaching the boys drill and habits of discipline, is of value to them in their general training.[53]

This brief summary of the Club's aims and the activities arranged to carry them out in 1888 captures the essential features of the recreational provision that settlements and missions thought suitable for the working-class youths, towards whom much of their energies were directed in their efforts to improve the spiritual and material conditions of the people among whom they had volunteered to live. Founded by Canon Barnett in 1884, the Settlement was intended to meet some of the social needs of the East End by bringing together socially aware university-educated unsectarian Christians to live in a community where, as he later put it, 'a condition of membership is the performance of a citizen's duty, a house among the poor, where the residents may make friends with the poor'.[54]

The attempts to run the Whittington Club democratically were a reflection of the helpers' own experience of taking part in running the public schools they had recently left. This was not always successful in clubs, as Eager has pointed out, and the Toynbee Hall Annual Report for 1902 noted that it was the managers of a club, rather than the way it was organised, that determined its value.[55]

The 1890 Annual Report contained the standard complaint about the scarcity of pitches from those who took football teams in London at the time. Could anyone lend the team a field within a six-penny return fare from Whitechapel, a helper wanted to know, so that the boys could continue to avail themselves of 'this first rate exercise'? There were few fields to lend or let within easy reach of Whitechapel in the 1880s, but his appeal was not made in vain. Two years later a report on the Whittington announced that the football team 'has had a special ground allotted at Forest Gate'.[56] The Sydney Club, another boys' club staffed by volunteers from Toynbee Hall, met at Rutland Road Infants School, Stepney, and offered boxing, wrestling, musical drill and gymnastics, as well as football, which in 1892, was played at Wanstead Flats.[57] Many of the clubs founded or supported by Toynbee Hall were located in schools and some, like the Old Northeyites in Limehouse, consisted of past pupils of a particular school, a form of elementary-school 'old boy' club which will be explored in Chapter 6.[58] Here it may be noted that Barnett, in enabling East Enders to form such clubs, so that a loyalty to their board schools might be encouraged in a way that resembled public-schoolboys' loyalty to their old schools, was advancing one of his aspirations for working-class life, namely, that it might develop a set of cultural institutions comparable to those of other classes. Barnett has been criticised for seeing the poor as lacking a culture of their own, with Whitechapel represented 'as a cultural void, into which his own culture had to be poured'.[59] This culture was imported by the settlers and transmitted to the local population by means of lectures, classes, art galleries, club and social work and by example. It may be wondered, therefore, what Barnett actually thought of football and the working-class adoption of the game. A few clues can be found in *Practicable Socialism*, a book published after his death that contains a selection of his writings and those of his wife, whose opinions on most subjects corresponded closely to his own. Holidays for the workman will be of little benefit if he spends them in sleeping and eating, Barnett wrote in 1911, 'or in exciting himself over a match or race where he does not even understand the skill'.[60] Games 'well played' fulfilled his demanding criteria for worthwhile recreational activities, 'and there is no more cheering sight than that of playing fields where young and old are using their limbs intent on doing their best'.[61] Henrietta Barnett disapproved of 'the football matches, which thousands watch, often ignorant of the science of the game, but captivated by the hope of winning a bet or by the spectacle of brutal conflict'.[62] Understanding the skilful or scientific element in the game was clearly considered to be of value, and participation rather than watching matches (or betting on them) was to be encouraged.

While historians of Toynbee Hall have given no attention to the significance that football might have had in the Settlement's work with boys and youths, an account written by a Prussian visitor who was a resident at Toynbee Hall in 1911–12 left no doubt about its importance.[63] In recounting the open air games that were such an important part of the Settlement clubs' programme at the turn of the century, he referred to football as fulfilling a role very much like that attributed to drill training at the Whittington Club described above. For football, he wrote, stood at the head of Club activities, and had great social value:

> Here for the first time the boy learns to subordinate his own will to the welfare of the majority. Each has his place and his duty, and woe to him whom an ungoverned temperament, or the ambition to shine, drives out of his proper place. Thus, the game becomes a training in discipline, and it considerably helps forward that public spirit without which a Club cannot live.[64]

Frederick Charles Mills was among the earliest of the Oxford graduates who responded to Barnett's call and his first assignment in the East End was to work with a group of boys in Wentworth Street. One of the activities he organised for the boys was a cricket match in the (already drained) moat of the Tower of London. Several other assignments were addressed with equal competence, and he had gained sufficient successful experience of working with boys to be able to buy a premises to open his own club in Ratcliff, near to where he had opted to live, and alongside Broad Street Board School, of which he was a manager. Club members, who had to be over 13, included boys with whom Mills had already worked and boys who were attending evening classes at Broad Street School. The club premises had originally been a ship's block, mast and tackle makers and the sail loft was used for practice by a drum and fife band, which was incorporated into the club. The band-master was a Mr Wells, whose son joined the Club and later gained international fame as the boxer Bombardier Billy Wells.[65]

Billy Wells also had a reputation as a runner and footballer and Fred Wright, whose article on the Club is summarised in the previous paragraph and whose father was football, boxing and gymnastics trainer at the club, recalls seeing Wells' picture in a photograph of the Broad Street Club football team taken around the turn of the century. Football was played at Broad Street from an early date, and the first sports entry in the Club Record Book for 1887 is the result of a match with the Eton Mission. Other activities recorded, besides football, included boxing, gymnastics, cricket, swimming, chess, drafts and billiards.[66]

Extracts from two letters to Fred Wright about Billy Wells, written in the course of his research into the history of the Highway Clubs, of which Broad Street was one, capture something of the flavour of the spirit of boys' club life that reflected that of the public schools attended by so many of the men that founded and staffed them. Tom Downing recalled that at Broad Street they had 'a wonderful club spirit instilled in us all by Mr Mills (bless him) and Billy Wells carried that with him in all his sporting ventures. A gentleman.' The second extract was written by Tom Ritchie, who, along with other lads from Broad Street, had gone to see Wells fight at the Wonderland in Whitechapel:

> I think everybody has admired Billy for the absolutely fair way he fought this fights — some said he verged on the quixotic — there was something of the old Corinthian spirit about it all. I can remember him helping to carry this Corporal Brown chap to his corner. I think he was like that — as Lord Desborough said at one of the Fed[eration of Boys' Clubs] finals at the Albert Hall — 'the amicable ferocity with which they attack each other amazes me'. The old club spirit to a T.[67]

The Oxford House Settlement, which opened in Bethnal Green at the end of 1884, had its origins in Keble College, Oxford, and was guided by principles similar to those of Toynbee Hall, except that it was more avowedly Christian. The Men's Club at Oxford House had a football team that played in the Clapton District League and when the Settlement's Boys' club, the Webbe Institute, opened in 1888, it, too, soon gained a reputation at football. Oxford House was also responsible for establishing the Repton Club, financed by the public school of that name, 'to touch a lower class of boys than the Webbe Institute' and which developed into the boxing club that is internationally known today.[68]

It was the better element of Bethnal Green youth, presumably, that was represented in the Webbe Institute team that was beaten by Fairbairn House Boys' Club in 1897.[69] The Fairbairn House Club was the youth section of Mansfield House, a Settlement that had its origin in F.W. Newland, pastor of Canning Town Congregational Church, making known the needs of the area to Mansfield College, Oxford. Students spent vacations with him and a settlement was decided upon, with Percy Alden appointed 'to do the pioneering work'.[70] Will Reason, Secretary of the Settlement, has left an account of how the first priority was seen as making friends with the people of Canning Town 'without either patronage on one side or subserviency on the other; to share in the joys and sorrows, the occupations and the amusements of the people'. This suggests an attitude to working-class culture rather more positive than that adopted by the Barnetts, and it is not surprising, therefore, that football featured in the Settlement's programme from its early days and that links were forged there between upper-class and working-class football. When the Mansfield House Men's team played Eton Mission in the Federation of Social Clubs' competition in 1894 the referee was the solicitor P.M. Walters, a Charterhouse 'old boy' and an Oxford University 'blue' who had represented England at football on many occasions.[71] In 1900 an audience of 150 turned up at the Fairbairn House Boys' Club to welcome the Corinthian G.C. Vassell, 'who gave us a most interesting lecture on "Football" with lantern illustrations'.[72]

Following its success in winning the London Federation of Boys' Clubs football championship in 1902, Fairbairn House's achievements in Federation and LFA competitions were such that the claim, made by the club in the 1920s, of 'long held unchallenged superiority in football among London Working Boys' Clubs' was substantially true.[73] When West Ham United agreed to play a match against Fairbairn House Old Boys to raise funds in 1935, the team selected by the latter included a number of established professional players, and the two ex-Fairbairn House players who were linesman for the game were former England internationals John Townrow and Syd Bishop.[74]

A leaflet headed 'Fairbairn House: Club Talks', dated 1912, treats the subject of team spirit and can be best summarised by quoting its key paragraph:

> The club spirit is a good spirit without being goody-goody or over modest. It is a frank, open and manly spirit. It likes a bout with the gloves and glories in the struggles of the cricket and football field; but it keeps our sport clean and shows us how to take defeat with grace.[75]

Substitute 'school' for 'club' and there is nothing here that could not be taken as part of a sermon by the headmaster of a Victorian or Edwardian public school looking forward with relish to the new cricket or football season.

Public-school missions and boys' clubs

As early as the 1860s, Uppingham opened a mission in North Woolwich, which later moved to Poplar, and in the following decade Rev. Dr Linklater persuaded Radley to support the parish of St Peter's, Wapping.[76] Noticing that children had nowhere to play but the streets, an early contribution of the Mission to the area was to levy a subscription on Radley boys each term to meet the rent on a playground alongside the parish school in Wapping. A missioner was later appointed and accommodation for visiting Radleians was provided in St Gabriel's House. The League of Hope and the Church Lads' Brigade, which had already been established in the area, were taken under the wing of the Mission, which soon became prominent in local youth football:

> The Mission runs two football clubs, and a year or two ago a strange thing happened. The First Eleven ran to the final in their league, only succumbing in the final to the Eton Mission Eleven! So it is not only at Henley where Radley meets Eton in friendly rivalry![77]

The Malvern College Mission to Canning Town also had the Church Lads' Brigade under its wing and the club's football match reports in the local press appeared under the name of 'Malvern Mission C.L.B'.[78] An interesting feature of the activities of this club was that the boys made their own football boots and kept them in good repair.[79] The Leys School Mission to St Luke's, Whitecross Street, on the edge of the City, also dated from the 1870s. The staff at the Club, which later moved to new premises in City Road, offered play opportunities for both boys and girls, and found 'lots of chances to teach a lad that certain things are "not cricket" and that "cheating" is not part of the fun'.[80]

Other public-school missions in the London area dating from the 1880s and having football teams in Federation competitions and friendlies included those of Harrow in Notting Dale, Felsted in Canning Town, Marlborough in Tottenham and the Charterhouse Mission in Southwark. Charterhouse had already moved from the City to its new building in Godalming by the time the School's Mission was established in the area around Tabard Street, Southwark, in the1880s. Confronted with the poverty of the area, the provision of games facilities were not the first call on the missioners' time, but when a new mission building was completed towards the end of the century it included, besides a church and gymnasium, a 'cage' on the roof immediately above the boys' club premises. Given the scarcity of open space in that overcrowded area, this came to be the centre of football training at the Mission, and Charterhouse 'old boys' known to have visited it included General Baden-Powell, once the school's goalkeeper and founder of the Boy Scouts, as well as England internationals C. Wreford-Brown and G.O. Smith and several of the Corinthian FC.

Football and the Eton Mission to Hackney Wick

Bishop Walsham How recommended Hackney Wick as the location for the Eton Mission to the London poor that was proposed following his talk at Eton in 1880. At a series of meetings in that year, the Mission Council's Executive Committee, which was chaired by the headmaster, J.J. Hornby and included Edmond Warre, the future headmaster, agreed that funds for the Mission should be raised in the manner that each house master saw fit but that contributions should be voluntary. The Council also unanimously accepted Bishop How's recommendation for the location of the Mission, appointed Rev. William Carter as missioner and set about finding a suitable site for his operations. An early indication of the part that sport might play in the Misson's work in Hackney Wick is found in the minutes of a meeting in October, when it was agreed to appoint a sub-committee 'to consider means for carrying into practice the suggestions made at a Council meeting with regard to the supply of old footballs, etc.'. An indication that there was a wish to involve the boys in the school in ways other than as contributors to the Mission's finances is clear from the decision taken to permit them to be equally represented with masters on the Committee – they already had a majority on the Council.[81]

In his history of the Mission, Tim Card suggests that Warre was a dominant figure in its foundation.[82] While there is no evidence of Warre directing the activities of the Mission in a manner to ensure that games might be employed in the moulding of the character of boys in Hackney Wick in the way that they were at Eton, there was scarcely any need for him to do so, given the sporting background of so many of the early missioners and helpers and their obvious commitment to the value of games.

Carter, the son of an Eton master, had been successful at games while he was at the school, gaining honours in the College Wall and the Mixed Wall.[83] The Hon. and Rev. Algernon George Lawley, who was shortly to join him as a curate without stipend, was the son of Lord Wenlock, and while not making the Football XI at Eton, was good at the game and returned as a member of 'old boy' teams selected to play against the school.[84] Charles Granville Kekewich, another early helper, was the son of a judge and had gained his Eton colours at shooting, while Ernest Milbourne-Swinnerton Pilkington, the son of a Yorkshire baronet, was active as a trainer in several sports at the Mission, including rowing, for which he had earned his colours at Eton in 1877.[85] Pilkington's book, an entertaining and informative account of activities with boys at the Mission clubs in the 1880s, notes that Carter's brother Hugh, who often came to help, was 'an Old Carthusian football player of note'.[86]

After an inhospitable beginning, Carter soon established himself in the area, and while an immediate start was made in preaching the Gospel to the people of Hackney Wick, the primary purpose of the Mission, social welfare work to ameliorate the dreadful effects of the poverty of so many of the local inhabitants, was seen as an essential preliminary or accompaniment to any religious endeavours.[87] Club work with young people, which was started in a single room, expanded to take in a wide variety of both indoor and outdoor activities, which included early morning swimming in the Hackney Cut. This was essential preparation for those who wished to do rowing, for the coaching of which sport several experts were on hand besides Pilkington himself. Old rowing garments were sent from Eton 'to enable them to experience the benefit of changing for athletic pursuits'.[88]

Carter later recalled that Edward Lyttelton, county cricketer, England footballer as well as future headmaster of Eton and chairman of the Mission, used to come to play cricket in Victoria Park, situated a stone's throw from the Mission, but did not think much of the facilities there. Arthur Dunn, another Old Etonian who was capped for England at football, often came to the Mission to teach the boys football, although, rather than strict adherence to FA rules, Carter recalled, what was actually taught was 'more the Eton Field game'.[89]

In his 'Memorandum relative to the Eton Mission', which was included in Pilkington's book, Kekewich attributed the success of the Eton Mission teams in matches to the boys' speed and the fact that, rather than relying on the 'usual Association style of passing' all the team went for the ball in the manner of the Eton Field game. He went on to explain that when the team abandoned that style of play and conformed to the more usual pattern prevailing in football at the time, they were less successful.[90]

That there was little room for debate about the respective merits of the street football that the young players brought with them to the Mission's clubs and that played on regulation pitches by the Old Etonians is clear from a passage in Pilkington's book, where he is discussing practice games in Victoria Park on Saturday mornings:

> I have known many a lad join our club and be exceedingly angry because his name was not at once put down to play in a match. By attending a few ordinary games we would prove to him that he did not know quite everything he thought he did; and if he was a good sort, he would set about learning the right game without further trouble.[91]

The game the boys knew, and from which the missioners felt their charges needed to be weaned away, was probably a version of traditional football. This was the game that had survived for centuries as 'part of a colourful mosaic of folk games and pleasures, wakes and fairs, festivals and revels, which formed the popular recreational culture of the common people'.[92] It survived from medieval times through the Elizabethan period, despite becoming illegal, through the seventeenth century where contests between villages, though lacking in agreed or formulated rules to regulate play, demonstrated a rivalry between teams that remains a feature of the game.[93] The adoption and regulation of the game by the public schools has been related in Chapter 1, and the likely survival of the traditional pastimes in the East London area has been suggested by the exclusion of the 'rough element' from the sports day at Upton Park FC noted earlier in the present chapter.

The facilities in Victoria Park, that Lyttelton thought were so poor, were used by cricket and football teams from the Mission. Kekewich found the space allocated to football in the park adequate, but with no organised system for laying out or booking pitches, games could end in chaos, with one match encroaching on to a pitch being used by two other teams. Through the influence of some official, presumably of the Metropolitan Public Gardens' Association, Kekewich was able to take two gardeners around the park with him and, using measuring instruments, to lay out and number nine pitches, which were then balloted for weekly by the teams that normally used the park for matches.[94]

By the end of the 1880s the Mission's expansion in the area had extended on to its present site alongside the railway, donated by a friend of Bishop How, with a temporary church for Sunday and some weekday evening services, a Sunday School, Band of Hope and Temperance Guild, a Working Men's Club, a Girls' Club and of course a Boys' Club, at that time located in nearby Gainsborough Road.[95] Either because there were still problems with the use of Victoria Park or because of the expansion of the number of those wanting to play football, boys from the Mission, under the care of Rev. E.K. Douglas, the missioner who succeeded Carter in 1889, were playing the game on Hackney Marshes in November of that year. They were ordered off the open space by the cattle and sheep drovers, however, and had their goalposts confiscated, following which Douglas appealed to the Metropolitan Public Gardens' Association to use its influence to get permission for his boys to use the Marshes for football. The Association went further and arranged a meeting at the Eton Mission, attended by How, Douglas and several other local clergymen, as well as representatives of the LCC and the Hackney District Board (the forerunner of Hackney Council), for the purpose of making representations to the Board of Agriculture to have the 337 acres of Hackney Marshes placed under the control of the recently established LCC as a public open space. A public enquiry was held at Hackney Town Hall at which the Earl of Meath gave evidence in favour of the scheme, and this along with the efforts of G.B. Holmes, Hackney's representative on the LCC, influenced the latter to grant two-thirds of the £75,000 required to purchase the Marshes from the Lord of the Manor and its other owners, the remainder coming from the Hackney District Board, the Lord of the Manor and private subscriptions. The Hackney Marshes were eventually dedicated as a public open space in July 1894, and have remained so ever since.[96]

The temporary church was replaced in 1892 with the present St Mary of Eton and the Mission's area became a separate parish the following year. Five years later the laying of the foundation stone for Eton House marked the Mission's status as a settlement as well as a mission, with the hope expressed in the annual report that the House was intended 'to draw together the East and West – to contribute its small share to the solution of the great social problem, which requires before all things mutual knowledge and charity'.[97] Sport and the right club spirit was very much to the fore in the Mission's work with adults as well as youths. On noting the success of the Working Men's Club in football and rowing competitions in 1897, F.H. Rawlins reminded the Mission Council at Eton, with Warre in the chair, of the successful efforts of the Old Etonians, not only in training successful teams, but 'in fostering the right spirit among the members of the Club, which was sometimes so sadly lacking'.[98]

Ten years later, in an attempt at defining the aims of the Boys' Club, Mr Ponsonby, the missioner responsible for work with young adults between the ages of fourteen and nineteen, emphasised the importance of the missioners' influence in the formation of the boys' character, 'and personal experience only serves to confirm the belief that the one foundation upon which character may be securely built is that of sincere religious conviction'. Attendance at Sunday School for club members was not compulsory, but it was expected.[99]

The continued prowess of the Club at football is evident in the annual reports, that for 1912, for example, noting that Club teams won no less than six trophies, including a share in the Senior Cup for the Working Boys' Federation, when they played for a total of two hours and twenty minutes against the Harrow Mission without a winner emerging.[100] How the Club became independent of the Mission and evolved eventually into the Eton Manor clubs that became prominent in many sports, most particularly football and boxing, from the 1920s up to the 1960s is outside the scope of this book.[101] The possible influence of football at the Eton Mission from the 1880s on the origins of elementary-school football in Hackney is one of the issues which is considered in the next chapter.

Conclusion

Reflecting on comments made by Cambridge undergraduates to Canon Barnett to the effect that public-school missions had been a failure, Eager felt that in youth work the best of them had achieved something of lasting value, in that they 'passed down to emergent democracy what was finest in the Public School spirit...It bred the spirit of unity, the true bond of social peace, in the hearts of young men who ventured and understood.'[102] The evidence from this chapter is that this claim, insofar as it related to sport, was substantially true. For while an element of snobbery was evident in Upton Park's reluctance to recruit players from the working-class area that adjoined their pitch, no such exclusiveness was apparent in the teams trained by Hogg and Kinnaird at the Hanover Institute or in the clubs run by the university settlements and public-school missions, where missioners, helpers and local youths regularly played in the same team. High ideals of sportsmanship were evident in all the teams associated with public-schoolboys, from those at Upton Park through the Hanover Institute and Polytechnic to those of the university settlements and public-school missions. The war against cheating at the Leys School's Mission has been noted, as have Corinthian footballers' visits to the Charterhouse Mission and the sporting response to defeats emphasised in the Fairbairn House leaflet. It was the 'manly spirit', according to the writer of the Fairbairn House leaflet, which, while relishing the struggle on the pitch or on the canvas, generates the good sporting attitudes. For, as Eager pointed out, if the cricket match between the boys of the Eton Mission and the Harrow Mission at Lords showed the same spirit as that between boys from the two public schools at the same venue in their annual encounter, it was because of the work of the missioners in their boys' clubs:

> The spirit of a team impartially selected, the idea of playing the game for the game's sake were not indigenous to boys bred in the mean streets of 19th century urbanism. The Public School men had to overcome the Win, Tie or Wrangle spirit, and inculcate the basic idea of sportsmanship to be taken up later by the elementary schools.[103]

Before proceeding to an account of how teachers in elementary schools set about their task, it may be appropriate first to consider what was meant by the 'transmission' of ideas like those of club spirit and sportsmanship from public-school educated young men to the boys in the clubs founded by missions and settlements.

In his conceptual analysis of the terms 'transfer', 'transmission' and 'transformation' as they apply to one generation passing its culture on to the next, Harvey Siegal makes the point that the last term is more appropriate when what is passed on by parents and teachers is 'in significant ways changed in the very educational activity of passing it on'.[104] Could the missioners, university settlement residents and their public-school educated assistants who helped train teams and organise matches between boys' clubs in late nineteenth- and early twentieth-century London, in challenging traditional attitudes to football in working-class communities by insisting on standards of sportsmanship and endeavouring to create a team spirit resembling that which prevailed in public-school games, be seen as transforming the game in a sense that satisfied Siegal's criteria? It would appear that they could. For, having examined the factors that determine the issue of whether educators should favour cultural transmission, which consists of passing on aspects of culture as they stand at a particular time, and cultural transformation, which entails questioning the existing culture, Siegal concludes that education should strive to transform rather than merely transmit culture 'when culture stands in need of transformation'.[105] The Old Etonians associated with the Hanover and Polytechnic clubs and the gentlemen at Upton Park FC transmitted the spirit of sportsmanship and *esprit de corps* mostly by example. The contribution of the missioners and settlers was more direct. They saw that the football they promoted helped in forming a link with those to whom they had come to preach the Gospel. But they also saw that in training teams, organising matches and favouring particular attitudes towards the game, they had been presented with the opportunity of transforming the culture associated with football to one that resembled their own.

Notes

1 E.M. Hogg, *Quintin Hogg: A Biography* (London: Constable, 1904), pp. 30, 34–5.
2 Old Etonian Association, *Eton School Register*, 1905–06, 2, p. 73.
3 Q. Hogg, *The Story of Peter: From Bethsaida to Babylon* (London: Horace Marshall, 1900), p. 424.
4 Hogg, *Quintin Hogg*, p. 37.
5 Anon., 'A short sketch of the rise and progress of the Institute' in *The Polytechnic Magazine*, May 1896.
6 Eager, *Making Men*, p. 244; *Eton School Register*, 3, p. 14.
7 C.J. Montague, *Sixty Years of Waifdom or, The Ragged School Movement in English History* (London: Woburn Press, 1969 edn), pp. 34–6, 234.
8 Montague, *Sixty Years of Waifdom*, p. 252; Eager, *Making Men*, p. 251.
9 Hogg, *Quintin Hogg*, p. 58.
10 Q. Hogg, 'Polytechnics' in *Journal of the Society of Arts*, 35, p. 857.
11 Quoted in Montague, *Sixty Years of Waifdom*, p. 255.
12 E.M. Wood, *A History of the Polytechnic* (London: Macdonald, 1965), pp. 73–5.
13 L.C.B. Seaman, *The Quintin School 1886–1956: A Brief History* (London: Quinton School, 1957), p. 25.
14 W.C. March, *History of the Polytechnic Football Club* (London: The Polytechnic, n.d.), p. ii. I am grateful to Brenda Weeden, Archivist, University of Westminster, for allowing me to consult this and several other items in the University Archives, and for discussing Quintin Hogg's work with me.
15 *Home Tidings of the Young Men's Christian Institute*, January 1880.
16 Sarah A. Tooley, 'The Polytechnic movement: An interview with Mr Quintin Hogg' in *The Young Man: A Monthly Journal and Review*, May 1895.
17 F. Dawes, *A Cry From the Streets: The Boys' Club Movement in Britain from the 1850s to the Present Day* (Hove: Wayland, 1975), pp. 34–5.
18 Anon., *"They Made the Day": A History of the First Hundred Years of the Polytechnic Sports Club and Societies* (London: the Polytechnic, *c.* 1976). Kinnaird's physically rough way of playing football was described as 'robust' by those who admired him. Sir Frederick Wall, *Fifty Years in Football* (London: Cassell, 1935), p. 28.
19 Booth, *Father of Modern Sport*, pp. 108–18.
20 Green, *Football Association*, pp. 82–6, 493.
21 B.O. Corbett, *Annals of the Corinthian Football Club* (London: Longman, Green and Co., 1906), pp. 246–50.
22 *Stratford Express*, 4 April 1868.
23 The population of West Ham more than doubled between 1861 and 1871. E.G. Howarth and M. Wilson (eds), *West Ham: A Study in Social and Industrial Problems* (London: Dent, 1907), p. 6.
24 The main searches were in *Post Office Directory of Essex, Herts, Middlesex, Kent, Surrey and Sussex* (1879), *Post Office London Directory* (1879), and William White, *History, Gazetteer and Directory of the County of Essex* (1863). For the West Ham Board of Health, see *Victoria History of Essex*, 11, pp. 100–3. For an account of how the Park was acquired for public use, see Dr Pagenstecher, *The Story of West Ham Park* (London: Wilson and Whitworth, 1908) and for the owners of the land before it came into the possession of the Gurneys, see W.R. Powell (ed.), *West Ham 1886–1986* (London: London Borough of Newham, 1986), p. 48.

25 The photograph was reproduced in R.R. Lewis, *The History of Brentwood School* (Brentwood: Brentwood School, 1981) but the name was wrongly captioned as 'F. Wilson'. The notes for the book, preserved at the school, however, confirm that the player was F. Wilton. I am grateful to Michael Willis, Brentwood School Archivist, for arranging for me to visit the school and for allowing me to consult these notes and other material relating to football at the school.

26 R.J. Beevor, S.M. Gerrard and F.D. Windsor, *Alumni Felstedienses* (Felsted: Felsted School, 1948), p. 67. Wilson's obituary is in *East Ham Echo*, 15 January 1909.

27 A.E. Douglas-Smith, *The City of London School* (Oxford: Basil Blackwood, 1965), p. 540.

28 R.B. Gardiner (ed.), *The Admissions Register of St Paul's from 1748 to 1876* (London: George Bell and Sons, 1884), p. 340.

29 Beevor *et al.*, *Alumni*, p. 124.

30 N.L. ('Pa') Jackson, *Sporting Days and Sporting Ways* (London: Hurst and Blackett, 1932), p. 34; Gibson and Pickford, *Association Football*, 3, p. 37.

31 '1881 Census Project' (Genealogical Society of Utah).

32 T. Brown, *The Ultimate FA Cup Statistics Book* (Basildon: Association of Football Statisticians, 1994), p. 106.

33 D. Lamming, *An English Football Internationalists' Who's Who 1872–1988* (Beverley: Hutton Press, 1990), p. 260.

34 P.C. Adams, *From Little Acorns: A Centennial Review of the Old Foresters Football Club* (privately printed, 1976). I am grateful to Gerald White, School Archivist, for arranging for me to visit Forest School and consult the school records. G. Stott, *The History of Chigwell School* (Ipswich: W.S. Cowell, 1960), p. 106.

35 Lewis, *Brentwood School*, pp. 138, 181; M. Craze, *A History of Felsted School 1554–1947* (Ipswich: W.S. Cowell, 1955), p. 202. From an account of life at the school by the historian G.G. Coulton, who was there in the 1870s, it would seem that, compared to many schools, the attitude to games at Felsted was fairly relaxed. G.G. Coulton, *Fourscore Years: An Autobiography* (Cambridge: Cambridge University Press, 1944 edn), p. 73.

36 In 1875 'a well-known member of the Wanderers' visited and improved the game at the school. *The Felstedian*, 11 (October 1876), p. 37. I am grateful to Nicholas Hinde, Old Felstedian Liason Officer, for arranging for me to visit Felsted School and to read back issues of the school magazine.

37 Lamming, *Internationalists' Who's Who*, pp. 186–7.

38 Ibid., p. 176.

39 Ibid., p. 28.

40 *Stratford Express*, 17 March 1883, 23 April 1884.

41 Beevor *et al.*, *Alumni*, pp. 91, 117, 118, 124; M. Messiter, *Repton School Register 1564–1910* (Repton: Old Reptonian Society, 1910), p. 187; Douglas-Smith, *City of London School*, p. 540; E. Beevor, R.J. Evans and T.H. Savory, *The History and Register of Aldenham School* (Aldenham: Aldenham School, 1948), p. 21. The Upton Park team list is in *Home Tidings*, December 1881.

42 Additional lists used for this paragraph were E.M. Jameson, F.S. Porter, A.F. Radcliffe, C.C. Rice, J.L. Stokes and A.H. Tod (eds), *Charterhouse School* (Guildford: Charterhouse School, 1932); E.K. Milliken (ed.), *Brighton College Register (1847–1922)* (Brighton: Brighton College, 1922); *The Lancing Register: Eton School Register*, 3.

43 For Lambrick, see *Crockfords Clerical Directory* (1896), p. 791; for Duthoit, J.E. Venn (ed.), *Alumni Cantabrigienses* (Cambridge: Cambridge University Press, 1944), 2, p. 364.

44 Letter from Donald Shearer, 26 March 1998.

45 Jackson, *Sporting Days*, p. 34.

46 '1881 Census Project'.

47 Six Upton Park players were in the Corinthians in the 1880s. Corbett, *Corinthian FC*, pp. 25–7.

48 Russell, *Football and the English*, pp. 25, 27.

49 That Upton Park was virtually a London regional side rather than a local club may be inferred from the fact that no less than seven of the first team missed the Club's match against Clapham Rovers in 1884 because they were playing for the London representative team on the same day. *Stratford Express*, 6 December 1884.

50 A new attendance record was set at West Ham United's Boleyn Stadium when West Ham SFA played Liverpool in the final of the English Schools' Shield in 1921. Thirty-five thousand people, 20,000 of them schoolboys, watched the match. *Stratford Express*, 21 May 1921.

51 *Stratford Express*, 25 October 1884.

52 Ibid., 1, 19 November 1884.

53 *Toynbee Record*, November 1888.

54 S.A. Barnett, 'University settlements' in W. Reason (ed.), *University and Social Settlements* (London: Methuen, 1898), p. 26.

55 Eager, *Making Men*, p. 200; *The Eighteenth Annual Report of the Universities' Settlement in East London, for the year ending June 30th 1902*, p. 20. I am grateful to C.J. Lloyd for finding me this and other items relating to Toynbee Hall in the Tower Hamlets Local History Collection.

56 *Toynbee Record*, November 1892.

57 Ibid., November 1889, February 1890, November 1892.

58 J.A.R. Pimlott, *Toynbee Hall: Fifty Years of Social Progress 1884–1934* (London: Dent, 1935), p. 79.

59 Meacham, *Toynbee Hall*, p. 60.

60 S.A. Barnett, 'Holidays and schooldays' in Canon S.A. Barnett and Mrs S.A. Barnett (eds), *Practicable Socialism* (London: Longman, Green and Co., 1915), p. 78.

61 S.A. Barnett, 'The recreation of the people' in Barnett and Barnett (eds), *Practicable Socialism*, p. 61.

62 Ibid., p. 91.

63 In his exploration of the 'attempted cultural importation' of the settlers to their clients, Evans does not take any account of the sporting dimensions of the settlements' work with boys or youths. Tony Evans, 'The university settlements, class relations and the city' in G. Grace (ed.), *Education in the City: Theory, History and Contemporary Practice* (London: Routledge & Kegan Paul, 1984), pp. 139–58.

64 W. Picht, *Toynbee Hall and the English Settlement Movement* (London: Bell and Sons, 1914), p. 66.

65 F. Wright, 'F.C. Mills and the Broad Street Clubs' in *East London Record*, 13 (1990), pp. 19–20.

66 'Broad Street Club, Ratcliff, Record Book 1887–1927', Tower Hamlets Local History Archives, TH 8192/2.

67 I am grateful to Fred Wright for this and a wealth of other information he has provided in connection with the clubs, including the two letters, which are cited with permission.

68 Anon., *The Oxford House in Bethnal Green 1884–1948* (London: Oxford House, 1948), pp. 30–1.

69 *Mansfield House Magazine*, December 1997.

70 J.M.G., 'Percy Alden, M.A.' in *Mansfield House Magazine*, July 1892.

71 Lamming, *Internationalists' Who's Who*, p. 259.

72 *Mansfield House Magazine*, April 1900.

73 Newham Local Studies Archives, VFE/WES/360.

74 Ibid.

75 Ibid.

76 Tozer, 'The readiest hand', pp. 323–4; Cooper, 'Public School Missions', p. 151.

77 Cooper, 'Public School Missions', p. 152.

78 The Malvern Mission C.L.B. beat local rivals St Mary's (Plaistow) C.L.B. to win the 1903 Battalion final. *Stratford Express*, 14 February 1903.

79 Cooper, 'Public School Missions', p. 125.

80 Ibid., p. 44.
81 Min. Eton Mission (Committee) of 23 March, 4, 23 June, 7, 25 July, 25 October 1880. These minutes, along with those for the Mission Council, are on microfilm at Hackney Archives. I wish to thank David Mander, Archivist at Hackney Archives Department and Mrs P. Hatfield, Archivist at Eton College Library, for help in tracing material related to the Eton Mission.
82 T. Card, 'History of the Eton Mission' (Typescript in Hackney Archives, 211 MAR), p. 2.
83 *Eton School Register*, 3, p. 69; *Eton College Chronicle*, 12 December 1867.
84 *Eton School Register*, 4, p. 45; *Eton College Chronicle*, 31 October 1878.
85 *Eton School Register*, 4, pp. 82, 84.
86 E.M.S. Pilkington, *An Eton Playing Field: A Reminiscence of Happy Days Spent at the Eton Mission* (London: Edward Arnold, 1896), p. 13.
87 M. Chapman, *St Mary of Eton with St Augustine, Hackney Wick (The Eton Mission): A History 1880–1980* (London: The Church, *c.* 1980), p. 14.
88 Pilkington, *An Eton Playing Field*, pp. 36–7.
89 W.M. Carter, 'The Eton Mission in Hackney Wick 1880–1891' (Typescript in Hackney Archives, 211/MAR), p. 14.
90 Kekewich piece is in Pilkington, *An Eton Playing Field*, p. 113.
91 Pilkington, *An Eton Playing Field*, pp. 82–3.
92 James Walvin, *The Only Game* (London: Pearson Education, 2001), p. 23.
93 Marples, *A History of Football*, pp. 19, 21, 24–40, 42, 63, 86–7.
94 Kekewich in Pilkington, *An Eton Playing Field*, pp. 114–15.
95 Chapman, *St Mary of Eton*, pp. 15–17.
96 Sir J. Hutton, *Dedication to the Public of Hackney Marsh* (London: LCC, 1894), pp. 3–6.
97 *Eton Mission: Sixteenth Annual Report*, p. 11.
98 Min. Eton Mission (Council), 10 October 1897.
99 *Eton Mission: Twenty Seventh Annual Report*, p. 20.
100 *Eton Mission: Thirty Second Annual Report*, p. 14.
101 I am grateful to Les Jolly for many informative letters about Eton Manor, which had ten football teams in the 1930s and to Graham Phillips for information on successful players at the club. I am also grateful to R. Gould, Manager, Villiers Park, Bicester, for allowing me to consult the records of the Eton Boys' Club.
102 Eager, *Making Men*, p. 225.
103 Ibid., pp. 209–10.
104 H. Siegal, 'Education and cultural transmission/transformation: Philosophical reflections on the historian's task', *Pedagogia Historica*, Supplementary Series, 2 (1996), p. 28.
105 Ibid., p. 40.

3 Elementary-school football in London, 1885–1900

Introduction

In Chapter 1 it was explained that while the introduction and development of drill and physical exercises in the elementary school in the late nineteenth century has been traced in considerable detail by several writers, there has been no equivalent treatment of the attempts to introduce and develop outdoor games in the same schools. George Sharples, writing in 1898, might have been exaggerating in his claim that the early SFAs sparked a movement 'which has done more for the real physical well-being of the boys of this country, than all the drill and calisthenic exercises yet introduced'.[1] There is no doubt, however, that the provision of outdoor games was of equal educational significance to the provision of drill and other physical exercises. Building on Chapter 2, where it was found that a climate favourable to games for working-class children had been established in some parts of London by youth workers associated with university settlements and public-school missions, the present chapter investigates the origins, growth and achievements of the first SFAs formed by elementary-school teachers in the London area in the 1880s and 1890s. It also examines the work of the LSFA, founded in 1892, which helped co-ordinate and extend the work of those SFAs.

The section "The First Elementary Schools' Football Associations" examines the traditional claim of the South London SFA to have been the first SFA in the country and considers the case for an earlier association in the East End. The section "The Work of the First SFAs" recounts how football was organised as an extra-curricular activity in elementary schools, how inter-school matches were arranged and leagues formed by the SFAs and how teachers confronted the many problems associated with these innovations. The section "The London Schools' Football Association" traces the origins and early development of the LSFA, in particular its role in standardising rules for schoolboy football in the London area, arranging inter-association competitions and selecting a LSFA representative side to play other cities. The section "London Schoolboy Football at the Turn of the Nineteenth and Twentieth Centuries" assesses the achievements of the LSFA and the SFAs affiliated to it at the turn of the century, focusing in particular on how the work of teachers taking teams was perceived and on problems associated with the provision of pitches.

The first elementary schools' football associations

Inter-school football matches took place in London elementary schools several years before SFAs were formed. There was a team at Battersea Park in 1877, for example, run by Major R. Stokoe and J.W. Melton, while W.J. Wilson introduced football to Oldridge Road, Balham after his appointment as headmaster of the school in 1882. These two schools and a handful of others, including Hazelrigge Road, Clapham and St Mary's, Balham, were playing inter-school matches from around 1882.[2] Encouraged by the success of these friendly matches, Wilson arranged a preliminary meeting at his school in September 1885 with a view to forming a SFA. While only three other schools were represented at the preliminary meeting, the inaugural meeting the following month drew representatives from ten schools, with a further five expressing an interest in taking part. A.J. Sargeant of St Mary's, Balham, had been appointed chairman and Wilson secretary at the preliminary meeting and in October it was agreed that the committee of the new organisation, which was to be known as the South London SFA, would consist of two representatives from each affiliated school. Membership was to be open to all voluntary and board schools in the South London area only, on payment of a fee of five shillings. Players' names had to be on their school roll and 'no Paid Monitor, Candidate or Pupil Teacher will be eligible to play in any match whatsoever'. An inter-school challenge trophy was introduced, with the fourteen entries divided into two geographical groups, East Lambeth and West Lambeth, for the first round only, with an open draw for the succeeding rounds.[3] The early work of the Association in providing opportunities for competitive football for South London schoolboys will be recounted in the section "The Work of the First SFAs" along with that of other associations, while the remainder of this section will examine the claim that South London was the first SFA in the country.

In his article on schoolboy football published in 1905, H.J.W. Offord made two important observations on the origins of the 'thoroughly good football' he saw boys being trained to play in elementary schools. One was that the first inter-district schoolboy match was played in 1888 and the other was that the South London SFA claimed the honour of being 'the pioneer school organisation'.[4] The first observation remains unchallenged: the match, between South London and Tower Hamlets schoolboys, was played at the Beaufort House ground in Chelsea, and details of the organisation of the event have survived in the minutes of the South London SFA.[5] Offord, a teacher at Stroud Green in North London who was himself active in promoting the game among elementary-school pupils at the time, was aware that his second observation – South London's claim to have been the first SFA – was more problematical. There were, he wrote, 'rumours of another association that, in those early days, operated in the district of Tower Hamlets'. What might this association have been?

The Tower Hamlets SFA was founded in 1888 and Oban Street School, Poplar, won its first championship, that for the 1888/89 season.[6] However, as the records of the Tower Hamlets SFA were destroyed by bombing during the Second World War and as no early handbooks have survived, there is no way of knowing if it was founded as a genuinely new association, a continuation of an older association under a new name or an amalgamation of older associations, one of which might have formed the basis of the rumours referred to by Offord. Local newspaper reports of the time indicate that the rumours might have had some substance.

The *East End News* in 1897 noted that the Tower Hamlets SFA's chairman, Sir Edmund Hay Currie, had held his post for 13 years, a length in office that would take the first year of the Association back to 1883 or 1884.[7] The *Football 'Sun'*, published on Saturdays, was the football section of the *Sun* newspaper. It carried a regular column on schoolboy football in London around the turn of the century, signed by 'Marcian'. It is clear from the content that while the writer was not a teacher, he approved of what teachers were doing for football and took every opportunity to highlight their work. At the beginning of the 1899/1900 season he quoted from the Tower Hamlets SFA handbook to the effect that the Association was then entering its sixteenth season. This, again, would place the date of origin at 1884 or 1885 at the latest.[8] These reports suggest that either the Tower Hamlets SFA was in existence well before 1888 or that some other association or associations organising schoolboy football within the area must have preceded it and must have been connected with it in some way. A report on the presentation of the Poplar SFA in the *East End News* in 1887 noted that the Association had been founded a year earlier, which would have made it 2 years older than the Tower Hamlets SFA. In his speech at the presentation, Major Welby, a prospective parliamentary candidate who had donated a trophy for the winning team, said that while the entry of eight schools for the competition was a good one, he had been told that at nearby Shadwell, 'where a similar association had been in existence for about three years', there had been an entry of ten schools for a similar competition.[9] Again, we are taken back to the years 1884 or 1885.

A search through local newspapers for 1884 and 1885 failed to reveal anything on the activities of a SFA in the Shadwell area, but, as schoolboy football events were very erratically reported before the mid-1890s, this could not be taken as disproving its existence.[10] No log books for schools that might have belonged to a football association in Shadwell have survived, and no other evidence for its existence, besides that given above, has come to light. While being far from conclusive, the evidence is certainly sufficient to prompt a reconsideration of South London's claims. The South London SFA's claim to be the oldest SFA still in existence remains unchallenged, although the South Londoners' stronger claim made in 1922 that their Association was 'the first of its kind' may have to be modified.[11]

The work of the first SFAs

While there may be some uncertainty about which SFA was the first to organise matches for elementary-school pupils, there is no doubt that several such associations were in existence in the London area by the time the LSFA was founded in 1892. Besides South London and Tower Hamlets, four other associations were represented at the LSFA's inaugural meeting: Finsbury, Greenwich, Marylebone and West Ham. Two other associations, those of Hackney and West London, were in existence at that time but did not send representatives to the meeting. Hackney did, however, take part in the LSFA's first competition in the 1893/94 season, as did Woolwich, an association that first sent representatives to a LSFA meeting in 1893.[12] In addition to these nine associations, there were smaller ones like those of Poplar, which, falling within the wider geographical area of Tower Hamlets, acknowledged the larger association's right to provide the team for LSFA competitions, and continued to work in harmony with it.[13] While football matches were played between elementary schools in parts of London not covered by the associations mentioned here, it is with the activities of these ten associations in the late 1880s and the 1890s that the remainder of this section will be mainly concerned.

All the early SFAs had the primary aim of providing opportunities for elementary schools to play football against each other in competitive situations, leading in all cases almost immediately to the formation of challenge trophy or league competitions. In the case of the Shadwell association, as has been noted, ten schools were said to have entered their competition, no other details of which have been traced. Fourteen teams were in the draw for the first South London SFA challenge trophy competition in 1885, eight were in the Welby Shield competition for Poplar schools in 1886–87, the same number were in West London's first championship four years later, twelve schools were in the first Hackney competition in 1892 and twenty-eight contested the Tower Hamlets SFA trophy in 1888/89, the first season the event was held.[14] The trophy for the South London SFA championship was paid for by voluntary subscriptions from affiliated schools, Nunhead Passage, Oldridge Road and Heber Road, for example, each contributing half a guinea towards its cost.[15] Major Welby provided the shield that bore his name for the Poplar competition.[16] Medals for the boys on the winning teams, and sometimes for the runners-up, seem to have been presented by several associations from the outset, with the South London SFA purchasing a die in 1887 to imprint the association's initials on all its medals.[17] Other associations followed suit in presenting trophies and medals, as, when a gentleman in Edmonton promised a set of medals for the best schoolboy team in the area in 1905, the local paper remarked that Edmonton was the only district that had not presented medals for schoolboy competitions.[18]

While the attitudes and achievements of Harry Earle and Cornelius Beal, the two prominent figures in the early years of the West Ham SFA, will be explored in their biographies in Chapter 5, here it may be noted that the idea to found a SFA in West Ham did not come from either of them but from Thomas Wyles, a teacher in Odessa Road, in 1888, although the official inauguration meeting did not take place until two years later.[19] Earle's Godwin Road won the first West Ham SFA championship in 1890/91 and Beal's Park won it the following season. Played on a league basis, the competition included three schools from Leyton, Cann Hall, Mayville Road and Newport Road, who continued to play in West Ham SFA competitions until the Leyton SFA was formed later in the decade.[20]

Playing full back for Park's 1891/92 team was the first of many players from the school who would go on to feature prominently in senior football at a high level. This was Charlie Dove, who later played with the Thames Iron-works in Canning Town, the club associated with Arnold Hills that was shortly to become West Ham United.[21] Canning Town took part in the West Ham SFA's third championship in 1892/93 and had the 12-year-old Dick Pudan among their players. After a playing career that included an appearance on the Newcastle team that lost the FA Cup final to Wolverhampton in 1908, he had a successful career in football management.[22]

Byron Street, the most prominent school in the early competitions organised by the Tower Hamlets SFA, had changed its name from Bromley St Michael's when it came under the control of the SBL in 1878. Its headmaster was Robert Wild, an opponent of the Revised Code of 1862 and a tireless advo-cate in the cause of improving the position of elementary-school teachers, who later became president of the National Union of Teachers (NUT).[23] Although the local press carried detailed reports on the educational achieve-ments of Wild on the occasions of his retirement in 1906 and his death in 1916, there was no reference in either to his interest in or attitude towards schoolboy football.[24] His known interest in the promotion of swimming, the fact that he was a past student of St Mark's College, Chelsea, where so many of the teachers involved in London schoolboy football at the time had been trained and his presence at the Poplar SFA's presentation evening in 1887, when his wife pinned the winners' medals to the football shirts the boys were wearing, suggest that he may have made some contribution to Byron Street's prominence in the early years of the Tower Hamlets SFA.[25] Beaten finalists in the Tower Hamlets SFA's first championship in 1888/89, Byron Street won the title for the two following seasons, but failed to retain it in 1891/92, even though they had in their team a boy who was to make a considerable mark in professional football in the years before the First World War.[26] This was Fred Bevan, who played on the right wing, the position he occupied for Millwall Athletic when he made his debut with the professional side in 1899.[27] His long career in the game included 2 years with Manchester City and five at Clapton Orient, where he was selected to represent the Football League in 1910 and was club captain in 1911/12 and 1912/13, when Orient narrowly failed to gain promotion to the First Division.[28]

The origin of the Hackney SFA was unusual in that the man who initiated it and became its first treasurer, Frederick E. Tozer, was a school manager rather than a teacher. James Hart, the first president, announced at the inaugural meeting that he was not much good at football but was a good 'looker on', while the first secretary, R. Cook, a teacher in London Fields, organised the first competition which was to take place during the opening months of 1892.[29] Reporting on the success of the competition in a letter to the *Hackney Gazette*, in March 1892, Tozer announced that the final between Wilton Road, Dalston and Mowlem Street, Bethnal Green had been arranged 'on a special ground granted by the London County Council near the drinking fountain in Victoria Park'. It may be wondered if this was one of the pitches measured out by Kekewich of the Eton Mission and his two assistants nearly ten years earlier, as related in Chapter 2. Another possible link between the Eton Mission and the Hackney SFA is the fact that the first known matches between elementary schools in the area featured the team from Sidney Road, located near to the Mission in Hackney Wick.[30] Wilton Road not only won the first final, but retained the trophy, presented by Sir Charles Russell, the local MP, every season throughout the decade with the exception of 1897/98, when they shared it with Rushmore Road, South Hackney. The work of J.R. Schumacher, the teacher who trained the team at Wilton Road, is examined in Chapter 5.

As the minutes of the South London SFA committee have survived for the period 1885–90, more is known about that association's activities, the teachers who organised them and the boys who played in the matches, than about those of any other SFA at the time. The competition organised by the committee, mentioned earlier, was won by W.J. Wilson's Oldridge Road, who beat Battersea Park in the final at Tooting Common in February 1886.[31] It was agreed to retain the same format for the challenge trophy the following season, when the entries increased to seventeen, one of them arriving by telegram in the course of the meeting but after the draw had been completed! It was agreed to accept the late entry and repeat the draw, an indication, perhaps, that the committee were eager to include the maximum number of schools.[32] One of the newly affiliated schools, Goodrich Road, Dulwich, beat Gideon Road, Lavender Hill, in the final the following season. The final two seasons later (1888/89), contested by the same two teams, was of particular interest in that it offered a glimpse of another link between football in the public schools and that in the elementary schools. It was refereed by P.M. Walters, an Old Carthusian and a member of the Corinthian FC. The minutes of a meeting at the end of 1888 noted the committee's agreement to invite him to take charge of the game, although there is no information on who was to make contact with him.[33] A later minute records that, besides refereeing the game, Walters had criticised each boy's play in detail, offered advice on how to improve it and had also expressed himself 'as being thoroughly delighted at the capital manner in which both teams played the game'.[34]

In the same season it was agreed to introduce a preliminary competition for all schools except Gideon Road, Goodrich Road, Oldridge Road, the Orphanage and St Mary's, Peckham. This was the committee's response to the inequalities between school teams that had become apparent in the first three seasons of the challenge trophy, when some teams beat others by scores in excess of twenty goals, which must have been demoralising to the losers. The winning team in the preliminary competition received a football and, along with the runners-up, was permitted to enter the challenge trophy with the exempted teams, while the remaining schools went on to compete against each other again for a junior trophy.[35] Despite financial constraints that compelled them to pen a letter to schools asking teachers to make a contribution to the Association's funds, members of the committee voted to spend two guineas on a trophy for the junior competition.[36]

Very little was recorded in the minutes of the South London SFA about the actual conduct of matches, although one entry noted that, when a complaint was received over a boy's rudeness in a school game, the committee agreed 'that a letter be sent to all members of the C'tee not present at this meeting, asking them to caution their boys as to their behaviour during any match'.[37] Nor was teachers' behaviour always beyond reproach. When Sarjeant complained about the conduct of a colleague who was in charge of the Blackheath Road team when his school met them in a fixture in 1890, the committee supported him and unanimously carried a motion that 'strongly condemns the action of the Umpire and boys of the Blackheath Road team'.[38] The umpire was presumably the teacher-in-charge and it is to be regretted that no details of the nature of his unacceptable conduct, and that of his pupils, was minuted.

Having organised an efficient inter-school championship, with a preliminary competition designed to minimise heavy defeats of weak teams by strong, the South London SFA committee next directed its attention to forming a district representative side and finding teams for it to play against. An East Lambeth against West Lambeth annual fixture was established in 1887, with teams selected from affiliated schools, with H. Cavill of Nunhead organising the team for the East and Wilson taking charge of that from the West.[39] This no doubt made selection of the team for the first representative match relatively easy. The match, against Tower Hamlets, was the first played between district schoolboy teams, as noted earlier. Following that match, contact was made with a teacher in St Mary's, Aston, with a view to taking a team to Birmingham to play a match during the NUT's conference in that city in 1889. Sarjeant was appointed to take charge of the team, but negotiations broke down when it was ascertained that the South Londoners were expected to pay all expenses for the trip.[40] As inter-school football matches had been organised in Aston and Birmingham for some years by 1889, it must be considered an impediment to the national development of schoolboy football that a fixture between boys from two of the major centres where it was practised at this early date did not materialise.[41] Instead, a match against Chatham schools was arranged for the Easter weekend.

South London played a return fixture against Tower Hamlets in 1890, but the most adventurous event in schoolboy football that year was South London's journey to Sheffield to play the local association, which had been founded the previous year. While the Sheffield FA had eventually modified its rules to conform with those of the English FA in 1877, the rules of the

Sheffield SFA were slightly different from those of the South London SFA in that the goals were lower and narrower and the ball was smaller. The South Londoners seem to have had no difficulty adapting to the changes, however, as they won the match 1–0 before a crowd of 10,000 at the Olive Road ground. The size of the crowd at the return match at the Kennington Oval was not recorded, but it must have been considerable, as the contribution made to the Teachers' Orphanage Fund amounted to £100, a sum equivalent to the annual salary of a teacher at the time.[42]

That a NUT charity should have been the recipient of the considerable sum raised at the match at the Oval and of the more modest amount made on the Chatham match the year before is not, perhaps, surprising, in view of the fact that nearly all the teachers who attended the inaugural meeting of the South London SFA were members of either the West Lambeth or the Lambeth branches of the National Union of Elementary Teachers which became the NUT from 1889. C.J. Chase from Basnett Road, who was on the first South London SFA Committee in 1885, was the incoming president of the Lambeth branch.[43] Other Committee members included H. Cavill, who was representing Nunhead, the school attended by the pupils at the Teachers' Orphanage at Peckham Rye and Major R. Stokoe, who was representing Battersea Park and who had been on the Orphanage's Administrative Council since 1878.[44]

'The educational authorities of the time looked coldly on the project', wrote the anonymous author of the South London SFA's souvenir history in 1935, 'and that willing and valuable support now so freely given was then altogether wanting'.[45] No details were supplied, but it is interesting to note that while the minutes record the names of those who sent donations and agreed to become vice-presidents, a local MP and a locally elected Member of the SBL 'regretted their inability to subscribe'.[46] It is perhaps difficult to understand why, given the SBL's advanced attitudes towards physical training, gymnastics and swimming in its elementary schools, as outlined in Chapter 1, its South London representatives should have shown so little enthusiasm for the voluntary efforts of teachers to extend the provision of children's physical and recreational activities. It was not the disapproval of games, however, that dictated the Board's elected members and school managers' reservations about their introduction in elementary schools. Rather, it was what Colonel Onslow, in an address to SBL managers in 1890, called 'the many insuperable difficulties which stand in the way of the majority ever getting a chance of playing these outdoor athletic games'.[47] The assumption must be that, fearing the obstacles that would confront any attempt to provide inter-school sporting events for children in its schools on a London-wide basis, taking into account the cramped conditions of the playgrounds in so many schools and the scarcity of pitches in the heavier populated areas, it was thought better to withhold official support for any initiatives in inter-school football. Always sensitive to accusations of overspending, the vast expense involved in providing facilities for games for all its pupils must have tempered the Board's approval of outdoor games. As will be shown in the section "London Schoolboy Football at the Turn of the Nineteenth and Twentieth Centuries", there were politicians, school board members and school managers, especially in the East End, who spoke positively of the value of football for elementary-school pupils and at least one HMI expressed his approval of school football clubs. This was A. Rankine, who, in commending the appointment of a new headmaster to Canning Town, a particularly difficult school under the control of the West Ham School Board, expressed his view that with his local knowledge 'the school promises to move forward. The successful establishment of a Football Club is already a step in the right direction.'[48]

The attitude of the SBL may usefully be contrasted with the position in the Birmingham area. From the early 1880s football and cricket clubs in elementary schools were encouraged by the Birmingham School Board, and while the Board did not have the power to allocate funding for equipment for these clubs, its officials took a lead in raising voluntary subscriptions for this purpose. To supervise the activities of the clubs, the Board established a Physical Exercises Committee, consisting of Board members and others with a knowledge of sport in the area and a commitment to its value to young people. The Committee had sub-committees for swimming, gymnastics, cricket and football. While the sub-committee for football was initially interested in competitions between schools that took the form of contests in individual skills like kicking and dribbling, by the middle of the decade these contests were taking the form of inter-school football matches.[49] While a SFA for elementary schools under the control of the Birmingham School Board was established in Birmingham in 1892, it came considerably later than those in London because the initiative, as far as can be determined, had been taken by the School Board. On the other hand, teachers in schools in the Birmingham area that were run by the Aston School Board, which showed less enthusiasm for school sport than its neighbouring Birmingham Board, got together in 1886 to raise funds for a trophy for a football competition for elementary schools under the Aston Board.[50]

The London Schools' FA

As district matches between SFAs, and between schools that were affiliated to different associations, became more frequent, there was occasionally confusion over minor points with regard to the rules of play. This led the officers of the South London SFA to arrange a meeting in October 1892 aimed at standardising the way inter-school and inter-district matches were conducted in the London area. The rules agreed by the representatives of the six associations at the meeting were mainly those of the South London SFA, to which reference has already been made, with an additional rule that set the age of boys eligible to play at under-15 on 1 September of the school year in which a match took place. Ages of pupils eligible to take part in matches will be considered in Chapter 4, in the context of the introduction of new competitions. Copies of the rules were sent to all SFAs in London for their comments. A more important outcome of the meeting was the establishment of the LSFA as an organisation to co-ordinate the running of schoolboy football in London. Representatives from South London took a leading part in the new organisation from the outset. Wilson was appointed secretary, Sarjeant was acting chairman until he was succeeded by the permanent appointment of Stokoe, who remained in office until his death in 1909.[51]

At a further meeting of the LSFA in December the rules were approved, the only amendments being that a minimum size for pitches was to be stipulated – 80 yards by 60 yards – and that a crossbar (rather than rope or tape) should be compulsory for inter-association matches. There was a discussion at the meeting about the possibility of a competition involving one or two teams from each association and of a match between sides from north and south of the Thames.[52] Nothing seems to have come of either, but at a meeting in July 1893 it was agreed to hold an inter-association competition the following season (1893/94). As five of the associations were situated to the north of the Thames (Finsbury, Hackney, Marylebone, Tower Hamlets and West Ham) and three were to the south (Greenwich, South London and Woolwich), Tower Hamlets was 'selected' to join the teams south of the river to make two qualifying groups of four. Group matches were to be played on a league basis, with the first and second placed teams going through to the semi-finals.[53] Wilson was able to secure a trophy from the Corinthian FC, which was called the Corinthian Shield. Twelve years later Offord, in his article in *The Book of Football* wrote that 'the ambition of every London schoolboy footballer has been to help his district to win the Corinthian Shield'.[54] Except for a gap of 6 years during the Second World War, the Shield has been contested by London districts every season from 1893/94 to the present.

The first winners of the Corinthian Shield were South London, who beat Woolwich in the final. Two of South London's four goals were scored by Tommie Fitchie, who, still only twelve, was eligible to play for the district for several more seasons. Born in Edinburgh in 1881, his family moved to London when he was nine and sent him to Hazelrigge Road, Clapham, where E.W. Foskett, who had been active in South London schoolboy football from 1888 or earlier, was the teacher who trained the football team. Fitchie joined West Norwood when he left school and had many offers to turn professional but refused them. He played as an amateur with Queen's Park (Glasgow), Woolwich Arsenal and Fulham. He earned four caps for Scotland and was in the Woolwich Arsenal team that reached the 1906/07 FA Cup semi-final, where the Londoners lost to Newcastle.[55] Also in the South London team was Herbert Rainbird, who signed as a professional for Tottenham Hotspur in 1902.[56] Percy Sands was a defender for Woolwich in the final and was to go on to defend for Woolwich Arsenal in many important matches, including that with Fitchie in the 1906/07 FA Cup semi-final. For many seasons he was able to combine the career of footballer with that of schoolmaster.[57] Jack Hills, who later scored for Clapton Orient in the London Senior Cup final in 1901/02, was also in the Woolwich team.[58]

Woolwich reached the final the following season, but under unusual circumstances. West Ham and South London met in the 'first' final, which ended in a draw, whereupon South London withdrew from the competition. West Ham's opponents in the 'second' final, played at the Queen's Club, West Kensington, were Woolwich. The winners, West Ham, were presented with the 'handsome shield' and three cheers were given for the Corinthian FC's encouragement of football in schools.[59] The reasons for South London's withdrawal have not been discovered, but it may well have been that, as became apparent later in the decade, the committee placed more importance on completing inter-school fixtures than on the performance of the district team. There could be no doubting South London's success the following season (1895/96), when, with Fitchie scoring exactly half of their thirty-six goals in the competition, the South Londoners easily beat Leyton in the final.[60] Both the aggregate number of goals and Fitchie's contribution to it were exceeded the following year, when South London again qualified for the final, this time to meet West Ham at the Crystal Palace on the morning of the FA Cup final. Many early arrivals among the supporters of Aston Villa and Everton watched the schoolboy match. They saw a drawn game, with goals from Stares (West Ham) and Fitchie (in his fourth season playing in the competition) and excellent goalkeeping by West Ham's Wilding, who was later to play for Clapton in two FA Amateur Cup finals.[61] South London won the replay, after what their Association's historian called 'a desperate finish'.[62] West Ham were back in the final again the following season (1897/98), this time against West London, whose win gave them the Corinthian Shield for the first time.[63]

In the Corinthian Shield, as in other football competitions, a good player can play for a poor team, and the East Ham side that was beaten 10–0 by Tower Hamlets on Millwall's pitch on the Isle of Dogs in 1899 had a boy named George Hilsdon at centre half. He later played for West Ham United and Chelsea and, in gaining the first of eight England caps as a centre forward in 1907, became the first ex-LSFA player to achieve this honour.[64] South London and West Ham again contested the final that season (1898/99), with the former winning the match, played at Woolwich Arsenal's Manor Ground in Plumstead. West Ham's local newspaper picked out Arthur Winterhalder from Odessa Road and Harold Halse from Park as their defeated team's two best players. Winterhalder went on to play for West Ham United and Preston North End, while Halse, having first, like Winterhalder, established a reputation in local amateur football with Wanstead FC, went on to gain the unique distinction of playing in three FA Cup finals with three different clubs, Manchester United (1909), Aston Villa (1913) and Chelsea (1915).[65]

Halse was in the Park team that won the first London championship for individual schools in 1899. First discussed in 1892, the rules of the competition, for which a trophy was secured from Sherif Dewar and which were introduced at the end of the 1898/99 season, allowed one entry only from each affiliated association. This was normally the school that won the association's championship, and the opening round of the Dewar Shield was not usually held until late in the season to enable each district to conclude its senior competition. With seven of the West Ham district side in the team, Park beat Eltringham Street, Wandsworth, South London's representatives, in the first final.[66]

As noted earlier, South London had a match with Sheffield in 1890 and the fixture became established as an annual event in the 1890s. The London game was usually played at the Oval, although when the Sheffield boys travelled south during the Christmas holidays in 1896, the match had to be played on the Baseball Ground, Balham, because the Oval was not available. 'The Sheffielders had evidently heard of him', wrote the *Football 'Sun'*, referring to Tommie Fitchie, whom they had closely marked throughout the game, which Sheffield won 5–1.[67] Given the long-established contact between the Sheffield and South London associations, it is rather surprising that it was Leeds rather than Sheffield that was chosen as the opponent for West London, Corinthian Shield Winners in 1897/98, in a match at Cambridge during the 1899 NUT Conference.[68] Billed as a clash between the north and the south, the West London boys won 4–0, but, despite the defeat, the Leeds SFA invited an all-London team to play them in a return match. As no date could be fitted in so late in the season, it was agreed that a LSFA team would go to Leeds the following season (1899/1900).[69]

Tottenham was the leading district in London schoolboy football in the 1899/1900 season, having won the Corinthian Shield by beating West London in the final, played at Captain James' Ground, Walham Cross. The victory was hailed by the local paper as 'a fitting prelude to the arrival of the Southern League Cup in Tottenham'.[70] With seven of the Tottenham district team attending Page Green and the same number of West London boys at Halford Road, these players were already familiar with each other's method of play when they met in the Dewar Shield final for individual schools at the end of the 1899/1900 season. Halford Road won the match 2–0. In a manner quite uncharacteristic of the reporting of schoolboy football matches at the time, the *Tottenham and Edmonton Weekly Herald* took the defeat in a poor spirit, unhappy that the final at Shepherd's Bush should have been played so far away from Tottenham and on a playing surface 'quite unsuited to the style of football for which the team are so well known'.[71] A tribute to the high standard of football played at Page Green and to Charles Cook, the teacher who trained the team there, was later written by William Pickford of the FA Council, so it is not perhaps surprising that four boys from the school were in the LSFA team selected to travel to Leeds.[72]

In its remarks on the LSFA team, the *Football 'Sun'* noted that only one player, Shelley, the captain, came from a school under the control of the SBL, roughly the area covered later by the Inner London Education Authority and represented in the ESFA's inter-county events today by the Inner London County SFA.[73] All the other boys attended either church schools in the 'inner' London area which were not under SBL control or went to schools in 'outer' London boroughs which had their own school boards. This was not to be typical of LSFA teams, however, and of the fifteen selected the following season, six came from schools run by the SBL. There were no South London players in the 1899/1900 team, presumably because they were not eligible on account of South London SFA not entering a team for the Corinthian Shield that season. This was because the number of fixtures involved in the Corinthian Shield would have taken up too many Saturdays and interfered unduly with their own inter-school competitions. Geoff Shelley, who later played for Clapton Orient, was among the outstanding players in the LSFA's 8–1 win over Leeds and a *Yorkshire Post* reporter wrote that one of the Londoners' goals 'could not be surpassed by a First League team'.[74]

London schoolboy football at the turn of the nineteenth and twentieth centuries

Though less than 8 years old at the turn of the century, the LSFA had established itself as the largest schoolboy football organisation in the country. SFAs taking part in the Corinthian Shield included East Ham, Finsbury, Greenwich, Hackney, Leyton, Marylebone, South London, Tottenham, Tower Hamlets, Walthamstow, West Ham, West London and Woolwich. Most associations regularly nominated a school as their representative in the Dewar Shield competition. A representative side had been selected and although it had played one match only by the end of the nineteenth century, representative matches were to become a regular feature in the LSFA's activities in the early years of the twentieth century and have continued to the present day, with almost 300 LSFA representative teams having played against cities, counties, provinces and countries. In addition each of the affiliated associations had at least one competition for schools within its district, and some had several, with leagues graded to provide evenly matched opponents. Schools in affiliated associations varied in number from the thirty that belonged to the South London SFA to less than ten each in the Walthamstow and Leyton associations.

   Given the large number of school and district teams and the fact that by the turn of the century most of the competitions had taken the form of leagues, which entailed far more matches than the early knock-out trophy events, there must have been a great number of teachers prepared to train school teams and organise and control matches. In one association alone, Tower Hamlets, there were six pitches in use on Saturday mornings in Victoria Park between the beginning of October and the end of March. With three matches often scheduled for each pitch, there must have been as many as thirty teams in action in the course of the morning, with, presumably, a teacher-in-charge of each team. A reporter from the *Football 'Sun'* visited Victoria Park on a Saturday morning in October 1899 and found an abundance of schoolboy players and a happy atmosphere.[75] Acknowledgement of the efforts of teachers occasionally appeared in Marcian's column in the *Football 'Sun'*, with particular credit given to those who organised and trained teams in destitute areas like the riverside parishes of the East End, as may be witnessed in this report at the end of 1899:

> I am glad to see such very poor scholars as Cable Street and at the Highway holding their own in the competitions, and it says very much for the self sacrifice of the teachers that such should be the case. It required some energy to raise a football team out of the very raw material at their disposal, and there are evidently some real sportsmen in the division.[76]

A note in the *East Ham Echo* a year later identified one of the frustrations of running a school team in such areas, a frustration often echoed today by teachers who run teams in inner-city schools. 'Sandringham Road', it ran, 'have very bad luck in their players. They come from an unsettled district, where there are constant removals, and it is always the best football boys who leave the area.'[77] But even in schools where the movement of families was relatively low, there were problems for teachers running teams when boys reached the age or standard that permitted them to leave school. Byron Street had a strong team in the 1894/95 season, but struggled to maintain the lead in the Tower Hamlets SFA league when seven of their first choice players left school between Christmas and Easter, 1895.[78]

Even without such problems, the demands on the time of teachers taking teams were considerable. In a report on a match played against a visiting team from Luton at the end of 1895/96, the *East End News* wrote that it was the last of the Christmas holiday fixtures played by Glengall Road, the hosts, others having been played against Rushmore (Hackney), Park (West Ham) and Hale Street (Tottenham).[79] A.H. McVea was a teacher in the Orphan Working School that had won the Marylebone SFA championship on several occasions in the 1890s and in the course of 7 years took the team in a total of 163 matches, but had to stop taking it 'because of the pressure of private work'.[80] Given the hours that must have been spent on football by McVea and the teacher in charge of the team at Glengall Road, it may be wondered if the story told about W.J. Wilson, the driving force behind the foundation of the South London SFA and the LSFA, is more than apocryphal. His many commitments to football left him few evenings at home. Having occasion to punish his young son for some misdemeanour before leaving for work one morning, the son, on the father's departure, enquired of his mother as to what right 'that man' had to punish him, evidently believing his chastiser to have been one of his mother's lodgers![81]

Teachers were rarely named in newspaper reports of matches unless they were LSFA officers, secretaries of local associations or the trainers of particularly successful school teams. W. Nugent's work is known, for example, because he was secretary of the Tower Hamlets SFA, and, in addition, trained some good teams at Marner Street, Bromley-by-Bow. Jack Hilsdon, one of his pupils, went on to play with Clapton Orient and his younger brother George, already mentioned, had played for Marner as an 11-year-old before the family moved out to East Ham in 1897. Another Marner player from the 1890s, Bill Bridgeman, went on to play for West Ham United and Chelsea and remained in professional football up until the First World War. The benefits of Nugent's football work for the boys was acknowledged by his headmaster in the school log book.[82] Pride in the school football team's achievements was evident at Oban Street, Poplar, where, on St George's Day, 1894, the boys 'wore their attendance and football medals', and at Glengall Road in the Isle of Dogs, where 'a particularly pleasing feature' of a gathering for parents at the school in 1896 was the presentation of the trophies for both the Tower Hamlets and Poplar championships.[83]

A more detailed examination of the work of a number of teachers engaged in promoting football is undertaken in Chapter 5, but here it may be considered whether there were any advantages to be gained by teachers besides the compliments they might receive from their headmasters or the satisfaction of seeing their pupils enjoy the fresh air or take pride in their achievements. 'Cases have been known', the *Football 'Sun'* wrote in 1898, referring to teachers taking school football teams, 'where such work has been the means of bringing substantial benefit in the way of promotion.'[84] The newspaper frowned upon this form of motivation for teachers who trained teams, but there were other motives that might have been thought only marginally more honourable. Among them was the wish to be associated with famous players. When George Hilsdon's goals for Chelsea brought him to the attention of the England selectors in 1907, *Football Chat* wrote sardonically that every footballing schoolmaster in East London was claiming the new international to have been 'one of his boys'.[85]

More generous appraisals of the work of teachers and what they were thought to be achieving through football may be gleaned from local newspaper accounts of SFA meetings and presentation evenings in the East End. Contrasting sharply with the poor responses teachers in South London received to their pioneering work in promoting football, these tributes to the work of teachers and the value of what they were achieving for East End boys in promoting football, did not of course represent the official policy of the SBL. They indicate, however, that several individuals with an interest and involvement in education under-stood the value of outdoor games many years before they became part of the elementary-school curriculum. They also offer evidence that some educationalists saw football as a means of transmitting to the elementary-school pupils some of the benefits of a public-school education.

At the 1887 presentation evening for the Poplar SFA, to which reference has been made earlier, Major Welby, having first recalled his own footballing days at Eton, told the boys that if they wished to get on in the world they must com-bine work and play. By playing such 'manly games' as football, he continued,

> England had been enabled to send her sons all over the world, and to bear the cold of Canada, the heat of India, and the varied climates of Australia, the Cape Colony, and other countries. (Cheers) It would be more than

sufficient return to him if those who had taken part in the competition for the shield would take into life with them pleasurable recollections of the game.[86]

After the boys had received their medals and the Major had presented Byron Street with the shield that was named after him, local Liberal MP Sydney Buxton moved a vote of thanks to his political opponent for his attendance and in the course of his speech referred to his electoral rivalry with Welby as 'their little game of football'. Turning to the achievements of the boys, he repeated Welby's sentiments on the value of games:

> It was always a great pleasure to him to see boys competing in manly games which had done so much to make Englishmen Englishmen indeed, victorious wherever they went, and respected all over the world. The Duke of Wellington once said that the Battle of Waterloo was won on the playing Fields of Eton. In Major Welby they had one who had been in the playing fields of Eton, and who would know how to beat the enemy – he meant, of course the foreign enemy, and not the enemy at home.[87]

At the meeting to celebrate its first season of activities in April 1889, the Tower Hamlets SFA's first chairman, Sir Edmund Hay Currie, who had also been the first vice-chairman of the SBL, attributed the success of the Association 'to the good feeling existing among the teachers'. He introduced Sir John Colomb, MP, who said the boys should be grateful to the masters who gave up so much of their time to train teams and organise matches and went on to draw attention to what he considered to have been the value of games. 'He looked to education to make good men', he was reported as saying, 'and outdoor games formed a very important part of education. The East London schools were following the good example set them by the great public schools.'[88]

Speaking at the Tower Hamlets SFA's presentation at the end of the 1896/97 season, the Hon. Lionel Holland, Old Harrovian, barrister and local politician, also paid tribute to the teachers, 'whose labours extended far beyond the curriculum of the classroom'. He went on to say that Lord Harris' remark that cricket had made Englishmen what they were, ought to be extended to include football. For football, he said,

> gave us a whiff of the health and vigour of country life which no other sport could do in the crowded metropolis. It stimulated both the mental and the physical faculties. The players were the gainers – as was also the country at large – as it made them better citizens, and it developed pluck, endurance, and skill of the first rank, preparing them for the roughs and tumbles of after life, and enabling them to strive manfully to the goals of their ambition.[89]

Speaking during the course of the same function at the end of the following season, local politician G.L. Bruce remarked that when he saw boys striving to master the skills of football, 'he could not help thinking what a training, both morally and physically, they were going through, which would make good men of them in days to come'.[90] A Mr Howard, who distributed the prizes on this occasion, emphasised that football was a game that brought out the best in a boy, who needed to be 'plucky and unselfish' to succeed at it. Football was also, he said,

> the means of drawing the children of a school closer together, and healthy emulation was fostered. The outcome of the discipline of the football field was that in a great many instances the best footballers were the best scholars, and it also made the lads self reliant.

No evidence has been found of teachers making similar pronouncements to those made by politicians on the physical, moral, social, militaristic and imperialistic aspects of their work in running teams and organising matches and it may be wondered how much they might have agreed or disagreed with the sentiments expressed. On the one hand, teachers may have invited the politicians to such events to hear them articulate sentiments they may have been too modest to claim themselves. On the other hand, they may have considered it to have been so much rhetoric they had to listen to in return for the support of politicians for their work in promoting outdoor games at a time when school boards were reluctant to make a commitment to them for reasons already noted.

Evidence might also be found in the politicians' pronouncements for Hargreaves' contention that teachers taking school football teams were contributing to an apparatus of social control akin to that of the public-school missionaries and the uniformed youth movements, all forming part of what he refers to as an 'athleticist technology' designed to promote social harmony by keeping youth, in particular working-class youth, under control. Having noted the promotion of drill in schools 'for disciplinary rather than therapeutic purposes', and the advance of competitive swimming in schools, Hargreaves continues:

> But the really significant way the state schools promoted sporting activity among working-class people was through the extra-curricular initiatives of teachers, who took on themselves the role of youth workers, as a strategy for controlling their pupils' free time, with the objective of making them more amenable to school discipline. In 1885 teachers were thus responsible for the formation of the South London Football League and by 1890 there were highly competitive schoolboy leagues up and down the country.[91]

A few reservations may, however, need to be made. The first relates to the moral, social, militaristic and imperialistic characteristics that the politicians saw that football was capable of developing in elementary-school pupils. These did not differ much from those that a public-school housemaster of the same period would have been pleased to see developed in his pupils as a result of their exertions on the playing fields. A second reservation is that, while Hargreaves may not be wrong about the South London teachers taking football teams in order to make the boys more amenable to school discipline, there is nothing in the minutes of the South London SFA for the period between 1885 and 1890, which have survived in full, to suggest that this might have been one of the objectives of the teachers who founded the Association and organised its first competitions, let alone the main one. And from an extract from the South London SFA handbook for 1899–1900, one of the few pronouncements written by teachers on the subject that have survived, it is clear that the imposition of school discipline was by no means a major aim in those teachers' declared perceptions of what they were trying to achieve in their work for schoolboy football. For, while proud of the success of their teams and of the money their Association had raised for charity:

> It is still more proud of the lasting good conferred upon the lads in the schools. The more cordial relations between school and school, and between teachers and taught, and the physical benefits derived, are apparent; but the game has no less surely enforced the lessons of courage, self-reliance, decision and unselfishness which must have made an impression on the 10,000 scholars interested in the South London Association.[92]

Not all the energy in the promotion of schoolboy football in London came from teachers and not all the teachers were men. There was a strong team at Princess Frederica, Kensal Rise, at the turn of the century, affiliated at that time to West London SFA, but shortly to become part of the newly formed Willesden SFA. The *Football 'Sun'* expressed surprise to learn that all the teachers in the school were women, something more unusual then than now. While not wishing to take anything away from the women, without whose commitment a school football team would have been impossible, the success of the team in competitions may have been due to the fact that the father of one of the boys in the team was the trainer at Queen's Park Rangers.[93] As noted earlier, the man who called the meeting where the Hackney SFA was founded, and who became its first treasurer, was a school manager. The Tower Hamlets SFA's treasurer was also a school manager. This was F.C. Mills, a manager of Broad Street School, whose work in founding the Broad Street Club was discussed in Chapter 2. Mills' first settlement work in East London was under the direction of Canon Barnett and it was probably through his influence that Toynbee Hall provided a trophy for the junior section of the Tower Hamlets SFA league.[94] As manager of a board school active in football, founder of a youth club that had its origin in the Settlement movement, the donor of a trophy for a schoolboy competition and, as will be seen later, an active member of a campaign for better playing facilities in the London area, Mills represented an important link between the Settlement movement in the 1880s and the SFAs of the 1890s.

While professional clubs like Tottenham Hotspur and Woolwich Arsenal and amateur clubs like Clapton, London Caledonians, Grosvenor, as well as the Surrey County Cricket Club at the Oval, were prepared to allow their grounds to be used for district matches, this use was usually restricted to major fixtures like semi-finals, finals or prestigious games like those between South London and Sheffield. There were some other successful attempts to secure private grounds. The Tufnell Park Syndicate that ran Caledonian Park in North London was reluctant to let the ground for Marylebone SFA matches because 'the great fear has always been that the younger spectators would get out of hand, and in some way damage the syndicate's property'. When the pitch was eventually let for schoolboy matches in 1899 it was found that spectators were well controlled and the Syndicate's fears unfounded.[95] Munster Road, a school prominent in West London SFA competitions, was adventurous enough to ask permission to play matches in the Bishop's Park in Fulham and received a reply from the clerk to the Vestry of the parish of Fulham saying the school could use the pitch on Mondays and Wednesdays between twelve and one o'clock when the ground is 'fit to play'.[96]

Most district and almost all inter-school matches took place on pitches in public open spaces like Peckham Rye, Tooting Common, Victoria Park or Wanstead Flats. In 1893 the *East End News* reported that the LCC was attempting to drive schoolboy footballers from Victoria Park and asked its readers to 'agitate for a reinstatement of schoolboy rights! They haven't a vote yet but will have in a few years' time.'[97] The ban was only temporary, however, and later in the decade, when Hackney Marshes was opened up for football through the campaign initiated by the Eton Mission, as related in Chapter 2, adult matches were relocated there and Victoria Park came to be used exclusively for schoolboy football.

The Rev. E.K. Douglas of the Eton Mission, who had initiated the campaign that led to Hackney Marshes being made available for football, was a member of the Eastern District Sub-Committee of the LPFS, which had been founded in 1890 'to encourage and keep alive within the London area the peculiarly English sports of cricket and football'.[98] Chaired by the Old Etonian and cricketer, the Hon. E. Chandos Leigh, the list of vice-presidents included C.W. Alcock, Quintin Hogg and Tom Pelham and the members included Percy Alden of the Mansfield Settlement, Canon Barnett of Toynbee Hall, F.C. Mills, who was representing both the Tower Hamlets SFA 'and Boys Clubs' and Harry Richman of Byron Street, at that time secretary of the Tower Hamlets SFA. Committed to the idea that the provision of playing fields was as important 'for the development of one who gathers what education he can in London streets as for the public school boy or undergraduate', the Society's four district sub-committees identified the need for increased facilities for games in almost every part of London. Funded by subscriptions and donations, and working in harmony with elected local authorities, the Society set about extending the spaces allocated to games in existing parks and open spaces and providing new playing fields where a pressing need was seen for these. Other benefits to footballers and cricketers of all ages were provided by the Society through schemes like that organised by the Eastern Sub-Committee, which persuaded the directors of the Great Eastern Railway to grant reduced fares from Liverpool Street Station to those using the Society's pitches at Chingford and Wanstead Flats.[99] This must have been of particular benefit to schools in the Tower Hamlets and West Ham associations, as the train from Liverpool Street to Forest Gate (for Wanstead Flats) stopped at Stratford and Maryland Point, stations easily accessible to many 'football' schools. Individual members also received support from the Society in raising funds for particular projects, as in the case of Douglas Eyre, who, at the beginning of 1896 reported to the Committee that he had received promises of £2,000 towards providing the playing fields in Walthamstow that now bear his name and on which LSFA matches continue to be played today.[100]

Judged as a link between the football brought to working-class areas by ex-public-schoolboys and that introduced into elementary schools by SFAs, the most significant figure in the LPFS was perhaps Lord Kinnaird. 'Football was his life from his earliest days at Eton', wrote Geoffrey Green about the man whose career as player, trainer and administrator spanned the period from early controversies over the laws of the game (he would have retained 'hacking') to agreement to hold the FA Cup final at Wembley, although he died just before the first final that actually took place there in 1923. Trainer of the younger team at Hanover United, as noted in Chapter 2, he came into the LPFS in 1890, 3 years before becoming president of the LSFA, a position he held until 1920. Though himself a product of the public-school traditions of football, he was sympathetic to the adoption of the game by all social classes. To be president of the LSFA and a campaigner for better playing facilities for cities at the same time as he was president of the Football Association was perhaps appropriate, therefore, for a man who, to quote Green again 'lived only for what was good in the game and in the brotherhood of men in the field of sport'.[101]

The great number of clubs using Regent's Park was noted by the Northern Sub-Committee of the LPFS in 1891, but there was no danger of over-use.[102] 'Take advantage of every spell of fine weather to play off your rounds', advised the Marylebone SFA's handbook for 1899–1900, 'the smallest shower may prevent play being allowed in Regent's Park'.[103] Matches were cancelled there at the end of 1899 because of the weather and with Parliament Hill Fields also out of use at the time, it is hardly surprising that, with football in the area virtually at a standstill for two months, the Marylebone team lost heavily to Tottenham in the Corinthian Shield early in 1900.[104] A new superintendent in Regent's Park improved matters to the extent that 4 years later it was reported that schoolboy matches were allowed to go ahead there even when referees had reservations about the suitability of the pitches for play![105]

Despite cancellations due to the weather and other reasons, most associations seem to have managed to finish most of their fixtures and it is rare to hear of a schoolboy competition at the time that was not completed. There can be little doubt that the work of SFAs was instrumental in increasing the demand for playing facilities in the London area. The increasing use of Peckham Rye by the South London SFA was likely to have been a factor that led to calls for an extension of the playing fields there, something that was achieved in 1894.[106] Many of the pitches used had been the venues for traditional pastimes. Cricket had been played at London Fields as early as 1802 and at Tooting Common, laid out by the Metropolitan Board of Works in 1875 and the venue for many South London SFA fixtures from 1886, the ancient privileges of the local inhabitants were retained 'in the use of the common for recreation and village sports'.[107]

Pitches for matches between districts in Corinthian Shield games and between schools representing districts in the Dewar Shield continued to be a problem on occasions, presumably because a team would be reluctant to permit opponents to travel across London unless the use of a suitable pitch was assured. Plashet Lane, East Ham's representative in the 1899 Dewar Shield, for example, had to withdraw because of 'the difficulty of securing a ground' and Tower Hamlets had to withdraw from the Corinthian Shield in 1897/98 because a suitable pitch could not be found for group matches, although Millwall came to the rescue the following season when the professional club's pitch on the Isle of Dogs was lent for a match against Walthamstow.[108] Pitches for schoolboy matches were often inadequately marked out, so much so that referees often refused to award penalty kicks, in line with a FA ruling that penalties should not be awarded when pitches were not properly marked. There was even concern that the penalty kick might disappear altogether from schoolboy football.[109]

Finally, as regards pitches available to schoolboys in the London area, it may be appropriate to explore the possibility of a relationship between schools taking a prominent part in competitions and their proximity to playing fields, something that was found to have been the case in Birmingham.[110] The lists of participating schools for Finsbury, Greenwich, Marylebone, West London and Woolwich in the 1890s are incomplete, as are details of the pitches used. While the names of the schools that took part in the early South London competitions are recorded, information on the pitches used for matches is sparse in the minutes because the home team for each game had to find a pitch, rather than have one allocated by the Association. Of the ten SFAs with which this chapter is concerned, therefore, relevant information is available on four only, Hackney, Poplar, Tower Hamlets and West Ham.

Of the ten schools that were regular participants in Hackney SFA competitions, three, Gayhurst Road, London Fields and Wilton Road were close to London Fields, where, as noted above, football matches were played from the early 1800s. Daubeney Road, Sidney Road and Gainsborough Road were alongside Hackney Marshes, officially open for football from 1894, and Rushmore Road, Lauriston Road and Mowlem Street were within easy reach of Victoria Park. Proximity to playing fields seems to have been less of a factor among the schools that were prominent in competitions organised by the Poplar and Tower Hamlets associations. Among the pioneering schools in football in these two overlapping associations, Byron Street, Oban Street and Marner Street were a considerable distance from Victoria Park, the venue for most fixtures, and Broad Street in Ratcliffe and Glengall Road in the Isle of Dogs were even further. St Leonard's Road, Bromley, was about a mile away and only Monteith Road and Atley Road could be described as conveniently situated for matches in Victoria Park.

West Ham reflects the position in Hackney rather than that in the Tower Hamlets and Poplar associations. Earle's Godwin Road boys had only a few hundred yards to walk to reach Wanstead Flats for training and matches and in fact almost all the schools that entered the first West Ham championship in 1890/91 were located in the northern half of the borough and within easy reach of the Flats. They were joined the following year by Park, which had its own pitch. Godwin Road and Park dominated West Ham schoolboy football throughout the period under consideration in this chapter, and might be taken as evidence that proximity to playing fields was an important factor, not only in participating in schoolboy football competitions but also in winning them. It needs to be remembered, however, that the teachers who took the teams in those two schools, Harry Earle and Cornelius Beal, were perhaps the two most enthusiastic in the borough: their teams were likely to have been of a high standard no matter where their schools were located.

Beal was secretary of the West Ham SFA when it was unable to have the fixture list for the 1898/99 season printed because of a deficit of £4 in the association's funds. To help him, South London agreed to play a friendly at the Old Spotted Dog Ground during the Christmas holidays to raise funds. A crowd of 1,000 came to watch, even though the weather was so bad that part of the roof of the stand was blown off by the wind.[111] Besides the cost of pitches, local associations had to budget for medals for winning teams and usually for the runners-up. When resources would not extend to this, local benefactors would sometimes step in. When Dr Clarke, an advocate of schoolboy football in the East End over a period of many years, heard that the funds of the Poplar SFA were not sufficient to purchase medals at the end of the 1894/95 season, he 'generously promised to provide medals himself' and even invited the winning team to tea at his house.[112] From the regret expressed by those approached by the South London SFA that they were unable to make donations, mentioned earlier, it may be inferred that a subscription to the Association's funds was either a condition of becoming a vice-president or that at least some kind of contribution to funds was expected. But a SFA could not function on such donations or inter-association matches like that at the Old Spotted Dog, arranged purely to raise funds. Their main source of income was the fee paid by each affiliated school. Much as affiliation fees were needed, however, they were not accepted indiscriminately. When Gideon Road failed to affiliate to the South London SFA in 1889/90, a committee member offered to pay the affiliation fee for them so that the school could be included in the draw for the cup competitions, to take place that evening. The committee refused the offer and the draw was made without Gideon Road. The commitment of the school to taking part was seen as more important than the affiliation fee.[113]

Besides paying an affiliation fee to their local association (which in turn paid an affiliation fee to the LSFA), individual schools had to find money for travel costs, hire of pitches and kit. Donations came from various quarters. When a local clergyman visited Oban Street in 1894 he made a gift of five shillings to the school football team.[114] Old Etonian and prospective parliamentary candidate Herbert Robertson visited London Fields in 1892 and 'presented the (school) Football Club with jerseys and a new ball'.[115] In the more prosperous area of Kensal Rise in 1898, the team at Princess Frederica's, 'by the kindness of their friends...are fully equipped with boots, shirts and knickers'.[116] But schools generally could not rely on such donations. Boys in many schools put on functions to raise money for their teams. 'A special lantern show for the Football Club' was recorded in the log book for Marner in 1897, for example, with an admission fee of one penny.[117] Parents and managers sometimes helped. An entry in the log book of Oldridge Road in 1887 recorded that a successful entertainment was put on by friends of the school 'on behalf of the Cricket and Football Clubs'.[118]

In addition to income from fees paid by its affiliated SFAs, the LSFA had honorary officials who made regular annual contributions to its funds. One of its vice-presidents gave a guinea (£1.05) and two others half a guinea each to the LSFA for the 1907/08 season. Lord Kinnaird, chairman of the FA and President of the ESFA, also contributed half a guinea. An entry of two guineas from Leopold de Rothschild, a patron of the LSFA, appears regularly in LSFA balance sheets in the early years of the nineteenth century. The same balance sheets show small returns from the 'gates' at Corinthian Shield matches. The clash between South London and West Ham in 1907/08, for example, showed a profit – 15 shillings and seven pence (78 p).[119] There were even smaller returns from individual school games in the Dewar Shield, but finals, especially between teams representing adjoining districts, could often attract substantial numbers. When Wilton Road (Hackney) played Eltringham Street (South London) in the semi-final of the Dewar Shield in 1909/10, a profit of only 5 pence (2 p) was made on the match, but the amount paid at the gate for the final between Wilton Road and William Morris (Walthamstow) the same year was almost £1 and that for the replay was more than half as much again.[120]

Surviving evidence suggests that the single greatest source of income for the LSFA was that from inter-city matches. When Edinburgh Boys came to play the LSFA team at Craven Cottage in 1907, for example, the professional club charged only a nominal amount for the use of the ground. Paying for the visitors' accommodation was nearly £60 and other expenses related to the game came to around £25. Nevertheless, as advance sales of tickets and takings at the gate on matchday came to £180, a large profit was assured. This was a particularly profitable fixture that season. The match against Glasgow Boys, played a month earlier at Woolwich Arsenal's Manor Road Ground, made a profit of just over £10.[121] Some matches made almost no profit at all for reasons outside the control of the organisers and on one occasion at least there was a substantial loss. The attendance was less than expected at Craven Cottage in 1910 because of the death of King Edward VII on the day of the match.[122] When a Glasgow side came to the same venue in 1912 the weather was so bad and the attendance so poor that the LSFA, hoping to pay the profits from the match into the Titanic Disaster Fund, in fact lost more than £46 on the fixture.[123]

Despite the continuous struggle for resources, schools and SFAs were proud of their financial independence. In 1900 the SBL introduced a regulation that made it necessary for all money for charitable purposes collected in schools to come under the control of a committee consisting of school managers and teachers. When a West London school management committee tried to interfere with funds collected at a football match, the LSFA took up the case and Thomas Pear, the secretary, was able to persuade Thomas Gautrey of the SBL that the regulation needed to be amended to exclude contributions to school football teams, cricket clubs and similar organisations.

Conclusion

The pioneering work of teachers in providing competitive football matches for elementary-school teams has been considered in detail in this chapter, based largely on the minutes and handbooks of SFAs and on local newspaper reports of games and presentation evenings. These testify to the amount of voluntary work undertaken by the teachers to bring about something they saw as being of value to their pupils. While early SFAs expressed regret at the lack of official support from school boards that they might have expected for such useful work on behalf of their pupils, they nevertheless persisted, confident, perhaps, that they were not in any way acting contrary to the wishes of their employers. Rather, the SFAs were supplying something that, in an ideal world, would have been provided by school boards. Indeed, many individual members of school boards, managers of schools, local politicians, MPs and local clergymen, especially in the East End, came forward to offer support in the form of complimentary speeches at presentation evenings, donations of trophies and medals and occasional contributions to the funds of school football clubs. It was as if school boards were saying that schoolboy football was a good thing when undertaken on a voluntary basis, but the prospect of providing it for all children in urban areas as part of a school board's educational provision was unthinkable because of the financial implications. They could also, of course, have been convinced that voluntary efforts were superior, and in the long term more productive than provision by school boards. That such a view was sustainable might have been illustrated in the case of Birmingham. The development of schoolboy football in that part of the city where it was initiated by the Birmingham School Board seems to have been slower than in the area under the control of the adjoining Aston School Board, where it was not, and it was with the latter rather than the former that South London SFA made contact in 1889 when it wanted to arrange an inter-city match against Birmingham.

Several links have been established between the football played in elementary schools and the organised football introduced into working-class areas by the university settlement and public-school mission movements. There is, however, insufficient evidence to suggest that SFAs were a product of the public school inspired movements and it was only in the activities of the LPFS that the two seemed to have been working together towards the common cause of providing more playing fields in urban areas. That public-school attitudes to games, imbibed by teachers at their training colleges, might have been one of the motivational factors that inspired teachers to promote schoolboy football is an issue that will be explored in considering the biographies of teachers in Chapter 5. Before doing so, however, some of the wider implications of the work of SFAs will be considered, in particular their role in helping to secure the acceptance of outdoor games as part of the elementary-school curriculum.

Notes

1   G. Sharples, 'The organisation of games out of school for the children attending public elementary schools in the large industrial centres, as voluntarily undertaken by the teachers' in *Special Reports on Educational Subjects*, 2. P.P. 24 (1898), p. 160. Sharples had founded the Manchester SFA in 1889.

2   South London SFA, *The Half Century: A Souvenir* (London: South London SFA, *c*. 1935), p. 13. I owe a debt to the late Fred Newton for providing me with a copy of this item and for sharing with me his memories of some of the pioneering teachers of South London schoolboy football, several of whom were still active in promoting the game when Fred began his own 70 years of service to schoolboy football in 1923.

3   Min. South London SFA, 30 September, 20 October 1885. I am grateful to Terry Richards for allowing me to consult the minutes and handbooks of the South London SFA.

4   H.J.W. Offord, 'Schoolboy football' in *The Book of Football* (Westcliffe-on-Sea: Desert Island Books edn, 1973), p. 151.

5   Min. South London SFA, 18 December 1888.

6   Tower Hamlets SFA, *Programme of Entertainment*. Printed for the presentation at the end of the 1892/93 season, the programme lists players and previous winners of the trophy. Tower Hamlets Local History Archives, Poplar Box 825.

7   *East End News*, 6 November 1897.

8   *Football 'Sun'*, 6 November 1899.

9   *East End News*, 10 June 1887.

10   The newspapers were the *East End News* and the *East London Advertiser*.

11   ESFA, *Handbook 1922/3*, p. 6.

12   Min. LSFA, 14 July 1893. I am grateful to Reg Winters for permission to consult the minutes and handbooks of the LSFA.

13 When Poplar SFA was unable to hold its own championship in 1898, its trophy was presented at the Tower Hamlets SFA to 'the best team in Poplar'. *East End News*, 9 April 1898.

14 Min. South London SFA, 20 October 1885; *Chelsea Football Club Chronicle*, 22 February 1911; *Hackney Gazette*, 21 February 1892; *East End News*, 10 June 1887, 25 March 1889.

15 Min. South London SFA, 20 October 1885.

16 *East End News*, 10 June 1887.

17 Min. South London SFA, 1 February 1887, 31 January 1888.

18 *Tottenham and Edmonton Weekly Herald*, 6 January 1905.

19 West Ham SFA, *Diamond Jubilee 1890–1950* (London: West Ham SFA, *c.* 1950), p. 6.

20 Cann Hall continued to take part in West Ham SFA competitions for some years after the Leyton SFA was formed.

21 The Park team is listed in *Stratford Express*, 31 October 1891. For Dove, see Hogg and McDonald, *West Ham United Who's Who*, p. 59.

22 For Pudan, see Hogg and McDonald, *West Ham United Who's Who*, p. 168.

23 For a brief history of the school in the nineteenth century, see *East End News* 12 February 1898. The school still exists as Langdon Park Comprehensive.

24 *East End News*, 26 June 1906, 11 February 1916. Wild was chairman of Poplar Swimming Club.

25 The referee and one of the umpires at the final of the first Tower Hamlets SFA championship final were from the Old St Mark's Club. *East End News*, 22 March 1889.

26 *East End News*, 21 March 1890, 20 March 1891.

27 Lindsay, *Millwall*, pp. 152–3.

28 Kaufmann and Ravenhill, *Leyton Orient*, p. 104.

29 *Hackney Gazette*, 14 December 1891.

30 The log book records the team as playing their matches 'with neighbouring schools'. Sidney Road School (Boys) Log Book, 27 March 1888. LMA, EO/DIV4/SID/LB1.

31 Min. South London SFA, 5 February 1886.

32 Ibid., 12 October 1886.

33 Min. South London SFA, 18 December 1888.

34 Ibid., 2 April 1889.

35 Ibid., 2 October 1888.

36 Ibid., 6 February 1889.

37 Ibid., 30 November 1887.

38 Ibid., 4 February 1890.

39 Ibid., 19, 31 January 1888.

40 Ibid., 12 March 1889.

41 D.D. Molyneux, 'The Development of Physical Education in the Birmingham District from 1871 to 1892', MA Thesis, University of Birmingham, 1957, pp. 222–6.

42 South London SFA, *Half Century*, pp. 14–15.

43 National Union of Elementary Teachers (NUET), *Seventeenth Annual Report 1886/7*, pp. 75–8, 158–63.

44 NUT, *The B. and O. Fifty Years Afterwards: 1878–1928* (London: NUT, 1929), pp. 84–5.

45 South London SFA, *Half Century*, p. 13. An almost identical complaint was voiced in the West Ham SFA, *Diamond Jubilee*, p. 6.

46 Min. South London SFA, 5 February 1889.

47 Col. G.M. Onslow, 'The necessity of physical culture and recreation' in W. Bousfield (ed.), *Elementary Schools: How to Increase their Utility* (London: Percival and Co., 1890), p. 75.

48 Rankine's report was copied into Canning Town School (Boys) Log Book, 12 April 1893. I am grateful to Sarah Harding of Newham Local Studies and Archives for finding me this log book.

49 Molyneux, 'Physical recreation in Birmingham', pp. 222–4.

50 Ibid., p. 226.

51 Min. LSFA, 11 October 1892.

52 Ibid., 13 December 1892.
53 Min. LSFA, 4 July 1893.
54 Offord, 'Schoolboy Football', p. 151.
55 For Fitchie's early career, see *Football 'Sun'*, 28 January 1890; for FA Cup semi-final see B. Joy, *Forward Arsenal* (London: Sportsman, 1954 edn), pp. 17–18.
56 Goodwin, *Spurs Alphabet*, p. 302.
57 Ollier, *Arsenal*, p. 55.
58 There is a profile of Hills in *Stratford Express*, 29 April 1911.
59 *Stratford Express*, 1 May 1895.
60 South London SFA, *Half Century*, p. 19; *Stratford Express*, 15 February 1896.
61 *Football 'Sun'*, 10 April 1897.
62 South London SFA, *Half Century*, p. 19.
63 *West Ham Guardian*, 2 April 1898.
64 George Hilsdon's granddaughter, Patricia Atkinson, kindly showed me one of his England caps at her home in East Ham.
65 Winterhalder and Halse were described as 'shining lights in a clever forward line' for Wanstead FC. *West Ham Herald*, 19 February 1905.
66 West Ham SFA, *Diamond Jubilee*, p. 8.
67 *Football 'Sun'*, 2 January 1897.
68 Ibid., 8, 15 April 1899.
69 Ibid., 9 October 1899.
70 *Tottenham and Edmonton Weekly Herald*, 30 March 1900. Tottenham Hotspur did in fact win the Southern League for the first time that season. P. Harrison, *Southern League Football: The First Twenty Years* (privately printed, 1989), p. 10.
71 *Tottenham and Edmonton Weekly Herald*, 4 May 1900.
72 Pickford's tributes appeared in *Football Chat*, 27 February, 8 March 1906.
73 *Football 'Sun'*, 11 November 1899.
74 *Yorkshire Post* quoted *Football 'Sun'*, 25 November 1899.
75 *Football 'Sun'*, 14 October 1899.
76 Ibid., 18 November 1890.
77 *East Ham Echo*, 23 November 1900.
78 *East End News*, 16 March 1895.
79 Ibid., 4 January 1896.
80 *Football 'Sun'*, 6 January 1900.
81 *The Year Book of the Battersea Club*, 1907, p. 9.
82 Marner School Log Book, September 1895. I am grateful to Mrs O'Keeffe, who, when she was head of the school, permitted me to read the log books.
83 Oban Street School (Boys) Log Book, 23 April 1894. LMA, EO/DIV5/OBA/LB1; Glengall Road School (Boys) Log Book, 3 June 1896. LMA, EO/DIV5/GLE/LB1.
84 *Football 'Sun'*, 3 September 1898.
85 *Football Chat*, 5 March 1897.
86 *East End News*, 10 June 1887.
87 Ibid.
88 *East End News*, 9 April 1889.
89 Ibid., 17 April 1897.
90 Ibid., 9 April 1898.
91 Hargreaves, *Sport, Power and Culture*, p. 62.
92 No copy of this South London SFA handbook could be traced. The extract from it was quoted in the *Football 'Sun'*, 14 October 1899.
93 *Football 'Sun'*, 2 December 1899. The Queen's Park Rangers' trainer whose son was in the Queen Frederica team was 'Jock' Campbell, described by the club's historian as 'the best known football trainer in the world' at the time. G. Macey, *Queen's Park Rangers* (Derby: Breedon, 1999), p. 7.
94 *East End News*, 16 November 1895.

95 *Football 'Sun'*, 9 December 1899.
96 The reply is in Munster Road School (Boys) Log Book, 6 October 1898. LMA, EO/DIV1/ MUN/LB1.
97 *East End News*, 5 May 1893.
98 *First Annual Report of the London Playing Fields Committee*, May 1891. 'Committee' in the title was changed to 'Society' in 1899. I am grateful to D.C. Northwood for permission to consult the LPFS's records at Boston Manor.
99 Min. LPFS, 2 June 1891.
100 Min. LPFS, 21 January 1896. See also Peters, *The London Playing Fields Society*, pp. 29–30.
101 G. Green, 'The Football Association' in Fabian and Green, *Association Football*, 1, p. 88.
102 *First Annual Report... LPFS*, p. 34.
103 *Football 'Sun'*, 4 November 1899.
104 Ibid., 24 February 1900.
105 Ibid., 23 June 1904.
106 Sexby, *Municipal Parks*, p. 179.
107 Ibid., pp. 211, 354.
108 *Football 'Sun'*, 11 March 1899.
109 Ibid., 9 September 1899.
110 Molyneux, 'Physical Education in Birmingham', p. 228.
111 *Football 'Sun'*, 31 December 1898.
112 *East End News*, 1 June 1895.
113 Min. South London SFA, 15 October 1889.
114 Oban Street School Log Book, 5 December 1894.
115 London Fields School Log Book, 19 January 1892. LMA, EO/DIV5/LON/LB/2.
116 *Football 'Sun'*, 3 March 1900.
117 Marner Street School Log Book, September 1897.
118 Oldridge Road School Log Book (Boys), 23 May 1887. LMA, EO/DIV9/OLD/LB1.
119 LSFA, 'Cash statement for the year 1907/8' in *Handbook 1908/9*, pp 24–5.
120 LSFA, 'Cash statement for the year 1909/10' in *Handbook 1910/11*, pp. 16–17.
121 Cash statements for both matches are in LSFA, *Handbook 1907/8*, pp. 27–8.
122 *Fulham Observer*, 13 May 1910.
123 LSFA, *Handbook 1912/3*, p. 10. I am grateful to Averil Aldrich for drawing my attention to the finances of SFAs.

4 Consolidating elementary-school football in London, 1900–1915

Introduction

This chapter examines the development of elementary-school football from the turn of the nineteenth and twentieth centuries, through the Edwardian era up to the First World War. The main focus of the chapter is on how changes relating to the organisation and control of elementary-school education and in attitudes towards the physical welfare of children influenced the development of schoolboy football. A subsidiary focus is on the football careers of four players who had been prominent in London elementary-school football. The section "The End of the School Boards" traces the effects on schoolboy football of developments in elementary-school education arising from the growth of higher elementary and central schools and the transfer of elementary education from school boards to municipal and local councils. The section "The Physical Welfare of Children and Outdoor Games in Elementary Schools" examines how concerns about the physical welfare of children and the success of SFAs created a climate of opinion favourable to the introduction of outdoor games into the elementary-school curriculum. In the section "Four Players", the football careers of four London boys of the period are traced from schoolboy through to adult football and an attempt is made to assess the benefits of their early introduction to the game in an educational context.

The end of the school boards

The need for the LSFA to change the age groups for its major competitions and offer a new event for older pupils in 1912 had its origin in the greater number of pupils in the London area who, due to the improved standard of schooling, were progressing more rapidly through the six Standards in the elementary schools. The issue of rapid progress through Standards was partly addressed by introducing additional 'specific' subjects, like mathematics and some of the sciences, into the elementary-school curriculum and by the formation of a seventh Standard in 1882. In schools where large numbers of children were staying on in the higher Standards, a form of 'higher' elementary education was being developed that was causing concern to the headmasters of the grammar schools and was being questioned by the auditors. In their final report of 1888, the Cross Commissioners pointed out the necessity of defining exactly where elementary education, payable out of the rates, ended and where secondary education, payable from taxes and parental fees, began.[1]

Grants from the Science and Art Department, rather than from the rates, provided the main funding of the higher elementary schools, although some rates went towards the costs of the lower Standards in such schools.[2] From 1890 the Education Department encouraged such schools and took the part of the school boards when the auditor imposed a surcharge on boards for contributing towards them out of the rates. With the return to power of the Tory government in 1895, however, the issue of higher elementary schools became entangled with the struggle between the new government and the school boards as to who would control secondary education.[3] The school boards were thought to be too radical by the Education Department.[4] Sir John Gorst was Vice-President of the Committee of Council of Education at the time and his first major step towards undermining the position of the school boards was in 1897 when, as a result of an enquiry into the courses of the Science and Art Department, he empowered the county and county borough authorities to co-ordinate grants from the Science and Art Department, thus recognising them as the appropriate authorities to organise secondary education.[5]

In his recent study of educational policy-making in this period, Neil Daglish has shown how Gorst had initially hoped the school boards might co-operate with his scheme to place elementary and secondary education under local authority control. This was unlikely to happen, however, as his scheme directly undermined the policies of those school boards which, in providing higher elementary education, hoped eventually to assume responsibility for secondary as well as elementary education. 'The higher grade schools', writes Daglish, 'thus became a pivotal point in the struggle over policy formulation.'[6]

The details of this struggle are beyond the scope of this book, but it may be noted that neither the SBL nor the LCC which succeeded it was able to secure recognition from the Board of Education for their preferred type of higher elementary education. Seen solely from the point of view of what London wanted and what it was permitted by the Board of Education, Richard Morley noted in his detailed study of elementary education of a higher type in London that the first 10 years of the twentieth century were 'a barren decade'.[7] The harmful educational consequences, especially for working-class children, of the Board of Education's neglect of these schools in favour of the grammar schools is recounted with eloquence and passion in Meriel Vlaeminke's recent book.[8]

The details of the form of higher elementary education thought to be the most suitable for London children continued to be a source of disagreement between the LCC and the Board of Education. Michael Moran, in a recent thesis, has shown that the LCC's decision to withdraw its schools (except those few which had already been recognised by the Board of Education as fulfilling its criteria) from the Government's 1908 scheme for higher elementary education was a productive one. The LCC's new 'central schools' were meant to serve those pupils in elementary schools who wished to stay beyond 14 and those in secondary schools who wished to leave before 16. The central schools' curriculum was designed to enable pupils on leaving to gain entry to industry or commerce or to embark on training at a Polytechnic or similar institution. Entry to central schools was by means of a child's performance in the same Junior County Scholarship Examination that determined entry to the secondary schools. Thus the new schools could be seen as alternatives to the secondary schools rather than competitors with them (as the higher grade schools had been) or subordinate to them (as the higher elementary schools had been).[9]

Establishing higher elementary schools in the London area that had not been under the control of the SBL was equally difficult. Seeking recognition for such schools was described by Councillor Anderson as 'uphill work' in his speech at the opening of William Morris Higher Elementary School in Walthamstow in 1906. The school was almost immediately to become prominent in LSFA competitions and the councillor's thoughts on who the school was for and what it might achieve are of interest. It was, he said,

> for the children and parents who could not afford the course at the secondary schools and wanted something between the elementary and the secondary schools. It was for boys and girls from 12 to 15 years of age...he ventured to say that the school would bring about co-ordination between the elementary and secondary schools in the town.[10]

Gordon and Aldrich have pointed out that, following the Code of 1904, an important function for future elementary schools would be identifying children who showed exceptional promise and preparing them for entry to secondary schools.[11] Under the LCC there was a threefold increase in the number of free secondary school places available to London children in the years between 1906 and 1919.[12]

The transfer of responsibility for elementary education from the SBL to the LCC marked no significant change in attitude towards the work of SFAs, which continued to organise inter-school and inter-district competitions independently of, but with the tacit approval of, the new education authority. A direct comparison of the attitudes of the SBL and the LCC towards games during school hours is problematic. This is because in the period leading up to the transfer of control of education from the former to the latter it was possible to interpret the Board of Education's policy towards games as an acceptance of them as part of a school's physical training programme. As will be seen in the section "The Physical Welfare of Children and Outdoor Games in Elementary Schools", some schools adopted this interpretation and taught organised games as part of the elementary-school curriculum from the first years of the twentieth century, even though the Board of Education's Code was not formally altered to take the change of attitude into account until 1906. In the new circumstances from that date, the LCC found itself in a position never enjoyed by the SBL, namely one where games were permitted during school hours.

The LCC's response to the new circumstances was positive. Almost immediately following the change in the Code it set about improving playgrounds, 'threw open LCC parks' and provided equipment for outdoor games for the use of elementary-school pupils.[13] In assessing the progress of organised games that had been introduced into its schools in 1907, the LCC noted in its annual report for 1907/08 that it intended in future, 'as far as is practicable and consistent with educational requirements', to have apparatus manufactured at the Council's manual training centres and at the School of Building in Brixton. On the broader issues, the annual report confirmed that the experimental scheme of organised games lessons of between half an hour and two hours long had been found successful and that such games would henceforth 'be included as a permanent part of the ordinary curricula of council and non-provided schools'.[14]

In the 'Application Form for Organised Games' issued to its schools, the LCC quoted Article 44(f) of the 1906 Code's regulations governing organised games for older children in elementary schools and added several of its own, of which two are of particular interest. One was that games should not be seen as a reward for good behaviour and the other was that matches between schools 'are not allowed at the time set apart for organised games'.[15] While one interpretation of the second of these regulations might be that more children would benefit from a lesson that did not take the form of an inter-school match, another might be that the Council felt satisfied that inter-school football was already adequately organised by the LSFA and its affiliated associations as an after-school activity and had therefore no need to be accommodated during school hours.

The upper age limit for the LSFA's inter-district championship (Corinthian Shield) and individual schools' championship (Dewar Shield) was under 15 on 1 September of the school year in which the competition took place. A second inter-district competition, this one for boys under 14, was introduced in 1901, with the *Football 'Sun'* newspaper, which had been covering schoolboy football matches in London since 1896, presenting a trophy, the Sun Shield. The number of boys staying on at school beyond the age of 14 was increasing in the course of the first decade of the new century, partly helped by the kind of higher elementary-school provision that became the subject of the controversies outlined above. But, inevitably, more boys stayed on in prosperous than in poorer districts, to the advantage of the former, when a boy as old as 15 and a half could have actually played in the Corinthian Shield if his fifteenth birthday had been in the September of one year and the final of the competition in March of the following year. And while in a more prosperous area it was generally the most able children who stayed on, in poorer areas it was likely to have been the more able who left early. In 1899, an entry in the log book of a West Ham elementary school regretted that so many boys left for employment at 13 and that it was, 'generally speaking, the brighter and more intelligent boys (who) obtain work during the first nine months of the year'.[16]

It is not surprising, therefore, that the successful proposal at the 1913 Annual General Meeting (AGM) of the LSFA to reduce the age limit for the Corinthian Shield from 15 to 14, to begin in the 1913/14 season, was brought forward by A.H. Mann and seconded by W. Boxall, both representatives from West Ham, one of London's most impoverished districts. The age limit for the Sun Shield remained at 14, but it was now to be contested by reserve teams only, with strict rules to ensure that players could not appear for both teams.[17]

Part of Mann's proposals for reducing the age limit for the Corinthian Shield was that a new competition should be introduced for Central, Higher Grade and Higher Elementary Schools, because many pupils, who had hitherto been eligible for consideration for Corinthian Shield teams, would henceforth be too old. It was agreed to call a meeting of representatives of such schools, where a decision was taken to hold an individual schools' championship competition for them, to commence in the 1913/14 season. Initially, and throughout the period covered by this thesis, there was no upper age limit for this event, but after the First World War it was decided that a boy was eligible 'until the end of the term in which he reaches the age of 16 years'.[18]

Sir Thomas Lipton, the grocery magnate and sponsor of yachtsmen, agreed to provide a trophy for the competition, which was contested in four geographical groups in the initial stages, with the four group winners contesting the semi-finals. Twenty-five schools entered, with Walthamstow Higher Elementary beating William Street (West London) in the final. The competition was very enthusiastically received, the LSFA annual report for the season noted. Not only had the age limit for the Corinthian and Sun shields been reduced, but many local associations had reduced the age limit for their own championships to fourteen. Several associations, however, in due course, were to introduce new competitions for older boys.[19] The presentation of the trophy and medals by the donor to the winning team in the LSFA's new competition for older boys was arranged to take place at the Lancasterian School, Tottenham, during the function that followed the inter-city schoolboy match between the LSFA and Newcastle SFA at the end of the season. A letter from Sir Thomas Lipton was read to the meeting, however, apologising for his absence, and stating that the manufacturers of the trophy regretted they had been unable to finish it on time for the presentation, but that they had provided a full-size photograph of it instead![20] The trophy found its way to Walthamstow in due course and at the LSFA's AGM in June 1914. Sir Thomas was thanked for his trophy and wished success in 'his endeavour to bring back the Americas Cup to the Old Country'.[21]

Half-way across the Atlantic to witness the performance of 'Shamrock VI', his latest yacht built in secret to offer another challenge to the Americans, Lipton's radio officer intercepted a message from a German cruiser to say that the First World War had begun. 'Shamrock' was docked in safety in Brooklyn for the duration of hostilities, but the Lipton Trophy for schools affiliated to the LSFA was contested each season throughout the War.[22]

The physical welfare of children and outdoor games in elementary schools

In his introduction to M.E. Buckley's *The Feeding of School Children*, published in 1914, R.H. Tawney wrote that public attention to the physical defects caused by malnutrition had been highlighted by the South African War, for such defects, 'which had been regarded with tolerance in citizens, appear intolerable in soldiers'.[23] There had been concern in the London School Board area from its earliest days about the adverse effect on the learning capacities of children who came to school inadequately fed. The Council for Self-Supporting Penny Dinners and the Children's Free Breakfast and Dinner Fund dated from the 1880s, the latter founded by the writer George Sims and Mrs E.M. Burgwin, head of Orange Street School in Southwark, where familiarity with the need was first hand. While the work of these two organisations rarely overlapped, increasing attempts by different bodies to address the problem in the last decade of the century led to a chaotic situation, with an estimated provision for only half of those in need.[24] Some who fell through the network of outside charitable provision made their own arrangements within the school, sometimes with the highest degree of sensitivity. At Guardian Angels' School in Mile End in 1902, for example, parents of some boys sent bread for distribution among the poorer pupils. No stigma was attached to receiving it as it was acknowledged throughout the school 'that a boy fed one week may be a feeder the next'.[25]

In the same year the Boys' Department of Canning Town School received £12 from the *Daily Mail* to relieve poverty in a school where 'About 20 to 25 are without boots or stockings & more were in possession of very bad boots.'[26] The Charity Organisation Society held that school meals for necessitous children 'were palliatives that encouraged fecklessness', as Hurt has put it, but by the turn of the century some form of state assistance was accepted as essential in addressing so vast a problem.[27]

The Royal Commission on Physical Training in Scotland in 1903 argued that school authorities ought to supervise the feeding of children who came for instruction and the Inter-Departmental Committee on Physical Deterioration reported the consensus from witnesses that the time had come for the state to recognise the need for adequate nourishment for schoolchildren and that it was cruel to expect them to learn if they were half-starved.[28] Pressure from the Trades Union Congress in particular, which was campaigning for 'state maintenance of schoolchildren', kept the issue in the public eye. In the first session of Parliament that followed the return of a Liberal Government to power in 1906, a Labour MP, W.T. Wilson, introduced a bill to provide for the feeding of necessitous children. The Select Committee appointed to consider the matter wanted to place many qualifications on the spirit of an act that, for the first time, as Simon puts it, 'implied acceptance by the community of responsibility for poverty'. But pressure from inside and outside Parliament, from the Labour movement in particular, helped see it through. Local authorities were henceforth allowed to spend from the rates to aid an organisation providing food for schoolchildren, charging parents where possible, but in necessitous cases where a child would otherwise be unable to take advantage of the education provided, payment from the rates would be allowed. As the legislation was only permissive, its implementation was gradual.[29]

As with the provision of school meals, progress in establishing the details of children's medical disabilities was slow, but a climate of opinion was created in which it was accepted that a school medical service was necessary, beginning with medical examinations. By 1906, as conservative an educator as Gorst expressed his approval of 'proper medical inspection'.[30]

Running parallel with concerns about the poor diet, poor and unsanitary housing, poor health and poor physique, overcrowding and overwork of a substantial minority of working-class children was the view that the physical deterioration it led to could be countered by a variety of measures. Besides those mentioned already, such measures normally included the provision of more fresh air for urban children and more opportunities for physical exercise. Campaigns like those of Lord Brabazon (Earl of Meath), which had been in existence since the 1880s when he donated equipment to gymnasia to be used by London schoolchildren, demanded increased open space in cities, supervised playgrounds and compulsory physical training.[31] The conviction that the air of cities was particularly harmful to children and the apparent benefits that fell to those who were sent to 'recovery schools' and 'vacation schools' in the pure air of the countryside helped create a climate of opinion favourable to increased physical education in and out of schools.[32] Physical exercises, drill and games, accompanied by adequate diet, were accepted as being of value to all children. Witnesses before the Royal Commission on Physical Training in Scotland in 1903 agreed on the great importance of physical training. Yet, as A. Watt Smyth was to write in his book on physical deterioration published the following year, 'its recognition as a prominent branch of a liberal education appeared to be theoretical rather than practical'.[33]

A great number of those concerned with the poor health of schoolchildren at the turn of the century saw physical exercise and fresh air, accompanied by adequate diet, as an essential factor in any programme of improvements. Why, then, were organised games, which could provide healthy exercise in air (of admittedly sometimes questionable freshness) not an acceptable part of the elementary-school curriculum, as they were of the curriculum of public and grammar schools?

From the large number of teachers who came forward to take school football teams outside school hours in competitions organised by the LSFA and the sixteen associations that were affiliated to it by 1900, it is reasonable to assume that, if one sport alone could attract so many teachers prepared to give up their free time to promote it, the scarcity of teachers competent to teach games cannot have been a reason for their exclusion from the curriculum. Small and inadequately paved playgrounds were part of the reason, but some pitches were available, like those in Victoria Park, which were designated for the exclusive use of schoolboys for Saturday morning matches.[34] Could these pitches, which could accommodate thirty schoolboy teams on Saturday mornings, not as easily have been acquired for use during school hours if games had been part of the curriculum in local elementary school at the time?

Alfred Percival Graves was the HMI responsible for influencing the newly appointed Minister of Education, Augustine Birrell, to take up the case for games in the elementary-school curriculum. He wrote in 1904 that while the lack of adequate facilities was indeed an issue, where these did exist, as in the case of the apparatus in playgrounds provided by Lord Brabazon, mentioned above, they were not used efficiently. This he blamed on the SBL's unsuccessful attempts to get 'ladies and gentlemen of leisure' to organise games in play-grounds on Saturday mornings. Graves' view was that the SBL's project would have had a better chance of success if it had been put under the control of 'the young athletes of the Public School Missions in London', a view which the success of the missionaries in so many other of their endeavours in the realm of sport, as outlined in Chapter 2, suggests may have been an accurate one. Furthermore, he saw Morant's Code of the same year, with its encouragement for organised games, as sufficient sanction for them to be played during school hours, and blamed local education authorities and teachers for not recognising this. Most of the latter, Graves felt, were still 'under the shadow of the old results system' which permitted them to spare no more than a few minutes in the morning and in the afternoon on activities other than 'the mental work of the time-table'.[35] He explained how things could be different by citing the example of games taught at Eltringham Street, West Lambeth.

Graves traced the physical improvements of the pupils at Eltringham Street to the appointment in 1889 of Mr Crombie, a headmaster committed to the value of games. To make his point, Graves cited the improved performances of the Eltringham cricket, football and athletics teams in South London schools' competitions. In addition, from being below the height of their opponents 6 or 7 years earlier, the Eltringham boys' average height had increased by more than three and a half inches (9 cm) to reach, presumably, what was considered the appropriate height for their age. More interestingly, he listed the curricular time devoted to physical activities at Eltringham Street. While drill continued to form part of the programme, football, cricket and rounders featured prom-inently among the organised games taught there.[36] In this, the school was taking advantage of an instruction issued by the Board of Education to HMIs in 1900, to the effect that games were an acceptable alternative to Swedish drill or physical exercises in meeting the requirements of the Code, although the Code itself had not been altered to take this into account.[37]

Two months before Graves' article appeared in the *Contemporary Review*, the Benevolent Purposes Committee of the NUT, at the annual conference in Llandudno, was presented with a plan for a national schoolboy football scheme by the Committee's secretary, T.P. Thomas. At this time a teacher in Llanwrst National in North Wales, Thomas had been active in the Tottenham SFA while teaching in London in the 1890s. It is not known if he nurtured the idea of a national association for elementary-school football while he was promoting the game in Tottenham schools, but, with Tottenham SFA teams playing in LSFA competitions, he would certainly have come in contact with W.J. Wilson, who is known to have been interested in the idea of a national body to control schoolboy football in the 1890s.[38]

At the Llandudno meeting, Thomas was invited to take charge of preliminary arrangements for his scheme. Secretaries of NUT branches and Benevolent Committee fundraisers were asked to supply the names and addresses of any SFAs in their areas. When these details were made available to Thomas, he circulated a set of competition rules to all associations. The circular included an invitation to send any proposals for rule amendments to him and to attend a meeting later in the year for the purpose of reaching agreement on rules for a national association. The meeting subsequently took place at the Birmingham Athletic Institute and was chaired by William McGregor, 'the Father of the Football League'.[39] The venue was an auspicious one in that the Institute, which opened in 1892, had played an important role in pioneering the view that the playing field was as appropriate a setting for the conduct of physical training of an educational nature as the gymnasium.[40]

Besides the LSFA and the Sheffield SFA, the associations represented at the meeting included those from Birmingham (founded in 1892), Liverpool (1891), Newcastle (1894) and Nottingham (1891).[41] At a further meeting five weeks later, the Council of the English Schools' FA (ESFA) decided that boys taking part in the Association's events would have to be *bona fide* scholars at elementary schools, defined as those 'working under the Elementary Education Code'.[42] A trophy was presented by the Benevolent Purposes Committee of the NUT for a national competition between associations. Before it got underway, Thomas wrote to the FA for permission to hold such an event. While no copy of his letter has survived, the reply from F. Wall, Secretary of the FA, has been preserved and it is of particular interest in the light of the decision taken by the FA in 1997 to concentrate the entire training of talented young footballers at professional clubs.[43] Noting that the proposed competition was to be between boys at school, Wall wrote that the consent of the FA was not required and added, significantly, that 'We do not wish to control Schoolboy football.'[44] Nineteen associations contested the event, which was won by the LSFA team, which narrowly beat Sheffield in the final.[45] Further evidence of the goodwill of the FA towards the work of the ESFA may be inferred from an announcement by B. Creswick, ESFA chairman, at a meeting at Llandudno, where the final was played. The result of his correspondence with the FA, he announced, was that the latter had decided 'to grant two sets of medals to the finalists'.[46] The FA Council, for its part, briefly recorded its decision to present the medals 'with a view to encourage the game among boys'.[47]

The trophy was transferred from the Benevolent Purposes Committee of the NUT to the ESFA and became known as the English Schools' Shield. It was in use until the 1938 competition, when it was replaced by the English Schools' Trophy, which is still contested today. At a meeting following the first final it was decided that no combination of SFAs like the LSFA could enter in future.[48] Accepting the ESFA decision gracefully, the LSFA annual report for the 1904/05 season expressed the hope that the individual associations affiliated to the LSFA would enter the competition 'and that London may be successful in retaining the title Champions of England through one of its many local Associations'.[49]

Associations affiliated to the LSFA entered the competition individually from the 1905/06 season onwards, and in the period reviewed in this chapter did so with notable success. In the nine times the Shield was contested from 1905/06 up to the First World War, London associations affiliated to the LFSA reached four of the finals and were represented at the semi-final stage of the competition on three other occasions. This, added to the record of the LSFA's representative side, which performed well in annual matches against Glasgow and Edinburgh during this period, suggests that the standard of schoolboy football was equal to the highest in England and Scotland, the implications of which will be explored in the discussion of professional football in Chapter 7.[50]

The increasing evidence that outdoor games were conducive to good health and the fact that schoolboy football had permeated elementary schools in all parts of the country – there were more than 100 SFAs by 1907 – prompted educationalists to move from Graves' assurances that games *could* be taught during school hours to a change in the Code that ensured that every teacher knew they had become an accepted part of the elementary-school curriculum. 'While the children of the rich play too much, the children of the poor do not play at all', wrote Gorst in 1906.[51] It is clear from his book, *The Children of the Nation*, that he felt that the 1904 Code was not sufficient to permit the introduction of organised games into the elementary-school curriculum on the scale he would have liked. He disapproved of military drill and welcomed the Swedish drill in the new scheme of physical training that was to be introduced in elementary schools.[52] He also approved of games, although it might have come as a surprise to teachers who had been taking schoolboy football and cricket teams in matches for many years to learn that the sport he favoured as most suitable for the elementary school was ju-jitsu, requiring, as it did, neither gymnasium nor apparatus.[53] Whatever form physical training might take, however, he felt there was only one way of making sufficient time for it on the elementary-school curriculum, a curriculum, which, he argued, was practically at the discretion of the Board of Education for schools which received government grants. The Board of Education, then, 'could ensure a proper devotion of time to physical training by the alteration in their codes and regulations'.[54]

In his autobiography, Graves has described how his scheme for introducing games into the Code took shape. Put briefly, he gained the approval of Birrell at the Board of Education for his scheme and in consultation with the Chief Inspector of Schools, Edmond Holmes, provision of a permissive, rather than a compulsory, character was introduced in the 1906 Code for games to be taught during school hours.[55] Games lessons during school hours were taken up with enthusiasm by the LCC, as noted in the section "Four Players". The NUT also supported the new provisions, which might have been expected, given the part played by NUT members in establishing elementary-school football associations both locally and nationally. In a foreword to the 1906/07 annual report of the ESFA, attention is drawn to the value of outdoor games in schools in relation to good health and character-building. E.A. Wix, HMI, is quoted as saying that 'much excellent unadvertised work' had for years been done by teachers to counter the effects of physical deterioration and that, given the difficulty of getting boys together after school hours, 'it is a matter for congratulation that organised games can now be properly taught as part of the ordinary school curriculum'.[56]

Girls' games

Because the subject of this book is the origin and influence of SFAs, their contribution to the acceptance of games 'as part of the ordinary school curriculum' has been emphasised in this chapter. There were, of course, other contributors, not least the pioneers of physical education in girls' elementary schools. Military drill was not considered suitable for girls and the only exercise girls in elementary schools were likely to experience in the period immediately following the 1870 Education Act was swimming. While 24 'girls over ten' attending Lewisham Bridge were presented by the local clergyman with tickets to attend Greenwich Baths in 1872, it was not until later in the decade that the SBL introduced physical education for all girls in elementary schools.[57] Through the SBL's appointments successively of Concordia Lofving and Martina Bergman of the Central Gymnastics Institute in Stockholm to train the teachers to spearhead the programme of physical education into girls schools, Swedish drill became the dominant form of the subject first in London and later throughout the country.[58] Confusingly, perhaps, the term 'drill' is often used in the log books of girls' schools when it is Swedish drill that is being described. 'Drill continues to be well taught' ran an entry in Daubeney Road Girls' School log book in 1895.[59] An entry for Bellenden Road in 1905 recorded that on the day after the girls had given a 'Drill display' at a medical congress in Russell Square, the Dean of a Woman's university in Japan visited 'for the purpose of inspecting the Drill taught in the school and of obtaining information on the methods used'.[60]

Shelia Fletcher has identified Bergman (later Madame Bergman-Osterberg) 'as the author of a distinctly female tradition in English physical education'.[61] The tradition impinged on the education of boys, however, in that while it was indeed exclusive to girls on its introduction to London elementary schools, by the early twentieth century, while military drill was still retained for boys,

Swedish exercises had also become a feature of boys' physical education as well as that of girls'.[62] Girls' games, similarly, were influenced by developments in boys' games. An Old Etonian manager of Windsor Road, Hackney, expressed his hope at the school's opening ceremony in 1899 that both the boys and girls might take a prominent part 'in Hackney sport and swimming'. A few months later 'Hockey for Girls' was listed among the sports encouraged by teachers at the school.[63]

Four players

This section consists of accounts of the footballing careers of four players who took part in schoolboy football in London in the period under review. The selection of two professional players good enough to have gained England caps and two prominent amateurs (one of whom later became a professional) ensured that the careers of the four players were well documented. In addition, one wrote a detailed account of his life in football and personal information from relatives of the other three offered insights into attitudes which were not always evident from published accounts of matches. The section explores how the four players might have benefited from an introduction to football in an educational context in London elementary schools and the extent to which the values that inspired the teachers who taught them the game were successfully transmitted to them.

Charles Buchan

The sub-heading to the first chapter of Charles Buchan's autobiography, *A Lifetime in Football*, reads, 'When boys were brought up the hard way'. As a pupil at High Street School, Plumstead, in the 1890s he played football on a stony army manoeuvring ground on the local common, an experience from which he claimed to have learned 'how to fall lightly without getting injured too badly'.[64] At his next school, Bloomfield Higher Grade, he was taught to head the ball correctly by his teacher, Mr Swallow, who directed boys to send suitable crosses in from the wings for Buchan to head past the goalkeeper. Master and boys must have looked back on the time as well spent, because Buchan was later known in senior football as the only player in the Football League who could regularly score goals by heading the ball downwards, from above crossbar height, into the net. He gained his first football medal at Bloomfield Road, when his school won the Woolwich SFA's Shield, played at Woolwich Arsenal's Manor Field Ground.

His secondary schooling was at Woolwich Polytechnic, which he attended with the intention of becoming a teacher. This was at a time when the pupil teacher centres were being abandoned in favour of educating future elementary-school teachers in secondary schools.[65] While playing with the Polytechnic team on Saturday mornings, he would also play for a club of the same name that used the school's ground in the afternoon. On occasions he would play a third match on Saturday, a playing schedule for a teenager that would be condemned by modern coaches but on which the young player felt he thrived, for, as he wrote later, 'The more football I got the better.'

Despite the FA's ban on Sunday football, Buchan also played for a Sunday morning team, in the course of which he was watched by Charlie Paynter, at that time assistant trainer at West Ham United, who, noticing that he was on the small side and rather frail, decided to wait to see how he developed rather than try to sign him. Buchan, meanwhile, was approached by Woolwich Arsenal, with whose reserves he played a few games in the 1909/10 season. He left in the aftermath of a dispute over legitimate expenses. He played with Northfleet in the Kent Senior League for the remainder of the season, at the end of which he was offered £3 a week to sign for Bury in the Football League. This was a considerable sum at a time when, as he notes in his book, an engineer, fitter, turner or carpenter, after 5 years training, would have been paid under £2 a week.[66]

While considering Bury's proposition, he was approached by Fulham, who offered to make provision for him to continue his training as a teacher while playing for the club as a professional at £1.50 a week. He held out for £2 a week, and when this was not forthcoming, accepted an offer of £3 a week to play with Leyton, at that time a professional club.[67]

Buchan's reflections on his time with Leyton offer two insights into his sympathies that suggest that, despite signing as a professional, he was deeply convinced of the values of the amateur game, values which it is reasonable to assume he imbibed at his schools. The first is that in recounting the players who had an influence on him at the time, pride of place was given to Harold Fleming, the Swindon Town amateur who was good enough to hold a place in the full England team. The second player to whom he acknowledged a debt was the Rev. K.R.G. Hunt, a master at Highgate School, a gold medallist at the 1908 Olympics and a future full England international, who was at that time with Leyton.

The young Buchan improved his positional sense through playing with Hunt and improved his ability to get around defenders through copying one of Fleming's tricks. This last skill was further improved by watching a schoolboy implementing it on Plumstead Common, where Buchan went regularly on Saturday mornings to watch schoolboy games before travelling over to Leyton to play in the Football League in the afternoon. Having seen the small schoolboy romp past a big defender at full speed by feigning to hit the ball hard at him and causing the defender to lose his balance, Buchan tried the move himself in his League match that afternoon. He found that it worked and later wrote that he 'continued to use it for many years and it seldom failed'.[68]

Buchan was transferred to Sunderland at the end of the 1911/12 season and went on to a long career in football at the highest level and, even before his playing career was over, had established a reputation for himself as a leading football journalist. His achievements on the field of play included appearances in two FA Cup finals, gaining six England caps and the successful operation of a tactical scheme, in association with Herbert Chapman, Buchan's manager at Arsenal, to counteract the effects of the alteration in the offside law that was introduced by the FA in 1925.[69]

In 1926 Buchan wrote a series of articles in the *Daily News* on how young players could improve their game and the following year was asked to join the staff of the same newspaper. For the rest of his life he was to remain one of the most influential figures in English football journalism. He was involved in the FA's first chaotic attempts at organising a coaching scheme. Having gone to the course in his capacity as reporter, he found that there was no one there with any coaching experience and accepted an offer to take one of the classes himself.[70] It was a task he was capable of undertaking as, apart from his experience as a player and his writing on coaching, he had taught Physical Education for some time when he was playing for Sunderland.[71]

Disappointed at the poor control, passing and positional sense of most of the boys at an English Schools' Trophy match he witnessed in 1954, Buchan argued strongly for professional coaches to help teachers in schools.[72] It took some years for his recommendations to gain acceptance by the FA and the ESFA. The realisation that the better players in particular could develop their skills best through the kind of professional coaching a school could not provide found concrete expression in the creaming off of the country's best 14-year-old players for professional coaching at Lilleshall. The Associated Schoolboy scheme and the professional clubs' Schools of Excellence offered a greater involvement of professional coaches with a wider selection of schoolboy players. The current arrangements for the coaching of young footballers, which came into force at the beginning of the 1998/99 season, permit the professional clubs' Football Academies and Schools of Excellence to control both the coaching and, in consultation with their parents, the matches that may be played by the boys. While Buchan might not have expected the coaching of young players to have taken the exact direction it has, and while, as a schoolteacher he might have reservations about the extent to which schoolboy football has been marginalised, there is a very real sense in which the current arrangements may be seen as the culmination of his recommendations for the football education of talented players.[73]

James Gordon

James Thornton Gordon was the son of Donald Gordon, who had served an engineering apprenticeship in Dundee before coming south in the early 1870s and settling in Barking, at that time a small town with a fishing fleet.[74] James was sent to Gascoigne Road Board School and made his first appearance with the school's football team in the 1898/99 season. The details of the origin of the Barking SFA could not be traced as the early records have not survived, but some information on its history have been gleaned through conversations with George Cash of the LSFA Executive and Andrew Beeching, grandnephew of Barking SFA's first secretary, William Chapman. A shield for the Barking SFA's championship was presented by Major Glenny in 1896.[75] While this indicates that schoolboy football was organised in Barking at an early date, the Association was not affiliated to the LSFA. This permitted boys from Barking to play for East Ham SFA, which was affiliated to the LSFA, in the Corinthian Shield competition.[76] It also, surprisingly, seems to have enabled three Barking schools, Gascoigne, National and North Street, to take part in the East Ham SFA championship. It was in a match report on this competition in the 1898/99 season that Gordon's name first appeared in his local newspaper.[77] Gordon was in his school team again the following season, when the boys reached the final of the Glenny Shield.[78]

On leaving school Gordon joined a local club, Barking Victoria, which played in the South Essex League and shared the Vicarage Field Ground with Barking FC (formerly known as Barking Rovers, then Barking Institute and, from the 1903/04 season, Barking Town and still existing today as Barking and East Ham), the other leading senior club in the area. A profile of Gordon, when he was Barking Victoria's captain in 1908, described the 22-year-old as a player who 'never resorts to shady tactics and is as popular off the field as on it'.[79] By 1910 he had changed clubs, as he appeared in the Barking Town team that was beaten finalists in the Essex Senior Cup.[80] He gained London caps and an Essex badge while with the club, and played a prominent part in the major amateur competitions.[81]

That Gordon was an important figure in Barking by virtue of his footballing achievements is suggested by the prominence given to his wedding in the local paper.[82] At the AGM of the club a few weeks later, a letter from Gordon was read saying he was going to play for Grimsby, for whom he appeared at the start of the 1910/11 season.[83] Wayne Gordon, James Gordon's grandson, has explained that his grandfather already had an older brother in Grimsby and it is possible that a trial for the professional club might have been arranged through him.[84] Relegated from Division Two of the Football League in 1909/10, Grimsby had to play in the Midland League for the 1910/11 season which, with Gordon a regular in the side, they succeeded in winning. Grimsby was successful in seeking re-election to the Football League for the 1911/12 season and played in Division Two until 1915, when Football League matches were cancelled for the remaining years of the First World War. Gordon had played with distinction for the club throughout most of this period until a serious knee injury in 1914 effectively brought his playing career at the top level to an end.[85]

On returning to Barking, Gordon renewed his contact with his old club and was its financial secretary for some years. When he died in 1959 the Chairman of the LFA was Arthur Drewry, who, years earlier, used to watch Gordon playing for Grimsby Town. On being informed of Gordon's death by the secretary of the LFA, who had been notified of the bereavement by the deceased's wife, Drewry concluded his reply by noting that Gordon had been a centre half of the highest standard and that he was 'an ornament to the game and to those of us who saw him play the memory of Jimmy Gordon is a pleasant recollection'.[86]

Charlie Warren

Charles Baden Warren was born in Berners Road, Wood Green in 1900. In 1907, owing to a change of fortune brought about by the death of his father, who had been a compositor on the *Daily Mail* and *Gentle Woman*, the family moved to more modest and rented accommodation in Gladstone Avenue. Charlie attended Noel Park Infants (1905–07) and White Hart Lane (1907–10), where he was one of four boys (out of 80 candidates) who was successful in the examination to enter Wood Green Higher Grade.[87] While he undoubtedly played football at his earlier schools, it was at the Higher Grade School that his prowess at the game first came to public attention.

Sport was probably in Charlie Warren's blood, as his grandfather, Robert Warren, was the publisher of the *Illustrated Sporting and Theatrical News* in the 1860s.[88] Charlie's older brother, Will, gained a LFA badge in 1912/13 and a London Junior cap the following season. He was a member of the St John's youth club (attached to the church of that name in Wood Green attended by the family), and later Old Johnians, patronised by players too old for the youth club.[89]

At Higher Grade, Charlie Warren was in the team that won the Tottenham SFA's challenge cup for 1912/13.[90] The following season he was selected for the Tottenham district side which, in the Corinthian Shield semi-final, was drawn against West Ham, a team that contained three schoolboy internationals.[91] Thanks in large measure to Warren, who successfully contained Margetts, the England schoolboy centre forward, Tottenham won and went on to the final where they lost to West London.[92] Partly as a result of his outstanding performance against West Ham, Warren was selected for the LSFA team that played Newcastle at Tottenham's White Hart Lane ground in April 1914.[93]

Charlie's three brothers had served at the front in the First World War and he himself joined the fifty-first Royal Sussex Regiment in 1918 and was selected to play for his battalion against wartime opposition that included Walsall and Norwich. When demobilised he joined the Old Johnians. In the 1920/21 season, with three of the Warren brothers in the side (Reg, Will and Charlie), the team won the Wood Green League and Charity Cup and the LFA Intermediate Cup.[94] In 1926 all three brothers were in the Old Johnians team that reached the final of the Tottenham Charity Cup. Having been selected for LFA representative sides on four occasions, Charlie was awarded a London Junior badge at the end of the 1923/24 season and when he played for London on three more occasions the following season, he gained his London Junior cap.[95]

He continued with the Old Johnians throughout the 1920s and 1930s until the ground in Wolves Lane was taken over for allotments as part of the

'Dig for Victory' campaign in 1940. He played for Broomfield early in the Second World War, and on returning from evacuation in Sussex after the War, continued with that club, first in the Nemean League and later in the Southern Amateur League, until retiring from football at the age of sixty-two in the 1961/62 season. The Southern Amateur League had its origin in the breakaway of a number of 'Old Boy' amateur clubs from the FA in 1907, a split that led to the formation of the Amateur Football Association (later Alliance). A feature of this League was that no cups or medals were awarded to winning teams.[96] Warren had played for an Alliance representative side at least once before the Second World War.

'During my career', he wrote, 'I have gravitated from left-half to centre-half; then to left back and finally to outside left, from where I scored seven goals in my last season.'[97] While it was with the fourth team that he scored the seven goals in 1961/62, given that he was 62 years old at the time, it was a remarkable conclusion to a remarkable football career.

Jack Tresadern

John Tresadern was born in Livingstone Road, Stratford, in 1891.[98] In an account of her father's early life compiled for the present writer before her death in 1996, Tresadern's daughter Poppy related how the young Jack, who had been a small and delicate child when he started at Napier Road Board School, West Ham, in the 1890s, had, by the age of thirteen, developed into an excellent scholar and an outstanding footballer.[99] His scholastic development had been helped by the interest taken in him by the school's headmaster, Mr Reynolds, who had given him extra tuition, and his footballing progress was partly due to the training of Harry Earle, under whose influence he came when he was chosen for the West Ham SFA district team in 1905.[100] Mr Reynolds wanted Jack to stay on as a pupil teacher at the school when he reached fourteen, but his father was insistent that he should leave at Christmas 1906 in order to get a job and contribute to the family income.

With his reputation in schoolboy football established through the West Ham district team, it is not surprising that within a year of his leaving school his name appeared in local club football with a team called Park Athletic, based in West Ham Park.[101] He played briefly with Wanstead FC, shortly before the club folded in 1911.[102] The following season (1911/12) he was in the Barking Town team that played London Caledonians in the London Senior Cup, when the *Stratford Express* applauded him on the 'unobtrusive' way that, despite his small stature, he tackled the Caledonian players on the right wing. Although he gave them no respite, 'not once were his tactics questioned by his opponents or the referee'.[103] The *East Ham Echo*, in drawing attention to the friendly spirit in which the match was played, noted how the Caledonian captain and Tresadern 'conversed together when the ball was at the other side of the field'.[104]

Tresadern's sights were clearly set higher than amateur football, for, following some games as an amateur with West Ham United, he was taken on as a professional before the start of the 1913/14 season. He played mostly in the reserves and had difficulty making any impression at the club until after the First World War. He enlisted as a private in the Army Service Corps for the duration of the War, serving in the Motor Transport Company of the Royal Garrison Artillary and was appointed to a commission as a second lieutenant early in 1918. He was promoted to lieutenant in 1919 and relinquished his commission the following year.[105]

At the end of his military career and with the Football League programme back to normal, Tresadern worked hard to establish his place in West Ham United's halfback line. A match report in 1920 noted his improvement and another at the beginning of the 1920/21 season drew attention to the capacity for hard work which had already been evident at Barking.[106]

He played an important role in West Ham's promotion to Division One of the Football League in 1922/23 and in the semi-final of the FA Cup against Derby County the same season the *Stratford Express* wrote that 'nobody on the field played better than Tresadern'.[107] He earned two England caps at the end of the season, but made no impact in either match and was not selected again. West Ham lost to Bolton in the 1923 FA Cup final, held at the new Wembley Stadium. Tresadern's football was interrupted by a foot injury early the following season and he struggled to keep his place in the team. He was transferred to Burnley at the start of the 1924/25 season for an undisclosed fee but which the *Daily Sketch* understood to have been £1,000.[108] Despite a promising start with his new club and playing as team captain on several occasions, he did not maintain his form and at the end of the season he was transferred to Northampton Town as player manager.[109] He broke his leg in a match at Brighton at the end of 1927, an injury that effectively ended his playing career.[110]

He was next appointed manager of Crystal Palace, a club, like Northampton Town, in Division Three (South) of the Football League.[111] When Tresadern had been two months at his new club, a letter in the *Croydon Advertiser* remarked on the excellent team work of the Palace players, 'which has been especially noticeable since the advent of Mr Tresadern as manager'.[112] Crystal Palace narrowly missed promotion at the end of the season, finishing second when only one team was promoted. While the club remained in the lowest division of the League throughout Tresadern's time there, his status as a highly regarded manager may be inferred from a tribute to him in the match programme of one of his rival clubs that applauded Crystal Palace for renewing his contract, because, 'For really good men the demand exceeds the supply.'[113]

Tresadern moved to Tottenham Hotspur in 1935. The club had been relegated to Division Two of the Football League the season before his arrival, despite having finished as high as third in Division One the season before that (1933/34). Tresadern's brief was to get the club back into Division One as quickly as possible. He failed to do this, and, despite guiding the club to several good FA Cup runs, he was criticised, as his daughter put it 60 years later, 'for not getting to the final'.[114] He was allowed to leave the club voluntarily at the end of the 1937/38 season, amid speculation that he was about to be asked to do so.[115]

He was appointed manager of Plymouth Argyle in 1939, but while he may indeed have gone there with 'a wealth of football experience behind him' as a historian of the club has put it, any ambitions he had for the club received a setback in the form of the Second World War.[116] For, such was the extent of enemy action against the south coast naval city that an early attempt to continue football even at the modest level of the Wartime South West Regional League (which the club, fielding many guest players stationed in or near Plymouth, had won in 1939/40) had to be abandoned after the fall of France in June 1940.[117]

Alan Ronson, Tresadern's son-in-law, has recalled how his father-in-law was so enthusiastic about restarting football on the badly damaged Home Park ground that he agreed to forgo his salary for one year after the War, claim half of it only for the second year and resume his full salary only in the third year.[118] His exertions to get the club running again included the restoration of the ground and travelling far and wide to recruit players.[119] Despite his efforts, Plymouth fared badly when faced on the field of play by clubs that had been less disrupted by the War. Tresadern resigned in 1948, not because of the poor performance of the team but, according to his son-in-law, because of an altercation with a director, who, on becoming chairman, disclaimed all knowledge of the 'gentleman's agreement' that had promised properly remunerated employment to Tresadern when the club was back on its feet.[120]

After a spell as a scout for Crystal Palace, he was manager of Chelmsford City for a while and then spent a longer period (1951–58) as manager of Hastings, a non-League club heavily in debt at the time of his arrival. He succeeded on getting the club back on a reasonable financial footing through a series of schemes, including 'Tresadern's Tanner Club', but mostly, his son-in-law has related, through the generosity of a benefactor who had seen Tresadern play at West Ham 30 years earlier.[121] He left Hastings in 1958 to become manager of Tonbridge and died from a heart attack on Boxing Day 1959. Recalling his short, but active and enthusiastic period in charge of the club, local journalist Mike Pinnock noted that the football at Tonbridge was 'being played with a spirit and will to win inspired by his incessant promptings'. In the same newspaper on the same day a columnist, in relating his last conversation with Tresadern a few days after Tonbridge had been beaten by Bath City in the Premier Division of the Southern League, perhaps sums up a lifetime's commitment to the game and its importance to him. When the columnist wished him a Happy Christmas, Tresadern replied that it *would* have been, 'if we had defeated Bath City'.[122]

Arsene Wenger, the current Arsenal manager, said in an interview in 1999 that he loved football and had to defend it against those who saw it merely as a source of business opportunities. 'If tomorrow', he continued, 'there's no money in the sport any more, I'd still be in football. Many other people would not.'[123] While three of the four players whose football careers were examined in this chapter actually played as professionals for part of their careers, what unites them most of all, perhaps, is the impression they all give that, had they never received a penny for their efforts, they would all have spent a lifetime in football. Their long and productive careers in the game as player (Warren), player and official (Gordon), player and manager (Tresadern) and player, trainer and football journalist (Buchan) suggest that their initiation into formally organised football at their elementary schools was such as to ensure their lifelong engagement with the game.

None of the four belonged to the really poor of late Victorian and early Edwardian London. The economic conditions of the Warren family were considerably reduced when his father died in 1907. Charlie's son has informed me that there was a strong family bond between the brothers as they were growing up, perhaps as a result of their changed circumstances, and has drawn attention to 'the fact that the children were good at sport helped to provide a ray of sunshine in their lives'.[124] Buchan's comments on the hard surfaces he had to play on as a boy have been noted, as has the way he put these early experiences to positive use in his adult football career. But his father seems to have been in regular employment and there are no suggestions of an impoverished childhood in his autobiography. The Tresaderns owned property in their street and in nearby Abbey Lane, which suggests they were far from being the poorest in their neighbourhood.[125] Jack Tresadern's experience of not being allowed by his father to pursue his chosen career as a teacher seems to have been put to positive use in that it may have provided motivation for his single-minded application to his second-choice profession. Not enough is known about Gordon's early life to compare him with the other three, but, given that his father had served an apprenticeship as an engineer before moving to Barking in search of work, similar circumstances (safely above the poverty level) may be assumed.[126]

While the direct influence of their elementary schools in giving the four players their first taste of organised competitive football is beyond doubt, the extent to which their teachers might have been responsible for the boys' acquisition of footballing skills and praiseworthy attitudes to the game is, inevitably, less clear. The log book for Gordon's Gascoigne Road for the period has survived, but the only reference to outdoor games records the presentation of medals to the team that won a football shield in 1901.[127] Warren's son cannot recall his father saying anything about the teacher who did the training at Wood Green Higher Grade, except that he was treated with great respect by the boys. With Buchan and Tresadern the picture is more complete. Buchan, in his autobiography, has given a vivid account of the training given to him by his teacher and Tresadern was fortunate enough to have come under the influence of Harry Earle when he was selected for the West Ham district team. Besides being one of the most successful trainers of schoolboy teams in the country for the two decades on either side of 1900, Earle had even written a manual on how to train young players. He was also committed to the amateur ideal and even when he lost his amateur status in unusual circumstances while at Clapton FC, still refused to receive money for playing in the Football League.

To what extent were the four boys' attitudes to the game determined by their elementary-school football teachers? So many and so varied are the influences of childhood that it is of course impossible to identify exactly what experiences, at any particular time, were most significant in the formation of a boy's character. That they had confidence in their own abilities from an early age was to be expected, given that they were all good enough to play for their schools and at least two for their districts. But the integrity, dignity and gentlemanly attitudes towards the game, dispositions with which all four players could be associated, reflect attitudes that were central to the game as promoted by SFAs.

Conclusions

The section "The End of the School Boards" in this chapter has demonstrated that changes in educational policy and in the administration of elementary education led to changes in the competitions organised by the LSFA and the associations affiliated to it. On the one hand, the upper age limit for competitions was lowered to that corresponding to the ages of the older boys in ordinary elementary schools, and on the other hand new competitions were introduced to accommodate those boys in higher elementary, higher grade and central schools who continued their education up to sixteen and beyond. In the section "The Physical Welfare of Children and Outdoor Games in Elementary Schools" it was shown how concerns for the physical welfare of children and the demonstrable success of SFAs throughout the country led to a climate of opinion favourable to the introduction of outdoor games as part of the elementary-school curriculum. Finally, in tracing the football careers of four London schoolboys from the period, it has been possible to identify some characteristics which may be traceable to the way in which they were taught the game at their elementary schools. A study of the teachers who taught the game and organised the schoolboy football competitions in which these and thousands of other boys played forms the subject of the next chapter.

Notes

1 E. Eaglesham, *From School Board to Local Authority* (London: Routledge & Kegan Paul, 1956), p. 28.
2 B. Simon, *Education and the Labour Movement 1870–1920* (London: Lawrence and Wishart, 1965), p. 191.
3 M. Sturt, *The Education of the People: A History of Primary Education in England and Wales* (London: Routledge & Kegan Paul, 1967), p. 406.
4 On the main thrust of party politics in 1870 and 1900, see P. Gordon, R. Aldrich and D. Dean, *Education and Policy in England in the Twentieth Century* (London: Woburn Press, 1991), p. 14.
5 Simon, *Education and the Labour Movement*, pp. 192–3.

6 N. Daglish, *Education Policy-Making in England and Wales: The Crucible Years, 1895–1911* (London: Woburn Press, 1996), p. 72.

7 R. Morley, 'The Development in London of Elementary Education of a Higher Type (1900–1910)', MA Thesis, London, 1961, p. 167.

8 M. Vlaeminke, *The English Higher Grade Schools: A Lost Opportunity* (London: Woburn Press, 2000).

9 M.P. Moran, 'Central Schools and the Reorganisation of Elementary Education, from 1902 to 1939, with particular reference to the London County Council and City of Manchester', MPhil Thesis, London, 1994, pp. 27–9.

10 *Stratford Express*, 12 May 1906. William Morris Higher Elementary won the LSFA's championship for individual schools (Dewar Shield) in 1908–09.

11 P. Gordon, 'Commitments and developments in the elementary school curriculum 1870–1907' in *History of Education*, 6, 1 (1977), p. 52; R. Aldrich, *An Introduction to the History of Education* (London: Hodder and Stoughton, 1982), pp. 83–4.

12 Maclure, *Education in London*, p. 91.

13 Graves, *To Return to All That: An Autobiography* (London: Jonathan Cape, 1930), p. 290.

14 *Report of the London County Council for the Year 1907/8* (London: LCC, 1909), pp. 95, 110.

15 LCC, 'Application Form for Organised Games' (1916). Public Record Office. PRO ED 14/97. I am grateful to Ann Morton for directing me to this item.

16 Hermit Road School (Boys), Canning Town, Log Book, 11 September 1899. Newham Archives and Local Studies Library.

17 Min. LSFA, 18 July 1913. After the First World War the age limit for the Sun Shield reverted to being one year younger than that for the Corinthian Shield and remains so to the present.

18 Min. LSFA, 15 January 1923.

19 LSFA, *Handbook 1914/5*, p. 20.

20 *Tottenham and Edmonton Weekly Herald*, 6 May 1914.

21 Min. LSFA, 22 June 1914.

22 A. Waugh, *The Lipton Story: A Centennial Biography* (London: Lipton International, 1952), p. 180.

23 M.E. Buckley, *The Feeding of School Children* (London: Bell and Sons, 1914), p. xi.

24 Buckley, *Feeding of School Children*, pp. 12–22; J.S. Hurt, *Elementary Schooling and the Working Classes* (London: Routledge & Kegan Paul, 1979), p. 106.

25 Guardian Angels R.C. School, Mile End, Log Book, 16 May 1902. Tower Hamlets Local History Collection.

26 Canning Town School (Boys) Log Book, 9 December 1902. Newham Archives and Local Studies Library.

27 J.S. Hurt, *Elementary Schooling and the Working Classes*, pp. 109–10.

28 Buckley, *Feeding of Schoolchildren*, pp. 28–9; Simon, *Education and the Labour Movement*, p. 281.

29 Simon, *Education and the Labour Movement*, pp. 281–5; Buckley, *Feeding of School Children*, pp. 39–44.

30 Sir J.E. Gorst, *The Children of the Nation* (London: Methuen, 1906), p. 54.

31 D.A. Reeder, 'Predicaments of city children: Late Victorian and Edwardian perspectives on education and urban society' in D.A. Reeder (ed.), *Urban Education in the Nineteenth Century* (New York: St Martin's Press, 1978), pp. 81–4; May, 'Curriculum Development under the School Board for London', p. 126.

32 R. Lowe, 'The early twentieth century open-air movement: Origins and implications' in N. Parry and D. McNair (eds), *The Fitness of the Nation: Physical and Health Education in the Nineteenth and Twentieth Centuries* (Leicester: History of Education Society, 1983), p. 93.

33 A.W. Smyth, *Physical Deterioration: Its Causes and the Cure* (London: Murray, 1904), p. 292.

34 Tower Hamlets and Hackney SFA played many of their matches in Victoria Park.

35 A.P. Graves, 'Physical Education in primary schools', *The Contemporary Review*, 85 (June 1904), p. 894. Graves was father of the poet, Robert Graves.

36 Graves, *Physical Education*, pp. 896–7.

37 McIntosh, *Physical Education*, p. 123.

38 *Football 'Sun'*, 5 December 1903.
39 Min. ESFA, 9–19 July, 29 October, 5 November 1904. I am grateful to Malcolm Berry, when he was Chief Executive of the ESFA, for permitting me to consult these minutes.
40 Molyneux, *Physical Recreation*, pp. 188–9.
41 Min. ESFA, 5 November 1904.
42 Min. ESFA (Council), 10 December 1904.
43 The new regulations are outlined in detail in (H. Wilkinson) *Football Regulations for Young Players: 'A Charter for Quality'* (London: FA, 1997).
44 F. Wall to T.P. Thomas, 6 October 1904. The letter is attached to Min. ESFA, 5 November 1904.
45 The LSFA beat St Albans, Northampton, Birkenhead in the semi-final and Sheffield in the final.
46 Min. ESFA, 24 May 1905.
47 Min. FA (Council), 14 April 1905. I am grateful to David Barber for allowing me to consult these minutes.
48 Min. ESFA, 17 June 1905.
49 LSFA, *Handbook 1905/6*, p. 14.
50 Between 1906/07 and 1914/15 the LSFA played Glasgow six times and Edinburgh once. LSFA, *Handbook 1992/3 (Centenary Edition)*, p. 25.
51 Gorst, *Children of the Nation*, p. 212.
52 On the introduction of Swedish Drill, see McIntosh, *Physical Education in England*, pp. 156–9.
53 Gorst, *Children of the Nation*, pp. 203–9. He practised what he preached and used to ride a bicycle to the Education Department. G.W. Kekewich, *The Education Department and After* (London: Constable, 1901), p. 103.
54 Gorst, *Children of the Nation*, p. 211.
55 Graves, *To Return to All That*, p. 289.
56 ESFA, *Handbook 1907/8*, pp. 3–4. Wix himself presented a trophy to the Herts and Luton SFA, which is still contested today. This information came from David Willacy, when he was the ESFA's Information Officer.
57 Lewisham Bridge School (Girls) Log Book, 15 August 1872.
58 Kathleen E. McCrone, 'Class, gender, and English women's sport, c. 1890–1914', *Journal of Sports History*, 18, 1 (Spring 1991), p. 161.
59 Daubeney Road School, Hackney (Girls) Log Book, 21 May 1995. LMA. EO/DIV4/ DAU/ LB/1.
60 Bellenden Road School, Peckham (Girls) Log Book, 21 July 1905. LMA. EO/DIV7/BEL/ LB/5.
61 Sheila Fletcher, 'The making and breaking of a female tradition: Women's physical education in England 1880–1980', *The British Journal of Sports History*, 2, 1 (May 1985), p. 30.
62 McCrone, 'Class, gender, and English women's sport', p. 162.
63 Windsor Road School Log Book, 8 November 1899. LMA. EO/DIV4/ WIN/LB/1.
64 Buchan, *A Lifetime in Football*, p. 10.
65 For an appraisal of the moves to retain the pupil teacher centres see W. Robinson, 'In search of a "plain tale": Rediscovering the champions of the pupil-teacher centres 1900–10', *History of Education*, 28, 1 (1999), pp. 53–71.
66 Buchan, *A Lifetime in Football*, p. 16.
67 For Buchan's career with Leyton, see D.I. Chapman, *Dubbed Boots and Shin Pads: A History of Leyton Football Club*, 2, 1889–1912 (London: The Author, 1999), pp. 31–3.
68 Buchan, *A Lifetime in Football*, p. 22.
69 For his ideas to counter the offside rule see Buchan, *A Lifetime in Football*, pp. 90–2.
70 Ibid., p. 123.
71 Ibid., pp. 61–2.
72 *News Chronicle*, 12 April 1956.

73 (Wilkinson), *Football Education for Young Players*.

74 I am grateful to Wayne Gordon, James Gordon's grandson, for information on the family's origins.

75 Barking SFA, *Handbook 1936*, p. 33. I am grateful to George Cash for finding me a copy of this item.

76 Frederick Kemp, for example, a pupil at Gascoigne Road, Barking, and a future West Ham United player, was in the East Ham district team that played Walthamstow in the Corinthian Shield in the 1899/1900 season. *South Essex Mail*, 18 November 1899.

77 *Barking Advertiser, 3 December 1898*.

78 Ibid., 24 March 1900.

79 Ibid., 25 January 1908.

80 Barking lost the final to the King's Own Rifles.

81 London FA, *Handbook 1934/5*, pp. 53, 54; Essex County FA, *Official Handbook 1995/6*, pp. 37, 40.

82 *Barking Advertiser*, 2, 23 April 1910.

83 Ibid., 28 May 1910.

84 Information from Wayne Gordon.

85 The information in this paragraph is based on a letter from Patrick Conway, Lending Services Librarian, Humberside County Council, to C.J. Appleby (one of James Gordon's grandsons), 23 November 1978, a copy of which was made available to me by Wayne Gordon.

86 Letter from A. Drewry, Chairman, FA, to C.W. Fuller, Secretary, London FA, 14 December 1959.

87 I am grateful to Brian Warren for supplying me with details of his father's early life.

88 Brian Warren has kindly provided me with a copy of a picture in the *Illustrated Sporting and Theatrical News* of 3 November 1866, showing Robert Warren in the ring with Jem Mace on the occasion of the newspaper presenting the boxer with a belt engraved with the ensignia 'Champion of the World'.

89 London FA, *Handbook 1934/5*, p. 65.

90 Brian Warren has kindly found me a photograph of the 1912/13 team.

91 West Ham lost the English Schools' Shield final to Sheffield. The schoolboy internationals were E. Goldsmith (the England schoolboys' captain), Margetts (later Leyton) and Hebden (later Queen's Park Rangers).

92 Officers of the West Ham SFA blamed their team's defeat partly on it taking place the evening following one of their English Schools' Shield matches. ESFA, *Handbook 1914/5*, p. 64.

93 *Tottenham and Edmonton Weekly Herald*, 6 May 1914.

94 London FA, *Handbook 1934/5*, p. 112.

95 Ibid., pp. 66, 67.

96 N. Ackland, 'The Amateur Football Alliance' in Fabian and Green (eds), *Association Football*, 1, p. 369.

97 His father's words were quoted by Brian Warren in a letter to me dated 4 May 1999.

98 Statistical and biographical works on West Ham United give Tresadern's place of birth as Leytonstone and his date of birth as 1892 or 1893. J. Northcutt and R. Shoesmith, *West Ham United: A Complete Record 1900–1987* (Derby: Breedon, 1987), p. 389; Hogg and McDonald, *West Ham Who's Who*, p. 204. Fred Wright's family history (Tresadern was a distant relative) gives the correct date (1891) and reproduces Tresadern's birth certificate as evidence. Fred Wright, *A Book of Wrights and Buckleys* (privately printed, 1994), p. 181.

99 Besides being indebted to the late Poppy Ronson, Jack Tresadern's daughter, I am also grateful to Alan Ronson, her husband, who kindly sent me his wife's notes about her father and later wrote down his own memories of Tresadern for me.

100 West Ham, Sheffield and Sunderland were the most successful teams in the early years of the English Schools' Shield.

101 *Stratford Express*, 26 October 1907.

102 For details of Wanstead FC and its relevance to the work of the LSFA, see Chapter 6.

103 *Stratford Express*, 6 April 1912.

104 *East Ham Echo*, 5 April 1912.

105 Letter from Miss L.F. Hearn, for Departmental Record Officer, Ministry of Defence, 10 March 1997.

106 *Stratford Express*, 7 February, 4 September 1920.

107 Ibid., 28 March 1923.

108 For injury see *Stratford Express*, 13 October 1923 and for transfer see *Burnley Express and Advertiser*, 1 November 1925, which quotes the *Daily Sketch*'s understanding of the fee.

109 In a profile of Northampton Town's new player manager the local newspaper noted, among other things, that Tresadern had been 'spotted' as a boy by Harry Earle. *Northampton Mercury*, 6 May 1925.

110 *Northampton Mercury*, 31 December 1926.

111 *Croydon Advertiser*, 25 October 1930.

112 *Croydon Advertiser*, 3 January 1931. The club had played six FA Cup games the previous season.

113 *Match Programme Clapton Orient vs Crystal Palace*, 10 March 1934. For Crystal Palace's record while Tresadern was manager see Purkiss and Sands, *Crystal Palace*, pp. 154–63.

114 His daughter remembered how Bill Nicholson, later Tottenham's manager, was an apprentice at the club when Tresadern first went there.

115 Goodwin, *Spurs*, p. 64. See also D. Turner and A. White, *The Breedon Book of Football Managers* (Derby: Breedon, 1993), p. 240.

116 W.S. Tonkin, *All About Argyle 1903–1963: The Plymouth Argyle Diamond Jubilee Book* (Plymouth: Plymouth Argyle FC, 1963), p. 43.

117 Ibid.

118 Tresadern's daughter's account: see Note 99.

119 *Western Independent*, 3 February 1946.

120 The official history of the club concedes only that the circumstances surrounding Tresadern's departure 'might suggest that the boardroom was not altogether blameless'. Tonkin, *All About Argyle*, p. 49.

121 Tresadern never revealed the identity of the benefactor.

122 *Kent Messenger*, 1 January 1960.

123 *Evening Standard*, 9 July 1999.

124 Letter from Brian Warren, 4 May 1999.

125 Electoral Registers, West Ham, Polling District Stratford High Street, Ward No. 3. Newham Archives and Local Studies Library.

126 Information from Wayne Gordon: see Note 74.

127 Gascoigne School Log Book, 22 May 1901. Valance House Museum, Dagenham.

5 London teachers and schoolboy football, 1900–1915

Introduction

This chapter examines the work of a number of elementary-school teachers active in the promotion of schoolboy football in the London area in the early years of the last century. The section "LSFA Council Members 1907/08 to 1914/15" discusses in general terms the characteristics of 104 teachers who served as representatives of local SFAs on the LSFA Council in those years. The section "LSFA Council Members from Lewisham, South London, West Ham and West London" explores in more detail what is known about the work of the representatives of four of these local associations. The section "Five Teachers" consists of five biographical studies of teachers prominent in schoolboy football at the time. Issues addressed in the chapter include the background, commitment and motivation of teachers. The relationship between a SFA's success and the stability of service of its officers is also explored, as is the extent to which a school's reputation at games might influence attendance and over-subscription.

LSFA Council members 1907/08 to 1914/15

The 104 teachers examined in this section represented the 15 associations that were in continuous affiliation with the LSFA from 1907/08 to 1914/15 (Table 5.1). Teachers in other associations, for example Ilford and Woolwich (the latter especially prominent in schoolboy football at the time), are excluded because they were not affiliated for the seasons 1909/10 and 1914/15 respectively. The dates were chosen because a complete run of the LSFA handbooks listing the Council members who represented each association between these dates has survived.

Perhaps the most striking aspect of the list is the continuity of service of teacher representatives on the Council. While in theory each association could have nominated three different teachers as representatives each year, making a total of twenty-four different teachers for each association, in practice no association's different representatives over the eight-year period came to even half of that number and apart from two associations, Acton & Chiswick and Greenwich & Deptford, which each sent eleven different

Table 5.1 Ranking order of SFA 'stability' between 1907/08 and 1914/15

Order	Association	Number of representatives
1	East Ham	4
1	West Ham	4
3	Lewisham	5
3	West London	5
5	South London	6
5	Tower Hamlets	6
5	Willesden	6
8	Hackney	7
8	Leyton	7
8	Tottenham	7
8	Islington	7
12	Hornsey	8
12	Walthamstow	8
13	Acton	11
13	Greenwich	11

representatives, none sent more than eight. No district had the same representatives for each of the eight years, but two, East Ham and West Ham, sent the same three teachers for six of the eight years. Besides those two districts, which were each represented by as few as four different teachers only over the eight-year period, Lewisham (5), South London (6), Tower Hamlets (6) and Willesden (6) also had a small number of different representatives.

Turning to the names of representatives, eight teachers, A. Quinn (East Ham), J. Hollick (Hackney), J. West (Lewisham), R.R. Crump (South London), C. Cook (Tottenham), E. Wenzel (Tower Hamlets), A.H. Mann and W. Boxall (both West Ham) remained on the Council for the whole eight-year period, while another, A.A. Newman (Walthamstow), was only prevented from doing so by his death in an air raid on London in 1915.[1] Several others served for six or seven years, among them J. Rose (Islington). When the LSFA team played Glasgow at Highbury in 1915, Rose was credited in the *Islington Gazette* with the match arrangements, and the reporter added that he had been by that time secretary of Islington SFA for 12 years.[2] The years of service given above relate only to the eight seasons under consideration. Many of the teachers had certainly been on the Council in earlier years and some of the long-serving representatives, like Wenzel, Hollick and T.J. Duke (Willesden), continued as representatives throughout the First World War and after.

In an attempt to ascertain if there was a correlation between the stability of local associations, as determined by the low number of teachers who represented the fifteen associations on the LSFA Council (Table 5.1), and the success of the fifteen associations, as determined by their performances in national and local competitions (Tables 5.2 and 5.3), two assumptions were made.

Table 5.2 Performances in English Schools' shield and in LSFA competitions 1907/08 to 1914/15

Season	English shield finalist (3 points)	English shield semi-finalist (2 points)*	Corinthian shield winner (2 points)	Corinthian shield runner up (1 point)	Sun shield winner (1 point)	Dewar shield winner (1 point)
1907/08		Woolwich	West Ham	South London	Woolwich	Leyton
1908/09		West London	Leyton	West London	Tower Hamlets	Walthamstow
1909/10			South London	Hackney	Lewisham	Hackney
1910/11	Tottenham		West London	Tottenham	Leyton	Lewisham
1911/12	West Ham		West London	West Ham	West Ham	West London
1912/13			West London	Acton	West Ham	Acton
1913/14	West Ham	West London	West London	Tottenham	West Ham	East Ham
1914/15			West London	West Ham	West London	West London

*In the English Shield, the 2 points for semi-finalists were not included for those teams that advanced to the final.

Table 5.3 Ranking order of 'success' of associations

Order	Association	Points
1	West London	18
2	West Ham	13
3	Tottenham	5
4	Leyton	4
5	South London	3
6	Hackney	2
6	Acton	2
6	Lewisham	2
9	East Ham	1
9	Tower Hamlets	1
9	Walthamstow	1
12	Greenwich	0
12	Islington	0
12	Hornsey	0
12	Willesden	0

The first was that having a small number of representatives on the LSFA Council over the eight-year period did in fact represent a barometer of stability. It could have been, for example, that the same people were elected annually because no one else was prepared to come forward. The small amount of evidence that exists in local association minutes suggests, however, that these positions were keenly contested and that re-election would only occur if the duties appertaining to the role had been discharged competently. Regularly re-elected representatives, therefore, suggests competent as well as committed officers in an association, which in turn suggests a stable and flourishing association. An adjustment from seven to five representatives over the eight-year period was made in the case of West London because two of that association's teacher representatives on the LSFA Council, J.A. Duley and S.F. Gill, were appointed to the post of secretary of the LSFA in 1909 and 1913 respectively. As this appointment gave them *ex officio* membership of the Council, two other teachers had to replace them as West London representatives. But the appointment of Duley and Gill (and that of T. Pear, another West London teacher, before them) to the most responsible position in the LSFA testifies to the strength and stability of the West London SFA rather than to its weakness, hence the adjustment.

The second assumption is that an association's success may be determined by its achievements in national and London schoolboy competitions rather than by, for example, the number of teams that took part in its internal schools' league or cup competitions or by the number of its boys who went on to play for senior clubs later in life. It is true that such additional information would provide a more sophisticated criterion of success than the rather crude one based on reaching the final stages of major competitions that is employed here. As details of local leagues and information on what became of former players are only partially available for a handful of associations, however, and as nothing at all is known about the internal competitions organised by some of the affiliated associations listed, a more sophisticated criterion of success than that used here is not possible at present. As regards the points system allocated to measure success, the criterion employed in awarding high points has been the difficulty of achieving the named stage of each competition. All the competitions taken into account were for districts, except the Dewar Shield, which was for individual schools, and it has been included because the playing strength of an association was often reflected in the playing strength of the school that was its representative in the Dewar Shield.[3]

The ranking order of the success of the fifteen associations (Woolwich is excluded because it was not affiliated every season over the 8 years) shown in Table 5.3 is based on the points allocated in Table 5.2 and does in fact correspond with what a subjective assessment would suggest about the respective playing standards of affiliated associations in the years between the turn of the century and the First World War, with one exception. This was South London, where performances during the eight seasons were uncharacteristically poor. In the eight preceding seasons, for example (1899/1900 to 1906/07), South London was in Corinthian Shield finals on no less than seven occasions, winning three of them and losing four, and in the eight seasons after the War (1919/20 to 1926/27), the district was again among the most successful in the country, winning national and LSFA titles.[4]

The back-to-back bar chart (Figure 5.1) suggests a moderately strong relationship between association 'stability' and association 'success', in that three of the five most stable associations were also among the five most successful on the field of play and in that the unstable associations had little or no success in competitions. East Ham is a conspicuous exception to the pattern of stable associations performing best in competitions. That the relationship is only moderately strong is not surprising, bearing in mind the other factors that would have determined competitive success like the total number of children in affiliated schools, the ability of teachers' training teams and the traditions of sport in an area, the existence of playing fields, the prosperity or otherwise of an area and the consequent diet and health of the boys and the average age at which they would have left school.

LSFA Council members from Lewisham, South London, West Ham and West London

This section explores what could be ascertained about the teacher representatives from a sample of four of the fifteen associations that formed the subject of the section "LSFA Council Members 1907/08 to 1914/15". The four SFAs whose twenty-three representatives are to be looked at more closely in the present section were chosen so that, broadly, the 'four quarters of London

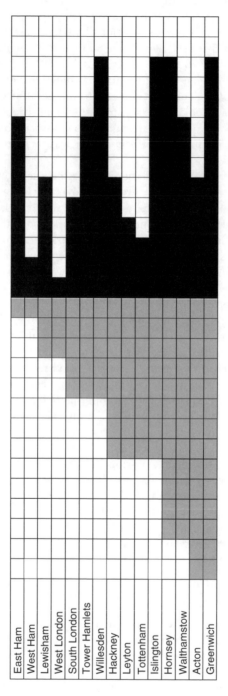

Figure 5.1 Back-to-back bar chart showing the relationship between the ranking order of the 'stability' of associations and the ranking order of their 'success'. 'Stability' is represented in grey and 'success' in black.

Note: 'Stability' and 'success' ranking order are represented by one box for first place in the ranking order, two for second, etc.

were included: South-west (South London), South-east (Lewisham), East (West Ham) and West (West London). Relevant information, in addition to the names of their schools and service on the LSFA Council, has been traced for thirteen of the twenty-three teachers as follows: Lewisham (2), South London (5), West Ham (3) and West London (3).

As striking as the continuity of service noted earlier in connection with the 104 representatives over the eight-year period is the longevity of service to schoolboy football that is evident from the biographical information that is available on the thirteen teachers. J.T. Ford, for example, appeared in the South London SFA fixture list as the teacher-in-charge of the team at Heber Road, Dulwich, as early as 1894.[5] A profile of W. Boxall in his local paper in 1909 noted that he was trained at Borough Road College and had been in charge of the boys' team at Manor Road, West Ham, for ten years by that date.[6] Boxall and A.H. Mann of Pelly Memorial took over the training of the West Ham district side from Harry Earle in 1912 and the magazine of the West Ham SFA reported in 1929 that Boxall was then in his final year as district team trainer.[7] This amounted to a total of thirty years of training schoolboy teams. S. Gill served the West London SFA, the LSFA and the ESFA for an even longer period. Having trained his first schoolboy team in 1898, he was still active as late as 1948.[8]

Another striking feature about the thirteen teachers is that, like the three named in the previous paragraph, many had responsibilities for the training not only of their own school teams, as might be expected, but of district teams, or, in the case of Gill, the LSFA representative side. W.E. Lucking, of Shillington Road, Battersea, for example, was responsible for the South London district side that won the Corinthian Shield in 1902/03 and the teams that were beaten finalists in the competition for the following three seasons.[9] Lucking was followed as district trainer by H. Britton. Trained as a teacher at St Mark's College, Chelsea, Britton guided his team to two Corinthian Shield final wins.[10] J.W. West of Sandhurst Road was trainer of the Lewisham team that won the Sun Shield in 1909/10 and J.W. Masters, trained at St John's and a teacher at William Street, was in charge of the West London team that reached the semi-final of the English Schools' Shield in 1908/09.[11]

Several of the thirteen teachers were involved in sport in other ways. Lucking and W.E. Child were referees, and Boxall played with the East Ham United team that won the Eastern Suburban League in 1902/03 and with the East Ham side that won the Walthamstow Charity Cup in 1907/08.[12] Child and Gill were both active in their local schools' swimming association and the former was described in 1912 as one of the oldest members of the Arlington Cricket Club but 'still one of their most reliable batsmen'.[13] Besides his involvement in football, swimming, cricket and tennis, Child was also the secretary of the West Ham Children's Hospital Fund, which encouraged children in schools to take an interest in the work of the hospital through raising funds and visiting patients.[14] He became headmaster of Custom

House in 1912 and after the First World War was appointed head of the Raleigh Institute, one of West Ham's controversial continuation schools.[15]

Four of the thirteen teachers had been secretaries of their local SFAs. Mann and R.R. Crump were secretaries of West Ham and South London respectively for all of the eight seasons, Gill was secretary of West London until he was appointed LSFA secretary in 1913 and F.H. Holland was secretary of Lewisham for at least two seasons. When it is borne in mind that all of the thirteen were full-time teachers and were sometimes engaged in promoting other sports besides football, it is scarcely credible that some of them found time for other praiseworthy pursuits unrelated to sport. A man who had been in Jimmy Hollick's class in Hackney Free and Parochial School has written that, besides his half century of service to the Hackney SFA, Hollick 'was mainly responsible for keeping my Scout Troop (14th Hackney, St John at Hackney) running' during the First World War and was also 'a tower of strength in Parish matters'.[16] At his funeral service in 1921, Mann, who helped train many successful school and district sides, was remembered by the vicar of his local church, St Peter's, Upton Lane, as having rendered great service to the parish over many years.[17]

This brief profile of a sample of teachers from four associations who served on the LSFA Council over the eight-year period suggests an enormous commitment of time and energy by those who chose to promote football in elementary schools at the highest level, something that will be reinforced in the more detailed biographies of the teachers who form the subject of the section "Five Teachers". In the present context, however, it may be appropriate to conclude by noting that the 104 teachers who formed the subject of these two sections consisted of less than a tenth of those engaged in promoting football in associations affiliated to the LSFA in the period under review.[18]

Five teachers

While the five teachers whose teaching careers, insofar as these relate to schoolboy football, form the subject of the present section were prominent figures in the promotion of the game in the London area in the period under review (1900–15), all five were also either training teams or organising inter-school matches, or both, during the last years of the nineteenth century. Four of the five continued with their commitment to school sport into the 1920s. All, therefore, conformed to the pattern of long service referred to in the last section as being characteristic of teachers that were involved in schoolboy football at the time. Of the five, one did not attend a teachers' training college or at least did not complete a course to qualify as a certificated teacher and the college of another could not be traced, if indeed he attended one. Of the others, two attended St John's College, Battersea and one St Mark's, Chelsea. The log books for the schools in which four of the teachers worked have survived for at least part of the time they were active in school sport.

W.J. Wilson

William J. Wilson, who was born in 1854, had been a pupil teacher at Brighton Central National before gaining admission to St John's College, Battersea, in 1874.[19] St John's had been founded by Dr Kay (later Sir Kay-Shuttleworth) in 1840 to address the problem of poorly qualified teachers.[20] A survey in 1910 revealed that as many as a third of the 2,200 teachers who had been trained at the college up to that date were employed in schools in the London area at that time.[21] St John's was one of several London training colleges where, in the course of the second half of the nineteenth century, increased attention was given to the value of games, something that derived in part at least from the increasing emphasis on games in the public schools.[22] Sport replaced gardening as the St John's students' main recreational pursuit towards the end of the century, with teams from the nearby St Mark's, Chelsea, offering formidable opposition on the playing fields.[23] Ernest Gray, the Conservative MP, who had been a student at St John's in the 1870s, later drew attention to the major part played by inter-collegiate sport in college life.[24] The football played at St John's at that time was guided by the Eton College rules, but through the energies of W.H. Gwynn, who was a student there in the mid-1870s, the rules of the FA were adopted by the college FC.[25] Many teachers trained at St John's reached prominent positions in football as players, referees and administrators and, of most relevance in the present context, as promoters of football in elementary schools. J. Fox, captain of the football team at St John's in 1872, became one of the leading referees in the country and served on the Council of the FA at the same time as Wilson.[26] George Sharples was in the college team a few years after Fox and his first year at Battersea coincided with Wilson's second.[27] When Sharples became President of the NUT for 1904/05, it was Wilson who wrote a tribute to him in the annual publication of the college's past students' club. From this we learn that Sharples supported the adoption of the association football rules introduced into the college by Gwynn. Afterwards, as a teacher, he was involved in running football teams in several schools in which he taught in Lancashire and Yorkshire. While in Manchester, Sharples was responsible not only for training an excellent team at his school and raising large sums for the Teachers' Orphanage through 'gates' at football and athletic events, but in founding the Manchester SFA he launched one of the most successful associations in national schoolboy football competitions from 1905 up to the present day.[28] Mangan and Hickey have identified Sharples as an 'influential diffusionist' of athleticist ideals.[29] While evidence might be needed to confirm that his main motivation was athleticism, however interpreted, there is no doubting his commitment to the value of schoolboy football and his tireless efforts to promote it.

Just before Christmas of 1875 Wilson was 'sent out' from St John's, as the College register put it, with a Second Class Certificate and secured his first post at Monnow Road, Bermondsey, as assistant teacher at £70 per annum.[30]

The log book for the school for that period has not survived, but he seems to have performed well as a teacher and made good progress up the salary scale, with his recommended increase of £5 in 1880, for example, the outcome of 'A Good Report'.[31] In 1882 he was appointed headmaster of Oldridge Road, Balham, in the SBL's Lambeth Division, at a salary of £130 per annum.[32] As the history of the South London SFA names him as one of the teachers who were running football teams in elementary schools before the South London SFA was formed in 1885, he must have began organising football at his new school very shortly after his appointment there.[33]

Mangan and Hickey cite extracts relating to drill, swimming, football and cricket from the log book of Oldridge Road as background against which the attendance at the school improved and the numbers on the roll increased. The extracts, together with a reference to Wilson in *The Schoolmaster* that he loved 'manly games' and liked his team to win matches, are seen as grounds for the claim that he 'was driven by a threefold desire to improve the health and fitness of the boys, teach them to enjoy games playing for its own sake and to develop in them a competitive spirit'.[34] While his log book confirms that Wilson's commitment to sport in his school was what might be expected of a headmaster interested in games, the entries offer little that might provide insights into his reasons for doing so. For while drill and swimming in school and football and cricket as outside-school activities are indeed referred to, such activities took place in hundreds of schools around London in the late nineteenth century. The log book of the school run by the man who founded the South London SFA and the LSFA and who was a leading figure in schoolboy football at the time, however, might be expected to reveal something more substantial on which to construct speculations about his motivation. In this, Oldridge Road's log book resembled those of most of the schools prominent in schoolboy football, the log books of which were examined in connection with this work and listed in the Bibliography at the end of this book. The existence of a school football team was often acknowledged, the name of the teacher who trained it was occasionally mentioned and details of success in competitions were frequently entered. It was rare, however, to find an entry that suggested reflection on what having a school football team meant in educational terms, why a teacher was devoting time to football training after school or what it was that the boys were expected to derive from playing the game. Entries like that at Marner, on the benefits of fresh air while playing football and that at Berkshire Road, on the benefits of games on teacher–pupil relations were the exceptions rather than the rule.[35]

It could have been, of course, that as games were played outside school hours, head teachers felt they were not an appropriate subject to record or reflect on in school log books. Or it could have been that, fearing that games were being given too much attention, teachers might have wished to disguise evidence of their influence. Or it might even have been that the arguments in favour of outdoor games were so well known as not to require justification any more than, say, music. Monteith Road in Bow, for example, won the Tower Hamlets SFA Junior Challenge Football Shield in 1895 and won first prize for school choirs at the Stratford Music Festival the following year. The log book entries that recorded both victories were of similar length, with no attempt made to justify the educational value of either.[36]

The relationship between school sport and improvements in attendance and enrolment is problematic. If it could be shown that a late nineteenth-century elementary school with drill and swimming on the curriculum and with a known and active advocate of inter-school games at its head had, *for that reason*, a better attendance record and a greater demand for its places than other schools, this would indeed constitute a considerable breakthrough in our knowledge of the attitudes of parents to games in the Victorian elementary school. But neither the log books of Oldridge Road nor those of any of the schools prominent in schoolboy football in the period under review show this. The factors determining improvements in school attendance are complex and, in the case of Oldridge Road, might not have been related in any way to the prominence given to games at the school. The percentage of attendance at schools run by the SBL had increased enormously during the first years of the Board's work, as would be expected from the great number of attendance officers that were employed to enforce it, the habits of regular attendance that were being formed and the increasing acceptance, among working-class parents in particular, of the value of the education the schools were offering. Inevitably, with an attendance level of over 80 per cent achieved by the beginning of the decade, increases in the rate of improvement declined during the 1890s. But there was still an overall percentage increase in attendance at London Board schools in these years, that had reached 89 per cent by the time the Board's work was transferred to the LCC in 1904.[37] It is clear that attendance at Oldridge Road was better than average; what we do not know is if the *rate of increase* was greater than average, and more importantly, if it was, whether or not games was a factor in causing it.

A survey of attendance at the ten schools most prominent in schoolboy football in Tower Hamlets between 1892 and 1903, for example, revealed that while the average school for the Division showed an improvement from 76.9 per cent in 1892 to 87.6 per cent in 1903, only five of the ten 'football' schools had a better improvement than the average, while the average improvement for the ten was less than that for the Division as a whole.[38] This suggests that prominence in games had little impact on average school attendance at the time, although it might, of course, have influenced attendance in the higher Standards, from which the teams were picked, or, more particularly, the attendance of the boys who actually played in school teams.[39] Similarly, evidence is needed to show that the increasing numbers who wanted to attend Oldridge Road (there are numerous references in the log book to the fact that the school was over-subscribed) were influenced by the school's reputation for games. The log book contains no such evidence. It might simply have been, for example, that the school was located in an area where the child population was rapidly expanding.

The minutes of the South London SFA and LSFA confirm the entries in the school log book that indicate that Wilson was a tireless advocate of outdoor games for elementary-school pupils. Scrutiny of the surviving minutes reveals the enormous energy he put into organising inter-school and inter-district football competitions, securing pitches, refereeing matches, making travel arrangements for venues as far away as Sheffield and Leeds, soliciting and purchasing trophies and medals and, perhaps, most time-consuming of all, arranging general, committee and special meetings, keeping efficient minutes of these meetings in his clear handwriting and following up the many decisions agreed but left to him to put into effect. Two brief examples may illustrate this. When a long discussion about the rules that should govern the South London SFA came to no conclusion at the preliminary meeting held at Oldridge Road in 1885, it was left to Wilson to get a list of rules to bring for discussion at the next meeting.[40] When the LSFA needed a trophy for its first inter-district competition in 1893/94, it was Wilson who approached the Corinthian FC to secure what became known as the Corinthian Shield.

Wilson's approach to the Corinthian FC rather than to a professional club for a trophy suggests a commitment to the amateur ideal. Whether he may rightly be seen as an embodiment of the games ideology associated with the public schools is another matter, unless every teacher promoting games with evident intensity is to be considered as such. His commitment was certainly intense. Indeed, his efforts in the cause of schoolboy football, as revealed in the minutes of the South London SFA and the LSFA that have survived, in newspaper reports and in his school log book, reflect an attitude to games that, in the intensity of his commitment to them, bore some resemblance to that of masters promoting games in public schools at the time. His one recorded pronouncement on outdoor games for boys, however, emphasised their value in improving the boys' physique. Part of Sharples' 1898 survey solicited information on what teachers saw as the benefits of elementary-school sports associations. Wilson's response emphasised that football provided healthy exercise during the winter months and that its benefits were evident in the improvements in the physique of old scholars who had played the game while at school when compared to those who had not.[41]

Wilson was also involved in the administrative side of cricket and his work in football was not restricted to schoolboys. In their profile of the fifty-three members of the FA Council in 1905, Gibson and Pickford wrote that Wilson, then on the Council as a member for the Surrey County FA, was 'a member of the great army of the teaching profession that plays so prominent a part in modern amateur football'. He was on the Council of the LFA for many years and a founder of the Old Londonians FC, one of the elementary-school 'old boy' clubs to be considered in Chapter 6.[42] He was also a well-known referee in amateur games and at the age of 69 was appointed Chief Steward at the first FA Cup final at Wembley in 1923.

When Wilson died 5 years later, the South London SFA's Executive Committee annual report contained a tribute which, besides drawing attention to his 40 years' service to football and his commitment to 'a clean English game', acknowledged his inspiration and help in a manner that suggests that he had continued to be active in the South London SFA until shortly before his death.[43]

T. Haydock

In 1923 the honour of president of the South London SFA was conferred on Tom Haydock, 'in recognition of services extending over a period of nearly 35 years'.[44] He is first mentioned in the minutes of that Association in 1889, when a complaint was made against him in his capacity of referee of an inter-school match.[45] At a meeting three weeks later it was recorded that the complaint 'could not be entertained'.[46] The confidence of the committee was well placed, as, while it is not clear if Haydock was a qualified referee at the time, he was to be so later and was to appear in LFA handbooks under its list of 'Registered Referees'.[47]

Haydock was born in 1865 and, having been a pupil teacher at Abbey Boys, Worksop, was admitted to St John's, Battersea, in 1884, 10 years after Wilson.[48] While there he played in the college football team, having previously been secretary of and played for Worksop FC.[49] He left college at the end of 1885 with a Second Class Certificate and was employed as a teacher at St George's Road, Southwark. That he played a high standard of football is evident from the fact that in the season after he left college, when he was aged around twenty-one, he appeared regularly in the Hotspur team that played at Wimbledon and succeeded in reaching the London Cup final, although Haydock did not actually play in the final.[50] He also appeared for the 'Past' of St John's, playing as a forward in the team that beat the 'Present' in 1892.[51]

Although Winstanley Road, where Haydock taught in the early 1890s, was not a major force in South London football, his team reached the final of the South London SFA junior championship in 1894/95, losing to Darrell Road. In 1897 Haydock was appointed assistant teacher at Deodar Road, Putney.[52] As the school was a relatively small one (there were only two assistant teachers in the Boys' Department) it was not prominent in competitions, but was nonetheless active at sport. The log book records the formation of a cricket club there in May 1898, the first summer after Haydock joined the staff.[53] The school, which changed its name to Brandlehow Road in 1901, was also active in swimming. When the Wandsworth Schools' Gala was held in October 1891, Haydock's name appears as one of the whips.[54] Haydock was obviously highly regarded in the school, as, when he left for his next post in 1902 after the relatively short stay of 5 years, he was presented with a gold chain on behalf of the managers.[55]

Haydock was appointed secretary of the South London SFA in 1893 in succession to Wilson and held the post until 1902. Apart from the normal duties pertaining to the post, Haydock made two particularly valuable contributions to the development of elementary-school football. The first concerned the fixtures between South London and Sheffield. Introduced while Wilson was still secretary, they were taken up with great enthusiasm by Haydock during his 10 years in office. The fixture had more significance than an annual outing for the best players and the most active teachers in the two associations. As well as establishing a strong relationship between two associations several hundred miles apart, the acceptance of each other's rules of play helped smooth agreement about rules for schoolboy football when a national body was formed in the following decade. In addition, the large numbers that paid to see the matches provided considerable funds for NUT charities.

Haydock's second major contribution to the promotion of schoolboy football was in the production of an annual handbook for the South London SFA from 1899. While the first issue has not been traced, many issues from the first decade of the new century are still in the possession of the Association and constitute an invaluable source on the early days of schoolboy football. These are the oldest handbooks traced for any SFA and if they were indeed the first of their kind, Haydock can be said to have set a standard that has not been bettered since. Besides typical features of sporting handbooks like lists of officers and winners of trophies, a review of the season past and fixtures for the season about to commence, the handbooks contained photographs of teachers prominent in the association, team pictures (both school and district), lists of boys who had played for South London and information on some of the boys who had gone on to make a mark in senior football. Later issues contained guidance on training young players and on how to run a schoolboy team.[56]

Haydock stood down from the office of secretary in 1902, possibly because in the same year he was appointed headmaster of Mitcham Lane in the West Lambeth Division of the SBL. As in the case of the log book of Wilson's school, that of Haydock provides ample testimony that he was an extremely good headmaster and that his school was held in high regard by the local inspectors and HMI. One of the latter, reporting in 1907, was particularly interesting in his account of the atmosphere in the school:

> The cordial relations which exist between the head teacher and his staff extend to the children in their charge, with the result that good discipline is maintained and good habits are being formed, not only without undue severity but also without apparent effort.[57]

It would be interesting to know if the headmaster's interest in and attitude to games might have contributed to this admirable atmosphere, but, as in the case of Oldridge Road, little is revealed in the log book that might help us understand how or why games were promoted in the school. There are entries indicating that the head teacher was absent from school occasionally to attend sports events in his own or other districts and that the boys took part in a physical exercise display, but no details were given of either and no attempt was made to show what value these activities might be seen to have for the participants.

One set of entries, however, does reveal something of the head teacher's attitude towards the issue of games during school hours, referred to in Chapter 4. On 6 April 1907 it was noted that Haydock was away all day at a conference on organised games and two months later the following entry appeared: 'If weather permits, the First Class Time Table will be altered from 3.25 p.m. and, as an experiment, Organised Games substituted.'[58] While the result of the experiment is not given in the log book, a future entry referring to the cancellation of an organised games lesson indicates, as might be expected from a head teacher so involved in the promotion of football, that games became part of the school curriculum once they had been given official approval.

Haydock became chairman of the South London SFA in 1909 and held that position until 1923, when he was succeeded by Foskett, referred to in Chapter 3 as Tommy Fitchie's trainer at Hazelrigge Road. Haydock was an active chairman and his attendance at committee meetings was exemplary, the annual reports showing him to have missed only 3 out of the possible 57 between 1912/13 and 1916/17. South London had some outstanding teams while Haydock was chairman in the years after the First World War, most particularly in 1921/22, when they won the English Schools' Shield for the first time, and in the previous season (1920/21), when what was thought by many to have been an even stronger side, was eliminated in the second round.[59] In 1923 Haydock was elected president of the South London SFA. He retired from teaching in 1925, but continued his active involvement with the work of the Association for another decade and was present when it celebrated its half-century in 1935. In the course of a tribute to him on the occasion of his retirement, it was said that there were few men who could 'more justifiably look back over such a lengthy period with the knowledge that the boys of our country, and particularly of South London, have reaped the fruits of his labours'.[60]

J.R. Schumacher

John 'Dick' Schumacher was a student at St Mark's College, Chelsea, in 1883 and 1884, featured prominently in the college football team and, after he left college, in the Old St Mark's team. This team played a high standard of football, but, having no ground of their own, had always to play away against opponents in London senior competitions. In the 1893/94 London Senior Cup, for example, Old St Mark's, with Schumacher at right back, came up against Tottenham Hotspur and, having earned a deserved draw at Northumberland Park, had to return to the same ground the following week for the replay. The replay was a significant match for historians of Tottenham Hotspur in that it was the first one held at their ground for which a printed programme was produced.[61] The result of the game was less memorable for the North London club, which was shortly to turn professional and was at that time drawing good crowds to its new ground, where it had moved from its original home on the Marshes in 1888.[62] With Jack Jull, one of the founders of the club, captaining the side and with Stanley Briggs, one of the great amateur players of the time playing at centre half, Tottenham lost heavily to the teachers. The defeat, a local paper wrote, 'fell as disaster on the district, and has absorbed the whole conversation in local circles'.[63]

Schumacher also played with Clapton FC, the club that had succeeded Upton Park as the most prominent amateur side in the East London area, appearing for them on the wing against Cambridge University in 1890 in a match that featured several international players, including H.A. Swepstone, the Clapton goalkeeper and A.H. Hossack, J.G. Veitch and M.H. Stanborough on the University side.[64] Despite appearing among such prestigious company and scoring twice in a Clapton win over London Caledonians, Schumacher seems to have been unable to hold his place in a team which was at that time playing at the very highest level of amateur football.[65]

As the log book has not survived for Wilton Road, Dalston, where Schumacher was appointed an assistant teacher in 1886, and as the minutes of the SBL confirming his appointment does not mention any previous employment, it is not possible to say at present if the post was his first in teaching since leaving St Mark's.[66] The school was built partly as the result of a deputation from local inhabitants requesting more school places for that part of the Hackney Division of the SBL, although a memorial arguing that there was no need for more places had to be considered by the Education Department before work actually began on purchasing the site.[67] The school was eventually opened at the end of 1886.[68] It is not known if Schumacher was engaged in training boys at the school at football in the years before the Hackney SFA was founded in 1891, but the fact that his teams were immediately successful in Hackney SFA events suggests that he might.

As noted in Chapter 3, the final of the first Hackney championship in 1892 was played in Victoria Park, with Wilton Road beating Mowlem. Wilton Road went on to win the competition outright every season for the remainder of the decade with the exception of 1897/98, when they tied with Rushmore, South Hackney. Tottenham Road won it in 1900, before Wilton Road went on to retain it for three consecutive seasons. The shield for the winning team in this competition seems to have been purchased by the association, unlike the trophies for other Hackney SFA competitions, which were donated by benefactors. Wilton Road also had a second eleven, which in 1903/04 won the Junior Division of the Hackney SFA. The cup for this event was donated by Horatio Bottomley and is still contested by Hackney primary schools today.[69] Yet another trophy was secured for Wilton Road, this one presented to Hackney SFA by Charles Russell, the local MP, when the second eleven was successful in the Intermediate League on several occasions.[70]

While very little about the progress of schoolboy football in Hackney is recorded in the *Hackney and Kingsland Gazette* in the 1890s, it is clear from the surviving result sheets that Wilton Road very much had things their own way in the senior competition throughout the decade. The introduction of a London Schools' individual championship (the LSFA's Dewar Shield) in 1899, therefore, would seem to have offered them an opportunity to pit their skills against the top schoolboy teams in London. Unfortunately, in the last match of the 1897/98 Hackney League, Rushmore beat Wilton Road, a result that left the two teams equal on points in the final table. As only one team from each district was permitted to enter the Dewar Shield, the Hackney SFA, as the *Football 'Sun'* put it, 'refused to make an invidious distinction and so nominated no school to represent it'.[71] Wilton Road were Hackney's representatives the following year (1899/1900), but were knocked out in the second round, and it was 1903/04 before the school made any mark in the competition. A surprise win over favourites Page Green (Tottenham) and an easy win against Oldfield Road (Islington) took Schumacher's side to the semi-final, in which they narrowly defeated Sherbrooke Road (West London) at Fulham.[72] In the final, Wilton Road held Higher Elementary (Ilford) to a draw, but in the replay at Ilford Sports Ground, the home team won 2–0.[73]

Six years later, by which time the *North London Guardian* had taken an interest in schoolboy football and Schumacher had been elected to the executive of the Hackney SFA, Wilton Road reached the Dewar final again.[74] Wins over Montem Street (Islington), Belmont Road (Tottenham) and Eltringham Street (South London) put Wilton Road through to the final against William Morris (Walthamstow) at Clapton Orient's ground.[75] Wilton Road were held to a draw, but won the replay at Wadham Lodge to claim the Dewar Shield and the individual schools' championship of London for the first time.[76]

There is evidence that the success of the Wilton Road teams was due to Schumacher. Speaking at the Hackney SFA's concert and presentation evening at the end of the 1903/04 season,

> Mr J.C. Dyke, the genial and energetic head of Wilton-road . . . modestly disclaimed credit for the football success of his team, stating that he had hardly to mention the name of Mr Schumacher, a name well known on every football field of the metropolis, to show that the work was in good hands or rather feet.[77]

Schumacher was well known on football fields not only because of his considerable ability as a player with Old St Mark's or his outstanding success as trainer of the Wilton Road boys' teams, but also because of his status as an able football administrator and as one of the leading referees in the country. He served on the council of the LFA, was for a time its refereeing secretary and was shortly to become one of its vice-presidents.[78] He was later to become a key figure in founding the Spartan League and was also chairman and refereeing secretary of the Isthmian League, two competitions that were to introduce to senior amateur football some of the aspects of league football that had proved so popular for professional players in the Football League.[79]

The details of his achievements as a referee are too numerous to enter into here, except to note that even when the demands for his services at the top levels of the game were at their height, he was prepared to referee schoolboy fixtures. Two weeks before he refereed the FA Cup final at Crystal Palace in 1912, for example, he took charge of the Leyton SFA's charity cup final.[80]

In conclusion, it may be appropriate to mention that he was willing to put his contacts with people of power and influence in the game at the disposal of schoolboy football. When an additional competition was introduced by the Hackney SFA in 1913 in the form of a charity event, the bronze shield for the winning team was 'obtained by the personal application of Mr J.R. Schumacher to prominent football personalities'.[81] It could not be established who these personalities were, and the programme notes to the 1937 final of the competition, held at Clapton Orient's ground, suggest that the benefactors might actually have been clubs rather than individuals. The Hackney Charity Shield, the notes read, 'is one presented years ago by Clubs of the First Division of the Football League, at the invitation of the late Mr Schumacher'.[82] Whether the approach had been to individuals or clubs, the competition for the Hackney Charity Shield raised as much as £3,000 by the time of Schumacher's death in 1933 – perhaps as much as £300,000 in today's money.[83]

H.T. Earle

Harry Earle's name first appeared in the log book of Godwin Road, Forest Gate, in 1887.[84] The school was at that time under the control of the School Board for West Ham and Earle was recorded in the staff return for the year as 'ex-P.T.'. He remained thus designated for the remainder of the period covered by this book, from which it might be assumed that he did not attend a teachers' training college.[85] An item in a report of the Education Committee of West Ham Council in 1920, when Earle had been in the Council's service for almost 33 years, indicates, however, that he might have done so for some time at least. The Committee reported that they

> had submitted to them an application from Mr H.T. Earle, an assistant teacher at Godwin Road Boys' School, to be placed in the same position as his fellow Certificated Teachers of similar service, and were informed that although Mr Earle passed part of the Certificate Examination he had been unable to complete his qualifications as a Certificated Teacher owing to domestic circumstances.

The Education Committee, 'in view of the exceptional circumstances', agreed to award him a set of three annual increases to bring his salary up to that of certificated teachers.[86]

His time as a pupil teacher, or at least part of it, must have been in the Tower Hamlets Division of the SBL, as a note in the *East End News* in 1895, commenting on Earle's football career, carried the information that he had played in the Tower Hamlets Pupil Teachers' team 'that won the football cup in 1887'.[87] Further evidence that he might have had associations with Tower Hamlets is the fact that his next known club was called Poplar Trinity (Poplar is an area within Tower Hamlets).

While the standard of football with the Pupil Teachers' team and with Poplar Trinity may not have been of senior club standard, that at his next known club, which he joined in 1889, undoubtedly was. This was Millwall Athletic which, founded as Millwall Rovers in the Isle of Dogs in 1885, was originally the works' team of Morton's jam and marmalade factory. By the time Earle joined it in 1889 the club had established itself as one of the strongest in the area by winning the East End Senior Cup in three successive seasons.[88] Although he was not in the team for all matches, Earle seems to have been selected for the more important games, playing as a forward in the first round of the FA Cup Qualifying Competition in 1890/91 and as a full back in the corresponding game the following season.[89] He was also in the Millwall team that was unlucky to lose by an own goal to Everton, at that time champions of the Football League, in a friendly played before a crowd of 5,000 in the Isle of Dogs.[90]

Earle had left Millwall by the time the club turned professional at the end of 1893. There had been speculations about the change to professionalism at the club for some time and this might have had an influence on his decision to leave and join the more rigorously amateur Clapton FC. He appears to have established himself quickly at his new club, appearing for them against Cambridge University late in 1893 and in the London Senior Cup and the London Charity Cup later in the season.[91] When the Southern League began the following season (1894/95) there were nine teams in the First Division, five of them professional (including Millwall) and four amateur (including Clapton). Clapton had a goalkeeping crisis in the second half of the season and R.H. Clark, the club's ex-centre forward, had to take over in goal as an emergency measure. He was injured for the fixture against Luton, one of the professional clubs, and Earle took his place in goal. He gained Clapton a draw with some excellent saves and had been, the local newspaper remarked, 'a most efficient substitute'.[92] He was more than that, as he made the position his own and went on to become one of the outstanding goalkeepers in the country over the following 10 years.

There was a football team at Godwin Road before Earle's arrival, probably run by the headmaster, Henry Herbert.[93] As was certain in the case of Wilson and likely in the case of Schumacher, Earle was engaged in training footballers at Godwin Road before his local SFA was founded. The school's log book records the case of a boy injured during a football practice at nearby Wanstead Flats, almost a year before the West Ham SFA was founded.[94] Both Earle and Herbert were at the inaugural meeting of the West Ham SFA on 30 September 1890, with the latter becoming the association's first chairman. Thirty years later, an unidentified man who had been a pupil at Godwin Road in 1890 recalled how Earle had gathered the school footballers together in his classroom to tell them that an inter-school football league was about to be formed 'and that he expected us to go in for it and win it'. His team did exactly that.[95] The following season Godwin lost the title to Park, a school which derived its name from West Ham Park (formerly Upton Park), and the trainer of which, Cornelius Beal, forms the subject of the next and last biography in this section. In subsequent years, right up to the First World War, these two schools were the dominant forces in West Ham schoolboy football, not only winning many titles between them, but providing a great number of players in West Ham district teams, many of whom later made a mark in senior football as professionals or as top level amateurs.[96]

Although Earle was at Godwin Road all that time, the school's success at football was not entirely due to his efforts. First of all, the school was only a few hundred metres from Wanstead Flats, with its excellent playing facilities for outdoor games. Second, the headmaster of the school was interested in games, as his acceptance of the chairmanship of the West Ham SFA testifies. Finally, the school was unusual in that it had two other teachers on the staff for a considerable part of this period who were interested in schoolboy football and in training schoolboy teams.

Walter Fields had been a pupil at Odessa Road, Forest Gate, and while there had learned his football on Wanstead Flats. He afterwards played with Dreadnought FC, based in West Ham Park, and was indentured as a pupil teacher at Godwin Road.[97] Besides his work at Godwin Road, Field, whose own football career was cut short by injury, followed Earle into Clapton FC later in the decade and was trainer of the junior teams there, many of which included ex-West Ham schoolboy players.[98] F.W. May had also been a pupil teacher at Godwin Road before going to college and returning as an assistant teacher in 1898.[99] In the 1904/05 season May took over the running of the school football team from Earle, whose training was then directed exclusively towards the district team. When the school won the coveted Dewar Shield for the first time in 1907, the School Management Sub-Committee recommended that the Education Committee's congratulations be conveyed to May and the boys.

The first match played by the West Ham SFA district side was against the adjoining area of Tower Hamlets in 1891. At first, West Ham district teams were selected by a committee of teachers on the basis of where a school was placed in the schools' league, with the leading team able to claim three places, the second placed team two and the remaining teams one each. Criticisms of the unsatisfactory way the team was selected came to a head in 1903/04. The committee was disbanded and the team was placed instead under the sole control of Earle. This led to the outstanding achievements of West Ham district sides in the English Schools' Shield, when the national inter-district competition was introduced in 1905. In an article in 1921, the magazine of the West Ham SFA recalled these changes and their consequences and offered an interesting insight into the attitudes the Association was trying to promote in schoolboy football. Earle's efforts, it said, had brought

> West Ham into prominence as a district where clever football was played, and where the game was played by boys who prided themselves upon their good sportsmanship. This reputation every player in West Ham should remember, as our good name depends not only upon the conduct of the boys representing West Ham, but upon the sporting behaviour of all players in all schools, and all our young spectators.[100]

Nor can there be any doubt that the success of the West Ham schoolboy teams on the field was attributable to Earle's training. In a 1908 interview with A.H. Mann, who had been secretary of the West Ham SFA since 1900, the *Stratford Express* made reference to the West Ham district teams' recent successes in the English and Corinthian Shield competitions, whereupon Mann 'modestly states, that these successes have been mainly due to the excellent coaching of Mr Harry Earle'.[101]

In contrast to entries acknowledging victories by the school team, run by F.W. May, in the Dewar Shield and Cook Cup (Essex SFA inter-schools' championship), achievements in which he clearly took pride, the headmaster of Godwin Road rarely made any mention of the district team.[102] The contrast was even greater with the enthusiasm shown by the headmaster for Earle's work with the school choir, which performed with regular success at the Stratford Music Festival and, in 1912, at the Paris Music Festival.[103] An obvious enthusiast for football, it could be that the headmaster felt that the Godwin Road Log Book was an inappropriate place to record the achievements of the district team, the boys in the team coming, as they did, from different schools throughout West Ham.

Earle retired as trainer of the West Ham SFA's district team in 1912. By that time his distinguished career as a player had also come to an end. Having made an outstanding contribution to Clapton FC as their goal-keeper, he fell foul of the FA when he accepted a present from the club supporters and was declared a professional when he refused to give it back. He played for a season with Notts County in the Football League, but his obituary in the *Stratford Express* in 1951 was adamant that 'despite his professional status, he never once accepted a pay packet'.[104] He got 'a most cordial reception' from the Clapton supporters when he returned with Notts County for a friendly against their team at the Old Spotted Dog Ground in 1905.[105] Whatever his feelings about his own situation might have been on that day, he must have been pleased to see that his opposite number in the Clapton goal, J. Wilding, who was to go on to play for the club in two Amateur FA Cup finals, had once been the West Ham SFA district team's goalkeeper.[106]

C.C. Beal

When a carter accidentally dropped a heavy truss of hay on Fred Bennett in 1910, causing Park's top scorer to fall and injure his knee, the local paper reported that Charlie Paynter, the West Ham United trainer, 'did wonders for the injured knee'.[107] Bennett, happily, recovered in time to lead his forward line to victory over Brownhill Road (Lewisham) in the Dewar Shield quarter final at the end of the week, but to defeat by William Morris (Walthamstow) in the semi-final shortly afterwards.[108]

It is of interest that the local paper should have given space to accounts of the fitness or otherwise of schoolboy players and that the West Ham United trainer should have made himself available to treat their injuries.[109] The contact between Park and the newspaper and between Park and West Ham United was almost certainly Cornelius Beal, who had been a teacher at the school, overlooking West Ham Park, for about 20 years by that time.

Beal had been a pupil and accomplished sportsman at St Michael's, Poplar, under the watchful eye of its dynamic headmaster, Robert Wild.[110] In 1878, when it came under the control of the SBL, the school changed its name to Byron Street and later to Hay Currie, in honour of the elected member for the Board who had been responsible for bringing Wild to the school, located in the Tower Hamlets Division.[111] Wild was an unrelenting opponent of the system of payment by results and played a significant role in its abolition.[112] Although the *East End News* carried detailed accounts of his educational achievements on the occasions of his retirement in 1906 and his death in 1916, there was no reference in either to his interest in or attitude to elementary-school games.[113] The swimming correspondent in the *Borough of West Ham Herald* commenting on the retirement, however, recalled that Wild had been his first swimming instructor and added that the number of children that he had taught to swim during his 44 years in Poplar must have been 'almost incalculable'.[114]

Byron Street was prominent in the early competitions of both the Poplar SFA and the Tower Hamlets SFA. When the school won the Poplar SFA League in 1886/87, Sydney Buxton, at the presentation evening, referred to the Byron Street victory as one 'which he felt sure Mr Wild, the headmaster, had done much to bring about'.[115]

Swimming and cricket were the sports at which Beal excelled. He also played football at a modest level with Toynbee Hall, a team attached to the University Settlement in Aldgate, to which reference was made in Chapter 2.[116] He does not appear to have attended the inaugural meeting of the West Ham SFA in 1890, but when his school joined the following season it made an immediate impact. With Beal in charge, Park defeated Earle's Godwin Road, the holders, in the first League match of the season, and held the lead right through to the end to win the competition. Park retained the title the following year, before Godwin Road, still run at that time by Harry Earle, took over as the most prominent team in West Ham schoolboy football for several seasons.[117] Beal was secretary of the West Ham SFA from 1897 until 1900, when he was replaced by Mann of Pelly Memorial which, under its previous name as West Ham Model, had been one of the founder-member schools of the West Ham SFA in 1890.[118]

Charlie Dove was full back in one of Beal's earliest Park teams, appearing for the school even before it entered for the West Ham SFA Challenge Trophy, as the original championship was called, and held the same position on the Park team that won the trophy in 1891/92.[119] On leaving school, Dove went to work in the Thames Iron Works shipbuilding company and played football with the Works' team. He was good enough to retain his place on the team when it later turned professional as West Ham United.[120] In the last football season of the nineteenth century, Park had another strong side, the school's first team winning the challenge trophy and the second eleven taking the junior trophy that had been introduced in 1893 for weaker schools and the reserve teams of those schools strong enough to contest the Challenge Trophy. This was the season in which the Dewar Shield was introduced and, in winning it, Park became the first individual champion of London. One of Park's outstanding boys that season was Harold Halse, the future England player, who was only 12 years of age when the season began.[121] Godwin Road was again the leading school in the early years of the new century, but by the end of the first decade Park was asserting itself again. This was in some measure due to the presence in the school team for two seasons of Sydney Puddefoot, the future West Ham and England forward. In 1913, when Puddefoot was showing the goalscoring potential that would lead to him becoming the first player to command a £5,000 transfer fee, the *Athletic News* wrote that he 'owes a lot to the training in the game he received at the Park School, West Ham'.[122]

The log book for Park survives from 1910, and while a teacher's most energetic years in promoting school sport might be thought to have been behind him by the time he had taught for 20 years, this seems not to have been the case with Beal. Numerous entries confirm his need to leave school to arrange matches in the various competitions, a reminder of the difficulties of coming to mutually agreeable arrangements about fixtures in the days when schools were not connected by telephone.[123] An entry that confirms more directly, perhaps, the school's approval of competitive games, might be that of 12 June 1911: 'Mr Beal left school at 9.30 to obtain the medals for the boys of the Football Team.' But such entries serve no more than to confirm what might be inferred from the school's active participation in inter-school sport for more than 20 years. Any entry, however brief, indicating what the school was trying to achieve by running teams and any comment on the benefits, mental and physical, that the boys might have derived from playing them was absent.

In contrast to this were the entries that related to the school's Nature Rambles, with Beal and other teachers taking classes to places like Hainault Forest and the Laindon Hills.[124] Some teachers even conducted Rambles on Saturday mornings, an expression of interest in their scholars that M.A. Watkins,

HMI, in his annual report on the school, believed 'cannot but have a good effect both on cultivating mutual sympathy and in developing the intelligence of the boys'.[125] That no similar expression of enthusiasm was entered in the school's log book in connection with Beal's extra-curricular activities on the playing fields between 1910, when the log book begins, and 1932, when Beal retired, seems a strange omission. Even the entry in the log book on the day of his retirement makes no mention of the hundreds of boys who, over a period of more than 40 years, had passed through his teams, several of them on the way to playing at the highest level of both amateur and professional football. 'He takes with him into his retirement', the headmaster wrote, 'the best wishes of the Education Committee and the appreciation of the Staff.'[126]

Conclusion

The section "LSFA Council Members 1907/08 to 1914/15" of this chapter found a moderately strong relationship between stable SFAs and success in LSFA competitions. The section "LSFA Council Members from Lewisham, South London, West Ham and West London" showed the great amount of work in promoting schoolboy football that was undertaken by many of the local association representatives on the LSFA Council, with many teachers committed to running teams in their school and district and organising inter-school and inter-district matches over a long period of time in addition to any duties their membership of the LSFA Council entailed. As the teachers whose work for schoolboy football was examined in more detail in the section "Five Teachers" were selected for their prominent contribution, it is hardly surprising that their workload and commitment compared favourably with the more active of the Council representatives. In terms of length of service, they far exceeded that of the Council representatives, all five serving for a period between 20 and 40 years.

All five teachers played football as young men, two at a modest level (Beal and Wilson), two at a senior amateur level (Haydock and Schumacher) and one at the top level of the game (Earle). Four of the five were prominent referees even before their football careers came to an end, with one (Schumacher) referred to in Fabian and Green's exhaustive *Association Football* as one of the three prominent referees in the country in the period before the First World War.[127] Schumacher's marital status is unknown, but the other four were married men with families, two of them, incidentally, having sons in the school in which they taught.

All five trained the teams in their schools to a high standard and it would appear that four at least of the five revealed more than an average enthusiasm for winning championship titles and trophies. (Not enough is known about Haydock's school teams to judge.)[128] In this, they were correctly teaching their charges what association football actually was, namely, a competitive game bound by strict rules and a game at which the boys' abilities could be improved by training. One of the five, Beal, had a reputation for an over-enthusiastic attitude towards the success of his teams, which might suggest that some of his attitudes were at variance with the Corinthian ideal that guided (and still guides) most schoolboy matches. Horace Panting became involved in schoolboy sport in West Ham a few years after Beal's retirement in 1932, but recalls that it was still said among teachers taking teams in the late 1930s that the reason the rules of the West Ham Schools' Sports Association were so long was that they had been designed to counter Beal finding loop-holes in them to the advantage of his teams.[129]

As students at St John's College in the late nineteenth century, both Wilson and Haydock would have been exposed to the attitudes towards games that prevailed there at the time. Schumacher would have been subject to similar influences at St Mark's and Beal's childhood headmaster and mentor, Robert Wild, had also been trained at St Mark's. Earle's time with the Tower Hamlets' Pupil Teachers' team would have placed him under similar influences, attached, as it was, to the University Settlement at Toynbee Hall.[130] The amateur clubs for which three of the five teachers played as adults would all have been guided by the Corinthian ideal: Schumacher's team consisted of men who had been trained as teachers at St Mark's, Haydock's Hotspur consisted almost entirely of teachers and Clapton, for which Earle and Schumacher had played, was known as one of the clubs in the London area most committed to the strict amateur ideal. The absence of autobiographical accounts from any of the teachers taking teams at the time and the weakness of elementary-school log books in identifying the reasons why teachers trained teams inhibits any categorical pronouncements about motivation. The other sources explored in this chapter, however, permit the conclusion that most of them appear to have been guided by a commitment to the value of football as beneficial to children's health and growth and saw the game as offering opportunities for character development through fair and friendly competition on the pitch.

Notes

1 LSFA, *Handbook 1915/6*, p. 22.
2 *Islington Gazette*, 24 April 1915.
3 One school from each association contested the Dewar Shield.
4 South London SFA withdrew from district competitions during the First World War.
5 The fixture list is among miscellaneous items in the South London SFA records.
6 *Stratford Express*, 4 December 1909.
7 *School and Sport* (previously called *The Hammer*).
8 *Bootle Times*, 3 May 1938; LSFA, *Handbook 1964/5*, p. 17.
9 South London SFA, *Half Century*, p. 23.
10 Ibid., p. 27.
11 Lewisham SFA, *Handbook 1910/11*, p. 10; *Fulham Observer*, 30 April 1909.
12 South London SFA, *Half Century*, p. 25; *Stratford Express*, 4 December 1909.
13 ESFA, *Handbook 1922/3*, p. 3; *Stratford Express*, 3 August 1912.
14 *East Ham Echo*, 17 January 1913.
15 Kim O'Flynn, 'Continual education and parental antagonism', *History of Education*, 27, 2 (1998), p. 165.
16 Letter from Frank Graham, 8 November 2000.
17 *Stratford Express*, 30 April 1921.

18   The figure of around 1,000 teachers is a crude assessment, based on an average of 50 teachers actively promoting the game in each of the affiliated associations over the period 1900–15.

19   Battersea Training College, Register No. 3. College of St Mark and St John Archives, J4. I am grateful to Alison Bidgood, Librarian, College of St Mark and St John, Plymouth, for permission to consult this and other items in the records of both colleges.

20   T. Adkins, *The History of St John's, Battersea: The Story of a Notable Experiment* (London: National Society, 1906), p. 42.

21   *Year Book of the Battersea Club*, 1911, p. 60.

22   While St John's, St Mark's, St Mary's and Westminster were prominent in sporting events in the late nineteenth century, it was at Borough Road College, among the London training colleges, that the emphasis on games seems to have been most evident. The Millwall footballer J.H. Gittins was on the staff there and among his duties was the supervision of special classes held to improve the physique of students who showed signs of underdevelopment. The two principals of the college in the closing years of the nineteenth century were committed to 'the moral and character training value of games'. G. Bartle, *A History of Borough Road College* (Isleworth: Borough Road College, 1976), p. 57. A recent article has identified staff appointed to London training colleges who might have been influential in promoting athleticism among their students. As these appointments were in the late 1890s and 1900s, the teachers trained by them would have had no influence on the origin and early development of schoolboy football in London, which, as shown in Chapter 3, had its origins in the early 1880s and was firmly established by 1900. J.A. Mangan and C. Hickey, 'Athleticism in the service of the proletariat: Preparation for the English elementary school and the extension of middle-class manliness', *The European Sports History Review*, 2 (2000), pp. 116–25.

23   Adkins, *St John's*, pp. 194–5.

24   *Year Book of the Battersea Club*, 1903, p. 59.

25   Paradoxically, Gwynn later found fame as a rugby player and an authority on that code.

26   Gibson and Pickford, *Association Football*, 3, p. 182.

27   Battersea Training College, Register No. 3.

28   W.J. W(ilson), 'George Sharples: President of the NUT 1904–5' in *Year Book of the Battersea Club*, 1904, p. 18; Sharples was elected secretary at the inaugural meeting of the Manchester, Salford and District Elementary SFA. *Manchester Guardian*, 14 July 1890. For Manchester SFA's success in schoolboy competitions see F.W.N. Hill, *The Story of the Manchester Schools' Football Association* (Manchester: Manchester SFA, 1989).

29   Mangan and Hickey, 'Elementary education revisited', pp. 87–8.

30   Battersea Training College, Register No. 3; *Minutes of the School Board for London* (*Min SBL* hereafter), 10 November 1875. A printed set of the minutes is available at the LMA.

31   *Min SBL*, 25 November 1880.

32   Ibid., 22 June 1882.

33   South London SFA, *Half Century*, p. 13.

34   Mangan and Hickey, 'Elementary education revisited', p. 76.

35   'The excellent spirit existing between the staff and the boys is exemplified by the results obtained in swimming, football and cricket ...'. Berkshire Road (formerly Windsor Road) School Log Book, 31 August 1906. LMA, EO/DIV4/BER/LB1.

36   Monteith Road (Boys) School Log Book, 10 May 1895, 3 July 1896. LMA, EO/DIV5/ MON/LB1.

37   Rubinstein, *School Attendance in London*, p. 112.

38   School Board for London, *Report of the School Accommodation and Attendance Committee: School Attendance Reports 1892 ... 1903*. LMA. I am grateful to Pat Ivin for drawing my attention to this source. The schools were selected on the basis of their prominence in the Tower Hamlets SFA League.

39   It was claimed in Birmingham in the 1880s and in Northampton in the 1890s that having school teams improved the attendance of the upper standards (Birmingham) and attendance of those actually in the teams (Northampton). M.I. Waterman, 'The history of the

Birmingham Athletic Club – Birmingham Athletic Institute 1866–1918'. Special Dip Ed Study, University of Nottingham, 1969, p. 17; Sharples, 'Organisation of games out of school', p. 164.

40 Min. South London SFA, 30 September 1885.

41 Sharples, 'Organisation of games out of school', p. 164.

42 Wilson represented Old Londonians on the London FA Council for 1896/97. London FA, *Handbook 1896/7*. I am grateful to D.G. Fowkes for allowing me to consult the LFA's records.

43 South London SFA, Annual Report, 1928/29.

44 South London SFA, *Half Century*, p. 8.

45 Min. South London SFA, 5 February 1889.

46 Ibid., 26 February 1889.

47 See, for Example, LFA, *Handbook 1902/3*, where he is listed as a registered referee, Class 1.

48 Battersea Training College, Register No. 4. College of St Mark and St John Archives, J5.

49 South London SFA, *Half Century*, p. 8.

50 LFA, *Handbook 1934/5*, p. 98.

51 *Schoolmaster*, 5 November 1892.

52 *Min SBL*, 8 July 1897.

53 Deodar Road School Log Book, 5 May 1898. LMA, EO/DIV/9/DEO/LB/1.

54 Newspaper cutting attached to the Log Book for 26 October 1901.

55 Brandlehow School Log Book, 16 May 1902. This is actually a continuation of the Deodar Road School log book, with the same LMA reference.

56 'Simple training for a school team' in South London SFA, *Handbook 1913/4*, pp. 13–16.

57 Mitcham Lane (Boys) School Log Book 1902–13. LMA, EO/DIV9/MIT/LB/3. The report is dated 26 July 1907 and is copied in the log book before the entry for 3 September 1907.

58 Mitcham Lane Log Book, 8 April, 4 June 1907.

59 The winning goal for Ebbw Vale against South London in the 1920/21 encounter was scored by Eugene O'Callaghan, later the famous Tottenham Hotspur forward. South London SFA, *Half Century*, p. 37.

60 South London SFA, Annual Report, 1925/26. Haydock was on the ESFA Council for five years and was also a vice-president of the LSFA. South London SFA, *Half Century*, p. 9.

61 What may be the only copy of the match programmes still in existence, and as such a coveted collectors' item, is securely lodged in the archives of the College of St Mark and St John. For this information and a reproduction of a newspaper report on the match see *Marjohn Today: The Journal of the College of St Mark and St John*, 6, 1999, p. 30.

62 P. Soar, *Tottenham Hotspur* (London: Hamlyn, 1995), pp. 14–18.

63 The quotation is from an untraced newspaper cutting filed with the match programme in the archives of the college of St Mark and St John. For Briggs and Jull see Goodwin, *Spurs Alphabet*, pp. 48–9, 214–15.

64 *Stratford Express*, 22 February 1890. The referee was T. Gunning, secretary of the London FA and on the staff of St Mark's College.

65 *Stratford Express*, 12 February 1890.

66 His salary on appointment was £95, but raised to £105 before he started work 'To bring salary to Grade', *Min SBL*, 2 December 1886, 24 March 1887.

67 For the deputation and memorial, see *Min SBL*, 10 July 1884, 27 November 1884.

68 *Min SBL*, 1 November 1886.

69 I am grateful to John Larter, Hackney Primary SFA Secretary, for showing me this trophy.

70 Information on competition results and trophies of the Hackney SFA appears on a hand-written sheet in the association's records. I am grateful to John Larter and David Grisdale for putting the Hackney SFA's records at my disposal.

71 *Football 'Sun'*, 11 March 1899.

72 Ibid., 5, 12, 19 March 1904.

73 *Football 'Sun'*, 26 March, 9 April 1904. Ilford Higher Grade School had also won the trophy the previous season, when it was publicly presented to the boys at a school

function. Ilford Higher Elementary School Log Book, 13 May 1903. Essex Record Office, E/ML 95/1.

74 Schumacher's election was in 1909. *North London Guardian*, 30 April 1909.

75 *North London Guardian*, 11, 25 March 1910.

76 Ibid., 6 May 1910.

77 *Hackney Gazette*, 22 May 1903.

78 LFA, *Handbook 1896/7* and Min. (Council), 21 May 1901; *Football Chat*, 19 May 1905.

79 P. Heady, 'The Spartan league: A short history' in M. Wilson (ed.), *The Spartan Football League* (privately printed, 2001), p. 2.

80 *Stratford Express*, 13 April 1912.

81 Source as in Note 71.

82 Les Jolly, who played for Glyn Road in the 1937 final, has kindly provided me with a copy of the match programme.

83 Schumacher's Obituary is in *Year Book of St Mark's and St John's Clubs*, 1933, p. lxxx.

84 Godwin Road School Log Book 1883–1895, 5 October 1887. I am grateful to the head teacher, Marva Rollins, for allowing me to consult the surviving Godwin Road log books.

85 Godwin Road Log Book, 26 January 1888.

86 *Report of Committees of West Ham Council: Education Committee*, 19 April 1920.

87 *East End News*, 28 September 1895.

88 Lindsay, *Millwall*, p. 8.

89 Ibid., p. 341.

90 E.W. Wilding, *Lions Through the Lens: A Pictorial History of Millwall Football Club* (Nottingham, 1989), p. 8.

91 *Stratford Express*, 25 November 1893, 27, 31 January 1894.

92 Ibid., 20 March 1895.

93 Godwin Road beat Cann Hall Lane in friendly at the end of 1885. *Stratford Express*, 28 November 1885.

94 Godwin Road Log Book, 11 November 1889.

95 *Hammer*, December 1921. I am grateful to Horace Panting for allowing me to use extracts he had copied from back issues, as I have been unable to trace a complete run of the magazine.

96 The careers of several of those players are referred to in Chapters 6 and 7.

97 Godwin Road School Log Book, 31 January 1888.

98 There is a profile of Field in *Stratford Express*, 20 November 1909.

99 May is listed in the Government Report on the school for 1894 (copied into Log Book on 8 February 1895).

100 *The Hammer*, November 1921.

101 *Stratford Express*, 26 December 1908.

102 Godwin Road Log Book, 2 May 1912, 15, 25 May 1914.

103 Ibid., 20, 21 March 1907, 4, 24, 25 June 1912.

104 *Stratford Express*, 5 October 1951.

105 Ibid., 17 October 1904.

106 Wilding was the West Ham SFA goalkeeper in the 1896/97 Corinthian Shield final at Crystal Palace. *Football 'Sun'*, 10 April 1997.

107 *Borough of West Ham Herald*, 25 March 1910.

108 William Morris was beaten in a replayed final by Schumacher's Wilton Road, as noted above.

109 Paynter was a future manager of West Ham United.

110 See profile of Beal in *Stratford Express*, 27 December 1909.

111 It still exists today as Langdon Park Comprehensive.

112 See his obituary in *The Schoolmaster*, 12 February 1916.

113 For retirement presentation see *East End News*, 26 June 1906; for his obituary see *East End News*, 11 February 1916.

114 *Borough of West Ham Herald*, 12 May 1906.

115 *East End News*, 10 June 1887.

116 *Stratford Express*, 19 April 1890.

117 West Ham SFA, *Diamond Jubilee*, pp. 6–7.

118 Ibid., p. 6.

119 Dove's name appears on the Park team list against St Bonaventure's (a school still prominent in Newham and LSFA competitions today) at the end of the 1890/91 season and in a Park side that played the rest of West Ham in October 1891. *Stratford Express*, 25 April, 31 October 1891. Beal attended his first West Ham SFA meeting in September 1891. *The Hammer*, 1, 2 (December 1921).

120 Hogg and McDonald, *Who's Who of West Ham*, p. 59. Dove also played for Millwall. Lindsay, *Millwall*, p. 398.

121 Halse, the son of a Stratford ironmonger, was born on 1 January 1886.

122 *Athletic News*, 20 January 1913.

123 See, for example, entries in Park School Log Book for 12 April 1911, 13 March 1912. I am grateful to S.A. Lachowycz, deputy head of Park Primary School, for arranging for me to read this log book.

124 Park Log Book, 21, 22 June 1913.

125 The report is copied in the Log Book, 2 May 1915.

126 Park Log Book, 30 June 1932.

127 Fabian and Green, *Association Football*, 2, p. 307.

128 All five trained teams that won their local SFA senior or junior championship.

129 Conversation with Horace Panting, 20 June 1997.

130 The great volume of records of Toynbee Hall recently deposited at the London Metropolitan Archives do not contain any that relate to the Settlement's important work with pupil teachers.

6 Schoolboy football and amateur football

Introduction

This chapter explores some of the influences of the LSFA, and the SFAs that were affiliated to it, on the development of amateur football in the London area in the years before the First World War. It examines in particular the contribution of the elementary-school 'old boy' teams, which were established from the 1890s onwards so that boys who played for their school teams could continue to play together when they left.

In a recent article, Matthew Taylor has expressed regret that, compared to the many studies of the professional game, there have been relatively few attempts 'to understand football as a participatory sport and to account for the very different motivations of, and problems facing those involved in recreational football'.[1] The relevance of this to the sources for the present chapter compared to those for the next, which is focused on the influence of SFAs on professional football, is that, while published lists of players have been compiled for most professional clubs, no such published lists are available for senior amateur teams.[2] Two of the four amateur FCs investigated in detail in this chapter have had their histories recorded in short publications. These are Dulwich Hamlet and Nunhead, the latter forming the subject of two publications, as well as part of a third.[3] While none of these works contains complete team lists, the most recent work on Nunhead contains a list of all players known to have played for the club between 1894 and 1940, with brief biographical details on a quarter of these.[4] The names of players who played in most of the amateur teams discussed in this chapter, therefore, have had to be gleaned for the most part from newspaper reports of matches, which often named only the more prominent players and in many reports, only the goalscorers were acknowledged. In contrast to our relatively detailed statistical knowledge of the professionals who emerged between 10 and 15 years after their schoolboy football careers, our knowledge of those who made a similar emergence into the top ranks of amateur football is somewhat limited, although the standard of football played by the latter might not have been much inferior to that played by the former.

Elementary-school 'old boy' clubs

The following entry in the log book of Hackford Road School, Stockwell, was written in 1899 by Robert Stokoe, the school's headmaster, who had been active in the South London SFA from an early date and was chairman of the LSFA from 1893 to 1909:

> Presented with a Cigar Case and Framed Photo of the Team by the Old Londonians Football Club, which contains several of our 'Old Boys' and which had such a successful season, winning the Surrey Senior Cup, and the County League Cup and Championship.[5]

Elementary-school 'old boy' clubs had their origin in the increasing number of schools which had football teams in the London area in the last decade of the nineteenth century and in the increase in amateur league football which occurred during the same period. The proliferation of these amateur leagues followed the success of the professional Football League, with its format of home and away fixtures, which had been introduced in the 1888/89 season. The growth of schoolboy football in London in the 1890s has already been traced in Chapter 3 of this study, and here the development of amateur league football will be traced with a particular focus on South London. This area was chosen because amateur football there was reported in detail in the *South London Press* and the surviving records of the South London SFA contain team lists which formed the basis for tracing links between schoolboy and adult football. While South London was a pioneering area in the field of amateur club football, it set a pattern which was followed in broad outline in other parts of London. A slight variation is evident in the East London area, where the amateur leagues were preceded by a knockout cup competition.

'Rambler', who wrote an extremely informative column on football in the *South London Press*, recalled in 1899 that in the previous decade the prominent clubs in South London football did not even belong to the LFA, implying that the LFA could not take the credit for the increasing popularity of amateur football in South London in the 1880s.[6] A check on the names of the six clubs he mentions against the list of affiliated clubs that appears in the LFA's *Handbook* for the 1882/83 season confirms that to have been the case: none of the six is listed.[7] There is no equivalent confirmation of his next assertion, namely, that in 1891 he himself suggested the formation of a league for amateur clubs in the South London area and that this led to the formation of the South London League. The fact that his first assertion proved correct, however, prompts one to have some confidence in his second.

The success of the South London League, according to 'Rambler', 'led to a great impetus being given to the sport and now to-day leagues are legion everywhere in the South (of England)'. This South London League, he continued, developed in size and influence up to 1894 and enabled the South London clubs who belonged to it to challenge the monopoly of the public-school 'old boy' clubs that dominated the LFA at the time. Whether through some conflict with the LFA or for some other reason, the South London League declined after 1894 and another league, called the Southern Suburban League, 'Rambler' wrote, 'practically caused its extinction'.

In East London, the amateur leagues that were to spread rapidly in the 1890s in a pattern similar to that in South London, were preceded by a knockout cup competition for which the East End Challenge Cups were awarded. Inaugurated in 1886, the Cups attracted an entry of twenty-two clubs in the senior section and thirty-eight in the junior section. An examination of locations of the participating teams indicates that the majority were local, a small number only coming from places outside East London.[8] One of the latter was Tottenham Hotspur, then an amateur side playing on Tottenham Marshes, which was knocked out in the semi-final of the senior competition by London Caledonians, at that time based in Leyton.[9] A feature of the junior competition was that three of the four semi-finalists were clubs connected with churches or church schools, a further indication of the role of churches in the early promotion of association football, referred to earlier in relation to the players at Upton Park FC in Chapter 2.[10]

By the date that 'Rambler' was writing his reminiscences, 1899, the Southern Suburban League was the main league for senior clubs in South London. There were several other leagues in the area which, surprisingly, 'Rambler' referred to as 'of minor importance in the locality'. As these provided regular league football for the smaller club sides, many of them elementary-school 'old boy' sides, these smaller leagues made an important contribution to the development of the amateur football that he consistently advocated in his columns. For, he concluded his article of reminiscences, although much had been achieved in amateur football in South London, much remained to be done, especially to keep football 'pure and unsullied from the stain of professionalism. We have not yet a paid team in our midst, and what is more do not require one. "The South London Press" has always kept amateurism to the fore.'[11]

Old Londonians, the club where Stokoe noted there were many ex-South London schoolboy players, was in the Southern Suburban League during the season in which the team won the Surrey Junior Cup. Besides Stokoe, W.J. Wilson, founder of the South London SFA and the LSFA, as recorded in Chapter 3, was also involved in the club and was its representative on the LFA Council in 1896/97.[12] The team was originally intended exclusively for young men who as schoolboys had represented South London SFA in district competitions, but from Stokoe's remark quoted above to the effect that 'several' of the players were ex-South London schoolboys, it is clear that some were not. Both backgrounds were represented in the Surrey Cup competition referred to above. One of the Old Londonian players was C. Knibbs, a teacher who had been trained at Cheltenham Training College and was then working at Hackford Road School, while in the final, one of the Old Londonians' goals was scored by H. Stanfield, who had been in the South London team that won the inaugural Corinthian Shield competition in 1893/94.[13]

Founded in 1905, the West London Old Boys' Club was similar to the Old Londonians in that its aim was to keep the 'old boys' from the different elementary schools in West London together so that they could make a mark in senior football. The club had four teams in 1913 when, according to the *West London Observer*, the first eleven was 'generally regarded as one of the best senior sides in London'.[14] This may have been something of an exaggeration, as, despite some good performances in the preliminary rounds of the FA Amateur Cup, the club never succeeded in reaching the competition proper. Several schoolboy players who had been prominent in West London's Corinthian Shield and English Schools' Shield successes appear in the matches reported in the *West London Observer*, some of them with a surprisingly short space of time between their schoolboy and senior football careers.[15] Clapton Warwick appeared to have had a similar role in Hackney to that of the West London Old Boys in West London, but seem to have had more success in competitions. Even when J. Gull and W. Swayne, two of the club's most prominent players, moved to a higher level of football with Clapton FC in 1910, Clapton Warwick still had a team strong enough to win the Middlesex Junior Cup in 1911/12 and 1913/14.[16]

Although little is known about the club and its players, Poplar Corinthians, which was originally in the Stamford Hill and District League and later in the North East London League, seems to have been attempting to harness the talents of ex-elementary-school players in Tower Hamlets for junior club football in a way that Clapton Warwick was doing in Hackney.[17]

The four clubs named so far had teams composed of young men who had attended different elementary schools in a particular area. More typical of the elementary-school 'old boy' clubs of the time were those founded for the past pupils of one particular elementary school and normally contained the school's name in the club's title. Eltringham Old Boys, the team consisting of past pupils of the school later used by HMI Graves to illustrate the benefits of outdoor games, was playing in the Clapham League as early as 1896/97.[18] Heber Old Boys, having begun in the Herne Hill League in 1900/01, then played with distinction in the Dulwich League, moving up from Division Two to the Premier Division between 1901/02 and 1904/05.[19]

A teacher prominent in schoolboy football was often associated with elementary-school 'old boy' clubs. Broad Street Old Boys, founded around the turn of the century, had their origin in a school that was prominent in Tower Hamlets SFA competitions at the beginning of the twentieth century; the teacher who took the team there, L. Williams, who had been trained at St John's, Battersea, was prominent in the running of his association for many years and also served on the Poplar Board of Works.[20] Walthamstow Grange owed its origin to the past pupils of Highams Hill.[21] The school was a founder member of the Walthamstow SFA and H. Belston, its first secretary, was a teacher there.[22] A.S. Orford, the founder of Old Newportonians in 1896, was complimented in the local newspaper many years later for having been responsible for producing many distinguished players at Newport Road, Leyton.[23]

Some of the clubs that began by drawing their players from the past pupils of only one school changed to taking them from other schools in the area, usually with a view to strengthening the team. Newportonians, for example, was good enough to win the Leyton League in 1898/99. By the time it won Division Two of the much stronger South Essex League in 1903/04, however, the team contained three future professional players, none of whom had attended Newport Road. These were Arthur Featherstone, who had been to the National, Barking; Frederick Kemp, who had spent part of his schooldays at Gascoigne, Barking; and Harold Halse, who had attended Park, West Ham.[24] In thus drawing on good players who had not attended the school for which the club was originally founded, Old Newportonians was similar to the first of the four elementary-school 'old boy' clubs to be examined in more detail below.

The London Junior Cup was introduced by the LFA for the 1886/87 season, four years after the inauguration of the London Senior Cup. The Junior Cup was intensely contested from the outset, for, besides the honour of capturing the trophy, victory was likely to ensure the status of a senior club to the winner. For an ambitious club, this helped gain entry to the London Senior Cup and the FA Cup the following season, as well as the opportunity of being considered to contest the better of the leagues, as, for example, the Premier Division of the Southern Suburban League, mentioned above.

Success in the London Junior Cup was therefore an important stepping stone to advancement up the football ladder for an ambitious club.

The results of the London Junior Cup finals between 1900 and 1905 were as follows:

1899/1900	Dulwich Hamlet beat Waverley
1900/01	Leytonstone Reserves beat Wingfield House
1901/02	Barking Institute beat Edmonton White Star
1902/03	Wanstead beat Asplin Rovers
1903/04	Asplin Rovers beat Clapham
1904/05	Page Green Old Boys beat Fulham Amateurs[25]

It is of interest that in the first six finals contested in the twentieth century, as shown above, five at least featured a contestant that was, at the time each final was played, a genuine elementary-school 'old boy' club.[26] The origins and contribution to London football of four of these clubs (Dulwich Hamlet, Wingfield House/Nunhead, Wanstead and Page Green Old Boys) will now be explored.

Dulwich Hamlet FC

Bernard Nurse has noted that the population of Dulwich around the turn of the century was particularly small compared to other registration sub-districts within six miles of Charing Cross. The local vicar at the time thought it could be classified into three distinct socio-geographical divisions. The wealthy lived to the south of the Art Gallery, the servants and tradesmen who depended on the wealthy for employment lived in the Village and the area to the north was occupied mostly by clerks who worked in London and their families.[27] It was appropriate, then, that when the SBL opened a temporary school at Dulwich Hamlet in 1884, on land obtained from Dulwich College, the first appointed managers should have included a gardener as well as the headmaster and chaplain of the College.[28]

It is clear that games were promoted from an early date, as one of the first entries in the school log book relates to alterations in the starting and finishing time of school caused by a football match.[29] It is surprising, therefore, that the school was not engaged in the activities of the South London SFA in the years between 1885 and 1890, a period for which the minutes of the Association have survived. Dulwich Hamlet is recorded in the Association's list of trophy winners, however, as having won the Junior Football championship for the 1893/94 season.[30] It must therefore have affiliated to the South London SFA sometime between 1891 and 1893. A printed sheet among the records of the South London SFA lists the names of all participating schools for 1894/95 and shows Dulwich Hamlet to have been in the Senior and Junior competitions, presumably with a reserve team in the latter. It also shows Mr Wheeler to have been the teacher-in-charge of both teams.

The school had a cricket club with fifty members in 1892, and, having won their division of the South London Schools' League in that year, the victory was celebrated in the school with thirty minutes of extra play.[31] The cricket team was run by C.T. Hunt, who taught there for several years and was acting headmaster before being permanently appointed to the post in 1901.[32]

In a foreword to the history of Dulwich Hamlet FC, written to celebrate the club's seventy-fifth season in 1967/68, the club president and ex-Dulwich Hamlet pupil, L.W. Bawcutt, comments on the difficulties the task entailed because many of the club records were destroyed in the Second World War.[33] In the history, Dulwich Hamlet FC's origin is traced to a cricket club formed by the 'old boys' of Dulwich Hamlet School.[34] In 1893, Lorraine Wilson, treasurer of the Cricket Club, was approached to form a FC to be named Dulwich Hamlet FC. As well as past pupils, older boys at the school, 'who had been well and truly imbued with the Hamlet spirit by Mr C.T. Hunt' were permitted to join and initially formed part of a second eleven.[35] The elementary school's close connection with Dulwich College seems to have led to the inclusion of some players associated with the College and there is also mention of players joining who had previously played for Westminster School. The general principle that the club was for past pupils of Dulwich Hamlet Elementary seems to have prevailed in the early days, however, as the history mentions that one of the important changes in the third season of the club's existence was that 'membership of the Club, hitherto reserved to Old Boys of the Dulwich Hamlet School, was now opened to local players'.[36]

The Club's historians do not comment on the reason for the club widening its membership, but a look at the progress of the team in its early years may suggest one. Making use of several venues in the Dulwich area in the first three seasons of its existence, the team was not making much progress, even at a local level. It may have been clear to the club management that any possibility of the team progressing higher up the football ladder was limited while membership was restricted to the past pupils of one elementary school only. If such was indeed the reason for the decision to remove the restriction on membership, it would seem to have been justified almost immediately. The team won the local Camberwell League in 1896/97 and the following season had an excellent run in the Surrey Junior Cup.[37] A brief look at newspaper accounts of the team's progress in the latter competition, however, indicates that its decision to widen membership beyond past pupils of the local elementary school did not lessen its commitment to young players who had made their names in South London schoolboy football.

Following its report on Dulwich Hamlet's 2–0 win over Townley Hall in the divisional final of the Surrey Junior Cup early in 1898, the *South London Press* added the following about the winning team:

> All the members are young and enthusiastic and work hard. Some of them are mere boys. Guy Bartlett is 15, E. Booker, 16, and Arthur Knight 17, while most of the others average about 20 years. Mr Lorraine Wilson must have been a proud man to witness the success of his boys, as he takes an almost fatherly interest in their weekly triumphs.[38]

The schoolboy details of Bartlett have not been traced, but Booker and Knight were both among the boys who joined the club while still pupils at Dulwich Hamlet. Booker later featured in a South London SFA handbook as the first of their ex-players to gain an Oxford blue, an opportunity that was opened to him by attaining first place in the Drapers' Company Scholarship in 1894.[39] Knight was in the first South London SFA team to win the Corinthian Shield in 1893/94, and went on to serve Dulwich Hamlet FC, as player and official, until his death in 1954.

Dulwich Hamlet beat Hendon in the semi-final of the Surrey Junior Cup a few weeks later, and after a drawn final against Commercial Athletic, a picture and profile of D. Wight, the Hamlet's full back and captain, appeared in the local paper. It recorded that while a pupil at Southampton Street he had 'won the London Schools Cup' and represented 'London' on seven occasions.[40] The information was not quite accurate because, as recorded in Chapter 3, the London championship for individual schools did not begin until the 1898/99 season and the first LSFA representative match, as explained in Chapter 4, did not take place until November 1899. Clearly it was 'South London' rather than 'London' that was referred to in the profile, and while Southampton Street did indeed win a trophy in the 1891/92 season, it was in fact the South London Junior championship, Nunhead Passage having won the Senior that season.[41] The profile of Wight concluded with the information that in the drawn Surrey Cup final with the more experienced Commercial Athletic he was the only one of the Hamlet boys who played up to his usual form.[42] He would have been about 19 years old at that time.

Two seasons later the Hamlet reached the final of the London Junior Cup, a more prestigious competition than the Surrey Junior Cup, and with 2 years' more experience behind them, more of the players were able to play to their full potential in the final, where they beat Waverley FC.[43] In the course of the following 15 years Dulwich Hamlet went from the strength to strength to become one of the foremost amateur clubs in the country, appearing in Surrey and London Senior Cup finals and reaching the semi-final of the FA Amateur Cup in 1908/09 and laying the foundations for winning the latter competition in the first season it was contested after the First World War. As in 1898, the attention given to the team in the local press as it made progress in the different competitions offers an opportunity to assess how much Dulwich Hamlet remained a club where ex-South London schoolboy players could, if good enough, gain entry to the highest level of amateur football.

Knight and Wight were in the team that won the London Junior Cup in 1899/1900 but Booker was not, presumably having moved to Oxford. The following season Dulwich Hamlet was established as a senior club and among the new players acquired was goalkeeper Jack Thompson. A profile of Thompson in the local paper towards the end of the season noted that he had attended Gipsy Road, an elementary school that was prominent in South London SFA competitions.[44] He was the first Dulwich Hamlet FC player to gain senior representative honours when he was selected for the London team in the 1901/02 season.[45] He served the club with distinction for many years and was good enough to represent the South of England against the North in the trial for the England amateur international team in 1908.[46]

The club was fielding three sides from 1900/01, with the first team competing in the Dulwich League, then the Southern Suburban League and, from 1907, the Isthmian League. The reserves played initially in the Second Division of the Dulwich League. Dulwich St Barnabas was a team affiliated to the club and consisted mainly of past pupils of Dulwich Hamlet, thus renewing the close contact between school and club that would inevitably have been weakened once membership became open. When it won the London Minor Cup in 1906/07, the local paper described Dulwich St Barnabas as 'a sort of third team of Dulwich Hamlet and is run under the influence of its officials, a sort of nursery for budding players'.[47] Dulwich Hamlet's centenary brochure lists the names of the boys who won the Minor Cup, and while it would seem that only one of them later played for the Dulwich Hamlet FC senior team, the idea of a nursery was revived after the First World War, with much more fruitful consequences for ex-South London SFA players, as will be indicated below.[48]

The teachers of Dulwich Hamlet remained as much involved with the club as the past pupils. C.T. Hunt, the headmaster of Dulwich Hamlet from 1901, was a founder member of the club and Mr Alford, 'one of the new recruits to the staff of the Hamlet School', was in charge of training the club team in 1899.[49] G.C. Wheeler, the teacher listed as running the Dulwich Hamlet team in the South London SFA competitions in 1894/95, was appointed secretary of Dulwich Hamlet FC around the turn of the century and retained that position until his death during the 1921/22 season.[50]

In the years leading up to the First World War, there were several prominent Dulwich Hamlet FC players who had originally made their reputation at football in South London SFA teams. George Shipway, for example, was one of Dulwich Hamlet FC's outstanding players for several seasons, gaining representative honours for London and several amateur international caps.[51] He had been captain of the South London SFA team that won the Corinthian Shield in 1906/07 and another member of that team, E. Renggar, also played in the same Dulwich Hamlet FC side as Shipway.[52] Occasionally, a Hamlet player had represented a district other than South London in schoolboy football, as in the case of J. Wilding, the goalkeeper who replaced Thompson in 1909.[53] He had been in the West Ham SFA team that was beaten by South London in the 1895/96 Corinthian Shield final, as noted in Chapter 3.[54]

Not all players at the club, however, had attended London elementary schools. A.L. Newman, who was among the first to join the club when membership became open and who featured prominently in the first team for almost a decade, joined the Hamlet shortly after he arrived in 1895 from Glasgow, where he had played junior football.[55] E.M. Smith, who besides being a player with West Norwood before joining the Hamlet, was also an athlete with South London Harriers, had been a pupil at Alleyn's School.[56] Liverpool-born C.F. Tyson, who was in the Hamlet's team that won the Surrey Senior Cup in 1908/09 and 1909/10, was a teacher at Alleyn's, and Hussein Hegazi, arguably the Hamlet's greatest player in the period before the First World War, began his football career playing for his school team in Cairo.[57]

If the claims for Hegazi to have been the club's greatest player before the First World War could be contested, few would dispute that the greatest player to represent the club in the years between the Wars was Edgar Kail. Born in Camberwell in 1900, Kail began his football career with Goodrich Road and was in the LSFA representative side that played Newcastle at Tottenham in 1914, a match referred to in the profile of Charlie Warren in Chapter 4.[58] When the War broke out later that year, Dulwich Hamlet FC withdrew from the FA Amateur Cup in December and, with many of the players volunteering for service, the club's pitch at Champion Hill fell into disuse.[59] Interviewed when the club's history was being written more than 50 year's later, Kail recalled the part played by him and other recent school-leavers in arresting the neglect of the ground and organising football on the pitch during the War. Among the youths who helped him were recent ex-South London SFA players F. Pilkington and W. Caesar.[60] In the first FA Amateur Cup contested after the First World War, that for 1919/20,

Pilkington, who had played for Kennington Road as a boy, was full back and Kail was inside right, with Shipway on his wing, in the Hamlet team that won the final.[61] Caesar, who had played schoolboy football with Aristotle Road, also appeared with distinction for Dulwich Hamlet in the 1920s and Kail's own long association with the club included another FA Amateur Cup triumph in 1931/32, several amateur caps and three full caps.[62]

This section concludes with a brief account of an event which, although it took place a few years after the end of the period covered in this study and it refers to the South London boys all of whom played for their schools after the First World War, is considered relevant as constituting the formal connection between Dulwich Hamlet and the South London SFA, for which most of the less formal connections described so far could be viewed as preliminaries. This was the formation and training of the Dulwich Hamlet Juniors in 1922, tasks undertaken by two schoolmaster members of the club, A. Hardy and E. Halley. The players initially consisted mostly of boys who had been in the outstanding South London SFA district sides of 1920/21 (which was thought unlucky not to have won the English Schools' Shield) and 1922 (which actually won it). Of these, the club history names no fewer than eleven that went on to distinguish themselves with the Dulwich Hamlet senior teams in the late 1920s and early 1930s.[63] That the association between the club and the South London SFA endured into the 1930s is clear from an editorial in an issue of the *South London Schools' Sports Magazine* for 1935. The Dulwich Hamlet Juniors for the 1934/35 season, it noted as 'under the able control of Mr E.W. Halley', contained no fewer than six players who had played for South London SFA teams in the past.[64]

Nunhead FC

The handbook of the South London SFA for 1906/07 contained a photograph and profile of C.W. Stein, one of its vice-presidents who regularly attended committee meetings. It explained how Stein, an associate of Lord Shaftesbury and other philanthropists, had been instrumental in founding a shelter for 'working lads and fatherless boys' in Central London in the 1880s. The profile also noted that Stein had been the founder of Nunhead FC (previously known as Wingfield House FC), where the team had been originally 'composed almost entirely of boys, who had gained their caps from the South London Schools' FA'.[65] It is to be regretted that the profile did not explain how a refuge for impoverished boys became a FC for unimpoverished ex-elementary-school boys in South London, as the records of the club, which might have given a detailed picture of how the change came about, were destroyed by a fire in 1936.

Acknowledging the difficulty presented to them by the destroyed records, the writers of Nunhead FC's fiftieth anniversary history in 1938 were only able to say that the refuge was located originally in Blackfriars before moving to Nunhead in 1894 and that the football team there was 'under the supervision and captaincy of Mr Prince, the steward of the house'.[66] What was not explained then or since was how and why Wingfield House changed its focus from refuge work with London's more unfortunate boys to the quite different kind of youth work that was entailed in working with school-leavers in a relatively affluent part of South London.

In the absence of contemporary evidence relating directly to the club, it may be assumed that the need for rescue work decreased through the efforts of organisations like that of Stein and through improving attitudes in late Victorian and early Edwardian London towards the physical and moral well-being of the poor, issues to which reference has been made in Chapter 4. Just as the success of the rescue work of Quintin Hogg, described in Chapter 2, coupled with other improvements in the lot of the poor, permitted him to develop the post-elementary-school educational work that led to the Regent Street Polytechnic, so Stein's rescue work at Wingfield House was able to move towards the provision of recreational facilities for youths whose circumstances were quite different from those towards whom his original philanthropic efforts were directed.

Although they do not state the exact year, the club historians of 1938, whose information was based on interviews with old members, indicate that some time between 1894, when Wingfield House moved to Nunhead, and the 1895/96 football season, the club was divided into two sections.[67] The implications of this for football were that one team, the Eastern Section, played in the Camberwell and District League and the Western Section took part in the Clapham League.[68] The Eastern Section was run by J.C. Marsh and the Western by E.W. Foskett.[69] Marsh's name could not be traced in the surviving records of the South London SFA, but as C. Marsh and H. Marsh were in the Wingfield House team, it may be assumed that he was a parent.

E.W. Foskett, the trainer of the Western Section, was a teacher in Hazelrigge Road, Clapham, and had been active in the South London SFA since 1886.[70] Recalling this 46 years later, Foskett wrote in the *South London Schools' Sports Magazine* that he had written reports on all matches played by his school team from 1885/86 to 1901/02.[71] His list of prominent players that attended his school during those years may therefore be taken as accurate, and three of the boys named are of particular relevance to Wingfield House. These are Tommie Fitchie, who scored no less than eight times with the Western Section team against Barnett's Brewery early in 1898, his brother W. Fitchie and F. Smith, both of whom appeared in the Wingfield House squad for a series of Easter matches in Essex in 1899, by which time the two sections of the club had amalgamated again to form one team.[72]

T. Fitchie was shortly to leave Wingfield House for West Norwood and later for a long and outstanding football career as an amateur player that included playing in two FA Cup semi-finals for Woolwich Arsenal and several full international caps for his native Scotland. He had many opportunities to turn professional. Playing for London against Cambridge University in 1899, for example, he was approached by an agent from Sheffield Wednesday who was trying to obtain his signature and who only left the ground when a LFA official threatened to report him to the FA for poaching![73] For 'Rambler' in the *South London Press*, Fitchie was 'the very beau ideal of pure and unsullied amateurism, especially when he declines to accept his legitimate expenses'.[74] He was interviewed by the *Football 'Sun'* at the beginning of 1899 and acknowledged that he had 'to thank Mr Foskett for all I know about the game'.[75]

In the interview referred to in the last paragraph Fitchie recalled that he was brought to London from Edinburgh by his family at the age of nine and that he was enrolled at Hazelrigge Road in 1890. While there he had represented South London SFA for four consecutive years and, as recorded in Chapter 3, had twice been in the school team that won the South London SFA champion-ship.[76] In a profile of E.A. Bramblery, the captain of the amalgamated Wingfield House team, it is noted that he was in the first Nunhead Passage team to win the South London SFA championship.[77]

Wingfield House won the Surrey Junior Cup in 1899/1900 and a comment in the local newspaper after the final confirmed that the majority of the players that made up the teams of both Wingfield House and Dulwich Hamlet were past pupils of South London schools who 'never seem to forget the many kindnesses of their mentors when undergoing instruction in mental and muscular education'.[78] A statement by Stein in the wake of an incident in which the reputation of the club was likely to suffer throws light on the high standards aspired to. His charges, he said, 'preferred keeping their good name to winning all the Cups in the world'.[79] Shortly afterwards another comment on the club in the local paper reveals the reasons behind the recruitment of ex-South London schoolboy players:

> The inception of Wingfield House was the outcome of much thought by Mr Stein, who noticed that the clever boy footballers on leaving school soon drifted away and became practically lost to the pastime. He conceived the idea of welding together a social club as well as a sporting one.[80]

Before the 1904/05 season began, Wingfield House amalgamated with Honour Oak FC, moved from Wavertree Road, Streatham Hill to the Ivy Ground, Forest Hill Road, and changed the name of the club to Nunhead FC.[81] There were signs, however, that the club wanted to widen its membership at least two seasons earlier. When Wingfield House won Division One of the Southern Suburban League in 1902/03, thus gaining access to the Premier Division and the status of a senior club, it was thought necessary to try to improve the team.[82] A note in the *South London Press* shortly after the final League match was played recommended that any good player thinking of changing clubs for the coming season might do worse than write to the secretary of Wingfield House.[83] It was significant, perhaps, that despite Stein's often repeated reminder that the club consisted of ex-South London schoolboy players, there was no mention of this in the appeal for new players to strengthen the team.[84] Stein's relationship with the South London SFA remained strong, however, for when a team representing the latter played Southend SFA at Champion Hill at the beginning of 1904, both teams were entertained afterwards at Wingfield House.[85]

The amalgamation led to immediate success, with the team, which had just survived in the Premier Division of the Southern Suburban League in 1903/04, winning the Premier Division the following season in a play-off with Dulwich Hamlet.[86] Commenting on this success, 'Ariel' in the *South London Press* remarked that 'Nunhead is now a little power in the South London amateur world.'[87]

Despite the acquisition of new personnel, most of the prominent players in the Nunhead match reports were those who had been in the club for some years before the amalgamation. Perhaps the most prominent of these was H. Stanfield, who had been in the South London SFA team that won the first Corinthian Shield competition in 1893/94.[88] A profile of Stanfield in the *South London Press* in 1904 pointed out that he had been with Old Londonians, the team run by South London SFA teachers Wilson and Stokoe for ex-South London schoolboy players, but had left it for Nunhead because it had 'not been progressive enough'.[89] If his ambition was to play in the top level of amateur football, it was fulfilled at Nunhead when the club was elected to the Isthmian League in 1908.[90]

By this time the club had moved to Brown's Ground, Nunhead, previously the home of the short-lived professional club, Southern United, a ground it was to occupy for the remaining years of its existence.[91] Nunhead ranked among the top amateur clubs in London in the years before the First World War, appearing in the London Senior Cup final twice and appearing in every London Charity Cup final between 1910/11 and 1914/15, winning three of the five. How many ex-South London schoolboy players were in these teams, or in the Nunhead teams that won the Isthmian League twice in the 1920s, is difficult to determine, as the more prominent players in South London SFA district sides, that is, those whose names appeared in match reports, seem to have gone to Dulwich Hamlet, as noted above. That Nunhead FC continued to recruit locally is suggested by a profile of their goalkeeper and captain, E. Mullery, in the *South London Schools' Sports Magazine* in 1935, when he was referred to as 'another Cormont Road boy who has played for Nunhead'.[92] There is every reason to believe, therefore, that the club continued to recruit among the past pupils of local elementary schools, even if the more high-profile South London schoolboy players gravitated to its near neighbour.[93]

Wanstead FC

Early in 1902, Forest Gate Perseverance FC, a team that was formed in the last years of the nineteenth century, changed its name to Wanstead FC. It is difficult to understand why, as, while there were several teams in the area that had 'Forest Gate' in their title, there was an equally large number that had 'Wanstead'.[94] For whatever reason, the team that began as Forest Gate Perseverance in the Leyton and District League in September 1901, finished the season as Wanstead FC in April 1902.[95] The League, in which Wanstead finished equal first with New Beckton, was for junior teams, the League secretary wrote in 1902, 'whose ground is within five miles of Leyton Station'.[96]

Of the players whose names appeared in newspaper reports of matches played by Forest Gate Perseverance or, from March 1902, Wanstead FC, four can be traced to West Ham SFA district teams. These are T. Moad and P. Weekes, who were in the West Ham team that won the Corinthian Shield in 1894–95, H. Halse, who was in the West Ham team that was beaten by South London in the 1896/97 Corinthian final and C.H. Pearce, whose profile in a local paper noted that he had 'started playing the game . . . while a scholar at Park School, where, under the able coaching of Mr C. Beal, he rapidly gained distinction'.[97] As Halse, Pearce and Weekes had attended Park and Moad had been to Godwin Road, it is not surprising to read in a local paper at the beginning of 1903 that the Wanstead team 'is almost entirely composed of old Park and Godwin boys'.[98] The dominance of Park and Godwin in West Ham SFA competitions has already been noted in Chapter 5.

Among Wanstead players complimented in press reports the following season was J. Wilding, goalkeeper in the West Ham SFA team that was beaten by South London in the replayed 1895/96 Corinthian Shield final. He played in the 1902/03 London Junior Cup final on the muddy Leytonstone FC pitch when Wanstead beat Asplin Rovers 4–1, a score that the losers claimed 'was not a fair result of the play'.[99] Wilding was not available for the Essex Junior Cup final the following week when Wanstead emphatically beat Maldon at Chelmsford before a crowd of 2,000.[100]

Victory in the Junior Cup enabled Wanstead to gain entry to the top division of the South Essex League the following season (1903/04), where opponents included established senior clubs like Leytonstone and Romford. This, as well as participating in the FA Cup and the London and Essex Senior Cups, established Wanstead as yet another senior club in the East London area. The highlight of the 1904/05 season was a visit abroad to play against the Football Club de Paris, where, 'like our noble ancestors at Waterloo, they fought and defeated them'. The East Londoners found the Parisians difficult enough opponents, however, and although goals from Halse (from a centre from A. Winterhalder, who played alongside him in the 1896/97 Corinthian Shield final) and Moad gave them a 2–0 win, they had to concede that the French 'have more than mastered the rudiments of the game'.[101]

Wanstead reached its zenith as a senior club the following season (1905/06) despite the fact that Halse, the club's outstanding goalscorer, was not always available. Reporting on a London Senior Cup tie at the end of 1905, a local paper bemoaned the fact that the Wanstead team was 'left in the lurch at almost the last moment by their crack goalscorer, Harold Halse, who went up north with Clapton Orient'.[102] The match he had gone to as an amateur with the professionals of Clapton Orient was a Football League fixture against

Manchester United. He was back the following week, however, 'bursting through the halves and backs in his own inimitable way' in an Essex Senior Cup win over Shoeburyness Garrison.[103] The following April, Wanstead played South Weald in the final of the Essex Senior Cup and in a match where 'Harold Halse was the bright star artist', the club became champions of Essex for the first time.[104]

While the Essex Cup was contested by experienced senior teams like Ilford, Leytonstone and Romford, Wanstead's win over Clapton in the West Ham Hospital Cup final the previous week was arguably a greater achievement. The competition, which raised large amounts for charity, was supported by local elementary-school teachers and pupils, and the Clapton–Wanstead final was in fact preceded by a curtain raiser between East Ham SFA and West Ham SFA.[105] An indication of the high standard of football that Wanstead were playing at this time may be gauged by the fact that in the Hospital Cup final that followed the schoolboys' match, no less than seven of the defeated Clapton side were in the team that won the FA Amateur Cup a year later.[106]

Wanstead's two scorers in the 2–0 win in the Hospital Cup final were Halse and Fry, both of whom left the club the following season (1907/08). The club struggled to survive at a high level of football after their departure, although the decline was slowed by the recruitment of several reputable players.[107] Many of these can be identified as having attended local schools, though not all of them had attended Park or Godwin Road. Walter Pearce, described by a local paper in 1907 as 'on present form, the finest left back in Essex' had been to Park, as had yet a third member of the family, Herbert Pearce, who was later to play as a professional with Fulham. A. Barclay had also attended Park, although he later went to the Coopers' Company School in Bow.[108] W. Watkins, goalkeeper from the end of 1908, had attended Parmiter's Foundation in Whitechapel.[109] The presence of Barclay and Watkins and of F. Redward, who had played for East Ham SFA as a boy, suggests that the club, in an attempt to compensate for the players it was losing to other clubs, was recruiting the best players it could find, irrespective of whether or not they had attended Park or Godwin Road. When the local paper announced that the club was disbanded at the beginning of 1911, it added that the reason was 'mainly through losing players and having unsuitable grounds'.[110]

While two changes of ground would not have helped a struggling club, it was the departure of leading players that caused the club to struggle in the first place and attendances to dwindle. A further problem was the location of the club in an area where there were several outstanding senior amateur teams ready to welcome disillusioned Wanstead supporters – and players.

The full number of outstanding Wanstead players who moved to other amateur clubs cannot be determined, but one example may be illuminating. When Ilford beat Walthamstow Grange in the Essex Senior Cup final in 1907/08, there were at least five ex-Wanstead players in the team. These were C. Pearce and H. Pearce, A. Barclay, T. Little and H. Carter.[111] Many had also joined the professional ranks. By the time the club closed down in 1911, Halse had already won a FA Cup winners' medal with Manchester United and was shortly to win another with Aston Villa. A. Winterhalder was playing with Preston North End in the First Division and T. Little was scoring regularly for Bradford Park Avenue in the Second Division.[112] H. Pearce was shortly to begin his professional career with Fulham.

It was perhaps ironic that, just before it folded, Wanstead should have gained the services of a player who made a mark on professional football comparable to that made by Halse. This was Jack Tresadern, whose career has already been considered in detail in Chapter 4.[113] His presence in the team was enough to confirm the continued commitment of the club to the recruitment of local players who had first made a mark in elementary-school football.

Page Green Old Boys FC

There was resistance in Tottenham to the implementation of the 1870 Education Act with regard to the provision of school places for all children who needed them, but with the population of the area almost doubling during the 1870s, the Education Department ordered that a local school board be established. Page Green was one of ten schools opened by the Tottenham School Board between its establishment in 1879 and its termination in 1902.[114] The school, which opened in 1882, became overcrowded when school fees were abolished in 1891, but stabilised with a roll of around 1,600 in the three departments by the turn of the century.[115]

The Boys' Department gained a reputation for football, cricket and athletics from the late 1890s, first locally, by winning the Tottenham Schools' Sports Association championships in these sports on several occasions and then more widely, with particular success at football in LSFA competitions. The latter included winning the individual schools' championship of London (the Dewar Shield) in 1900/01 and 1901/02 and providing most of the players for the Tottenham SFA team that won the Corinthian Shield in 1899/1900 and 1901/02.[116] The school, in addition, provided many players for the LSFA representative sides that played other cities, and had no less than five boys in the London team that played Leeds in 1901, a record number from an individual school that has not been surpassed in the intervening 100 years.[117] Although the school produced many outstanding individual players who later reached the highest level of amateur football, the school's success, the local paper claimed in 1901, when Page Green beat an Eltringham Street side which contained six South London district players, was not due to any individual, 'but to the fine spirit that pervaded the work of the whole team'.[118]

The *Tottenham and Edmonton Weekly Herald* announced at the beginning of the 1901/02 season that a Page Green Old Boys' FC had been founded. W. Falconer, full back in the Tottenham team that lost to South London in the Corinthian Shield final six months earlier, was made captain, while two other district players, W. Steljes and E. Dobson, held the posts, pro tem, of secretary and assistant secretary respectively. In the first match played, the *Herald* noted, as many as eight of the Old Boys' team had represented Tottenham in the Corinthian Shield.[119] Although his name did not appear in the *Herald*, on this occasion, an important figure behind the scenes in the formation of the club would seem to have been C. Cook, the teacher responsible for the Page Green School team as well as trainer of the Tottenham SFA team and, at least for some matches, of the LSFA representative side. At the second AGM of the club in 1903, E. Dobson said of Cook that he was 'the prime mover in connection with the inauguration of the Page Green Old Boys' and had not missed a single meeting of the club committee up to that time.[120]

At the same meeting Dobson said that membership of the club was open only to 'former scholars of Page Green school', although many other good players wanted to join. Other speeches reported from the AGM noted the beneficial effects of the young players taking part in committee meetings and that while the club was ambitious to become a senior one, it had no desire to seek fame in professional football. There was a reference to the club not only maintaining the friendships of schooldays into adult life, no doubt an aim of all 'old boy' clubs, but more intriguing was a reference to maintaining 'the style of play' of the school team. This might have been an allusion to the spirit pervading the school team that has been mentioned above or to the actual team formations that were successful in schoolboy football. When Page Green Old Boys' Reserves surprisingly knocked Edmonton Thistle out of the Tottenham Charity Cup in 1903/04, for example, the *Herald* remarked that the 'old school combination, Fred Lewis behind Stan Dobson' had been an influential factor in the win.[121]

Following success in local leagues, Page Green Old Boys' achievements reached a wider public with a successful London Junior Cup run in 1904/05. With several high-scoring wins in the early rounds leading up to the semi-final against Clapham Reserves, there was considerable interest shown by the local paper in the progress of the team. When the formation for the semi-final was announced, the *Herald* drew attention to the fact that the players were 'all old scholars of Page Green School'.[122] When they won the semi-final, the same paper congratulated the team on an achievement that 'reflects credit not only on Page Green (School) but on our Schools' Associations generally'.[123]

When Page Green Old Boys won the final against Fulham Amateurs, further attention was given to the club's 'unique position among the junior clubs of London – probably England' in that all the players had attended one school.[124] As regards the standard of play, the *Herald* thought it 'one of the best junior cup finals ever played'.[125] More objectively, perhaps, 'An Old Contributor' in *Football Chat*, a paper that covered amateur and professional football with particular emphasis on the London area, thought that it had been as good or better than many senior games he had seen.[126]

After a promising start as a senior club in the 1906/07 season, the team was unable to maintain its position at the top flight of senior football and by the 1909/10 season was again contesting the local West Green and District

League for junior teams.[127] Success in Division One of the Middlesex and District League in 1911/12, however, enabled the club to return to senior status in the Premier Division of the same League the following season.[128]

Throughout most of its existence, Page Green Old Boys had a reserve team, and some seasons a third team, playing in various minor league and cup competitions in the north London area. In 1912, the club's under-17 team was playing in a league that is of particular relevance to the issues explored in this chapter. This was the Old School Boys' League, founded in 1911 as a result of meetings between elementary-school teachers who trained teams in Tottenham. Tottenham Hotspur FC, no doubt impressed by two consecutive English Schools' Shield runs by Tottenham SFA in 1909/10 and 1910/11, when they reached the last eight and the last two respectively, showed great interest in the Old School Boys' League.[129] The League, which attracted entries from eight 'old boy' teams of Tottenham elementary schools and was contested by boys between the ages of 14 and 17, kicked off in September 1911.[130] Page Green Old Boys finished well down the League behind winners Belmont Old Boys.[131] This is hardly surprising, as by this time Belmont had, for several seasons, eclipsed Page Green as the leading school in Tottenham SFA competitions.[132] Up to the outbreak of First World War the Old School Boys' League continued to carry out its original aim, namely, 'to keep together the boys who show such promising form in the school team'.[133]

Page Green Old Boys secured an enclosed ground at Fairfield Road, Edmonton at the beginning of the 1913/14 season, but, despite an appeal to old scholars of Page Green to support the club, attendances were poor.[134] By this time, however, there were players in the team who had not attended Page Green as schoolboys, although all those in this category who have been traced had attended other elementary schools in the area. Most conspicuous of these were C. Hannaford and F. Rogers. Hannaford had been the outstanding player in the Tottenham team that reached the quarter-final of the English Schools' Shield in 1909/10, while a pupil at Belmont Road. Rogers, who had been a pupil at Stamford Hill, was in the Tottenham SFA team that reached the English Schools' Shield final the following season and, like Hannaford, had gained an English schoolboy international cap. From this it may be assumed that on the club's second attempt to maintain itself at the top level of amateur football, it had abandoned the rule that players should have attended Page Green as schoolboys.

By the time the 'second' Page Green Old Boys' senior side had brought the team to national prominence by reaching the last eight in the FA Amateur Cup in 1915, the First World War was already in progress. Indeed, two of the selected team were unable to get release from military duties to play in the match, one of them having signed up in the very week of the quarter-final.[135] An indication of the strength of the Page Green Old Boys'side may be inferred from the fact that the team it held to a draw in the quarter-final before going out in the replay was Clapton, which went on to win the Amateur Cup that season.[136]

Conclusion

This chapter has not attempted to quantify the contribution of the LSFA to the development of amateur football in the London area from the 1890s to the First World War, as such a quantification would require, in addition to the clubs already examined here, a further study of hundreds of minor and junior clubs as well as a great number of senior clubs like Clapton, Leytonstone or West Norwood, which, while not having their origins in the provision of football for ex-elementary schoolboys, had in fact a considerable number of such players in their teams.[137] Nevertheless, the examination of four ex-elementary-school 'old boy' clubs in the years before the First World War suggests that its influence, if it could be fully discovered, would prove to have been considerable. In addition, the fact that the rise of local amateur leagues in South London coincided with the first years when South London boys were leaving school with the experience of having played league and cup football with their elementary-school teams suggests that there was a relationship between the two. As very few names of the boys who played in these early schoolboy fixtures have been recorded, however, and as little is known about the make-up of the early local league teams, evidence is not available to make any more than a claim that it was possible that the availability of ex-schoolboy players made amateur leagues more likely to succeed.

In the case of the elementary 'old boy' clubs it was shown that all four achieved the distinction of reaching the bottleneck of the London Junior Cup final, and that the wins achieved by three of them enabled them to attain the status of senior clubs, with the fourth, Wingfield House (later Nunhead), attaining similar status following a win in the Surrey Junior Cup in 1899/1900. All four progressed beyond the bottleneck to make their marks as major senior clubs for varying periods of time. The least enduring was Wanstead, the closure of which was attributed partly to losing players to other senior clubs in the immediate area. Like Wanstead, Page Green Old Boys failed to attract the kind of attendances that would put the club on a solid financial foundation. There were continuous complaints about its poor financial state and, although it survived the First World War, it had no pitch on which to play its London League fixtures when that competition resumed in the 1918/19 season. Although a final date for its closure or possible amalgamation with another club has not been found, there is no further mention of the club in the *Tottenham and Edmonton Weekly Herald* after 1920. By 1915, however, Page Green Old Boys had already made a substantial contribution to the growth of senior amateur football in the Tottenham and Edmonton areas, not only because of its achievement on the field, but by the inspiration it provided for other elementary schools in the area to form 'old boy' teams and play in the Old School Boys' League. Of the two south London clubs, Dulwich became the more prominent in senior amateur football nationally and the more overtly associated with ex-South London schoolboy players. Nunhead was nevertheless a major force in amateur football up to and after the First World War and may have had as many ex-elementary and ex-council schoolboys on its books as Dulwich Hamlet, but, for reasons that have been explained, these could not always be traced and identified.

Reference was made in the introductory chapter to the recent questioning of the extent of the influence of public schools in the spread of association football in the period before 1880. Focusing on the period after 1880, the findings of this chapter do not confirm the dismissal by 'Rambler' of the influence of the public-school Old Boy Clubs in promoting the game, but they question the extent of this influence. In Chapter 2 it was shown that the direct public-school influence on the football played in many working-class areas of London was considerable. Chapters 3, 4 and 5 identified the influence of elementary-school teachers as key figures in the promotion of amateur football in the period from the 1880s to the First World War, in some cases building on the work of the public-school missions and university settlements. While an element of the public-school attitude towards games, originating in their training colleges, was retained in elementary-school teachers' promotion of football, other reasons for promoting games, like concern for the physical welfare of children in overcrowded cities, were also identified. Some elements of the public-school attitude to games were retained, but in a diluted form. This chapter has shown that many elementary-school teachers took their commitment to promoting football beyond the school team. In founding and in some cases running FCs for their ex-pupils, these teachers extended their influence from schoolboy into adult football. While, more than a century later, it is difficult to unravel the various strands that influenced the growth of amateur football throughout the London area in the late nineteenth and early twentieth centuries, this chapter has provided further evidence of the significant role and influence of elementary-school teachers in ensuring that association football became the national game.

Notes

1 M. Taylor, 'Football archives and the historian', *Business Studies Archives*, 78 (November 1999), p. 9.
2 *Who's Who of the Football League 1888–1915* (16 parts) and *Who's Who of the Football League 1919–1939* (15 parts) (both Basildon: Association of Football Statisticians, n.d.).
3 Anon., *Dulwich Hamlet*; Anon., *Nunhead*; Dave Twydell, *Gone But Not Forgotten*, Part 4 (Harefield: Yore Publications, 1984); Blakeman, *Nunhead*.
4 Blakeman, *Nunhead*, pp. 68–78.
5 Hackford Road School (Boys) Log Book, 29 May 1899. LMA, EO/DIV3/HAC/LB/1. Stokoe was treasurer of the South London SFA (1894–1909) and chairman of the LSFA (1893–1909). South London SFA, *Half Century*, p. 65; Min LSFA, 4 July 1893.
6 *South London Press*, 23 September 1899.
7 LFA, *Handbook 1882/83*, p. 2.
8 I am grateful to James Creasy, who has provided me with a complete list of all teams that took part in both the senior and junior sections of the East End Challenge Cup for 1886/87.

9 In the final, London Caledonians drew with Millwall Rovers (later Millwall Athletic, today Millwall, the professional club).
10 The competition was actually won by Waverley. The three other semi-finalists were West Ham Church Institute, Old St Paul's and St Augustine's.
11 The first professional club in south London was Southern FC.
12 LFA, *Handbook 1896/97*, n.p.
13 *South London Press*, 28 January, 18 March 1899.
14 *West London Observer*, 5 September 1913.
15 H. Bull (Peterborough Road), for example, who was prominent in the West London and LSFA representative sides in 1910/11, was in the West London Old Boys team that beat Slough in an FA Cup qualifying tie three seasons later. *West London Observer*, 3 October 1913.
16 Middlesex County FA, *Official Handbook 1997/98*, p. 34. Clapton Warwick was based in Clapton in Hackney, while Clapton FC, while retaining the name of the area in which it was founded in 1878, moved to Forest Gate in 1887. *Stratford Express*, 17 September 1887. Between leaving the People's Palace School, to which he had won a scholarship from Newington Green, and joining Clapton Warwick, Gull played with Newington Green Old Boys, another elementary-school 'old boy' team. *Stratford Express*, 15 April 1911. At Clapton F.C. Gull replaced Walter Tull, as centre forward. Tull was educated at an orphanage in Bethnal Green, where it has been assumed by his biographer that he 'would have been trained into the Methodist ethos of Muscular Christianity'. There is no record of the Orphanage taking part in Hackney SFA competitions at the time Tull was there. He later became one of the first black players to attain moderate success in professional football, before meeting his death as an officer in the First World War. P. Vasili, *Colouring Over the White Line: The History of Black Footballers in Britain* (Edinburgh: Mainstream, 2000), pp. 40–55. For Swayne's move to Clapton FC, see *Stratford Express*, 2 September 1911.
17 The team was managed by Dr Clarke, for many years chairman of the Tower Hamlets SFA. *East End News*, 27 March 1903.
18 *South London Press*, 16 January 1897. For HMI Graves and outdoor games see Chapter 4.
19 Ibid.
20 Broad Street won the Tower Hamlets SFA senior league in 1901/02. *East End News*, 18 April 1902. For Williams on the Board of Works see *Year Book of the Battersea Club*, 1897, p. 38.
21 W. Taylor, 'Sport in and around Walthamstow', p. 21. This is a copy of a contribution to a brochure on the Wadham Lodge Sports day of 1927, the original of which has not survived. I am grateful to Jo Parker, Social Studies Librarian at the Vestry House Museum for drawing my attention to this item.
22 Walthamstow SFA, *Diamond Jubilee Handbook*, p. 6.
23 The information on Newportonians FC comes from the Clapton Orient match programme (*Oriental Notes*) of 12 October 1907.
24 For Featherstone's school, see West Ham United match programme, 7 December 1907; for Halse's schoolboy football career with Park see Chapter 3; for Kemp playing for the same schoolboy team as James Gordon see Chapter 4, Note 76.
25 The chart is based on LFA, *Handbook 1934/35*, p. 125.
26 Barking Institute had its origin in the past pupils of Barking National School.
27 B. Nurse, 'Planning a London suburban estate: Dulwich 1822–1920', *The London Journal*, 19, 1 (1994), pp. 54, 61. The vicar was Howard Nixon of St Barnabas, and his opinion was offered to one of Charles Booth's researchers.
28 *Min SBL*, 2 August 1883.
29 Dulwich Hamlet School Log Book, 21 April 1884. I am grateful to Miss Diana Bell, head teacher, Dulwich Hamlet Primary School, for allowing me to consult the school's log books and for information on the present school.
30 South London SFA, *Half Century*, p. 62.
31 Dulwich Hamlet Log Book, 13 April, 5 September 1892.
32 Ibid., 9 June, 26 August 1901.

33 Anon., *Dulwich Hamlet*, p. 4. Bawcutt was in the South London SFA team that won the Corinthian Shield in 1902/03. South London SFA, *Handbook 1905/6*, p. 39.

34 Anon., *Dulwich Hamlet*, p. 8.

35 Ibid., p. 9.

36 Ibid.

37 *South London Press*, 3 April 1897.

38 Ibid., 5 February 1898.

39 Anon., *Dulwich Hamlet*, p. 9. An indication of the high academic standards at the school is that two of the four Drapers' Company Scholarships that year were won by Dulwich Hamlet boys, the other going to H. Blewett. Dulwich Hamlet School Log Book, 8 February 1894. Booker's success in winning his Cambridge Blue seven years later was celebrated, jointly with the passage of Lord Roberts through the area, with an afternoon's holiday at the school. Log Book, 22 May 1901.

40 *South London Press*, 19 March 1898.

41 South London SFA, *Half Century*, pp. 61–2. The final of the 1891/92 South London SFA's Junior Cup was, by coincidence, one of the few schoolboy matches reported in the local paper that season, and Wight was named as one of the prominent players in the Southampton Road team. *South London Press*, 2 April 1892.

42 There was a second drawn game before Commercial Athletic eventually won 3–0. *South London Press*, 9, 30 April 1898.

43 *South London Press*, 17 March 1900.

44 Ibid., 2 February 1901.

45 Anon., *Dulwich Hamlet*, p. 11.

46 *South London Press*, 31 January 1908.

47 Ibid., 11 May 1907.

48 *Dulwich Hamlet Football 100th Anniversary Club Centenary Brochure 1893–1992*, p. 1.

49 *South London Press*, 16 December 1899.

50 For Wheeler's obituary, Dulwich Hamlet FC, *Handbook and Fixture List 1922/3*.

51 Anon., *Dulwich Hamlet*, p. 14.

52 South London SFA, *Handbook 1907/08*, photograph and caption opposite p. 9.

53 Wilding replaced Thomson in the FA Amateur Cup tie against Upton Park (a different Upton Park club to that examined in Chapter 2 of this book). *South London Press*, 8 January 1909.

54 *Football 'Sun'*, 10 April 1897.

55 Newman was in the team that won the Surrey Charity Cup in 1902/03. *South London Press*, 21 March 1903. There is a profile of Newman in *South London Press*, 19 March 1904.

56 He was a contemporary of W.T. Folks, who later played with Clapton in the 1904–05 FA Amateur Cup final. *South London Press*, 28 October 1899.

57 I am indebted for information on Tyson and Hegazi to Jack McIlroy, whose profiles of the two players appeared in the magazine, *Hamlet Historian*, 2 and 3 (Summer and Winter, 1998).

58 *Tottenham and Edmonton Weekly Herald*, 6 May 1914.

59 The Hamlet's resignation from the FA Amateur Cup is noted in *South London Press*, 18 December 1914. The Isthmian League, in which the first team had been playing since gaining admission in 1907 when several teams withdrew to join the Amateur Football Association (later Alliance), had already ceased activities for the duration of the War.

60 Anon., *Dulwich Hamlet*, pp. 15–16.

61 Details of the 1919/20 campaign form the subject of a booklet produced to build a new covered stand at the Champion Hill ground. Jack McIlroy, *The Story of a Season: Dulwich Hamlet 1919/20* (The Club, n.d.).

62 Lamming, *Internationalists' Who's Who*, p. 147.

63 Anon., *Dulwich Hamlet*, p. 23.

64 South London Sports Association, *South London Schools' Sports Magazine*, December 1935.

65 South London SFA, *Handbook 1906/7*, p. 8.

66 Anon., *Nunhead*, pp. 3–4. The club closed down at the beginning of the Second World War and formally folded in 1942. Twydell, *Gone but not Forgotten*, p. 7.

67 Anon., *Nunhead*, p. 4.

68 Ibid., p. 5.

69 Ibid., p. 4.

70 Foskett's name first appears in the South London SFA Minutes for 12 October 1886.

71 *South London Schools' Sports Magazine*, April 1931.

72 Ibid., 19 February 1898, 1 April 1899.

73 *South London Press*, 18 February 1899.

74 *Football 'Sun'*, 22 February 1902. Fitchie's refusal to consider a professional career would have to some extent have been influenced by his business interests, which in 1904 were with the Fetter Lane firm of A.G. Spalding and Brothers. *South London Press*, 5 April 1904.

75 *Football 'Sun'*, 28 January 1899.

76 This was in 1895/96 and 1896/97. South London SFA, *Half Century*, p. 61.

77 This was in 1889/90, the first of four consecutive wins by Nunhead Passage. South London SFA, *Half Century*, p. 61.

78 *South London Press*, 24 March 1900.

79 Ibid., 19 January 1901.

80 Ibid., 6 April 1901.

81 Honour Oak was itself an amalgamation of two other football clubs, St Aidan's and Dulwich Village. Anon., *Nunhead*, p. 9.

82 *South London Press*, 18 April 1900.

83 Ibid., 25 April 1903.

84 Stein's reminder was repeated at the Wingfield House AGM a month later. *South London Press*, 23 May 1903.

85 Ibid., 16 January 1904.

86 Ibid., 16 April 1904, 29 April 1905.

87 Ibid., 29 April 1905.

88 South London SFA, *Handbook 1905/6*, p. 39.

89 *South London Press*, 5 February 1904.

90 When Nunhead played Clapton in the Isthmian League early in 1909, H. Stanfield was inside forward, while his brother, C. Stanfield, later a professional with Bury, was centre forward. *Stratford Express*, 9 January 1909.

91 Two photographs of what was left of Brown's Ground in the 1980s are in Twydell, *Gone but not Forgotten*, p. 8.

92 *South London Schools' Sports Magazine*, March 1935.

93 A difficulty in determining the extent of the ex-South London schoolboy involvement in Nunhead FC teams in the 1920s and 1930s is that, when the most prominent district players were going to Dulwich Hamlet, the names of the less prominent district players and those who featured only in individual school teams rarely appeared in newspapers.

94 For example, Wanstead Amateurs, Wanstead Avondale, Wanstead Park and Wanstead Wesleyans.

95 The club was listed as Forest Gate Perseverance in the League Table in February 1902 and as Wanstead when the next Table appeared three weeks later. *Stratford Express*, 15 February, 8 March 1902.

96 *Stratford Express*, 30 April 1902.

97 West Ham SFA, *Diamond Jubilee*, pp. 8–9. Pearce's profile is in *Stratford Express*, 16 January 1909.

98 *Borough of West Ham Herald and South Essex Mail*, 10 January 1903.

99 *Totttenham and Edmonton Weekly Herald*, 3 April 1903.

100 Wanstead won 7–1.

101 *Borough of West Ham Herald and South Essex Mail*, 28 February 1905.

102 Ibid., 9 December 1905.

103 Ibid., 16 December 1905.
104 Ibid., 21 April 1906.
105 Ibid., 14 April 1906.
106 Clapton beat Stockton in the 1906/07 final. *Stratford Express*, 3 April 1907.
107 The club finished near the bottom of Division One of the South Essex League in 1907/08, 1908/09 and 1909/10.
108 For W. Pearce see *Borough of West Ham Herald and South Essex Mail*, 26 January 1907. There is a profile of Barclay in *Stratford Express*, 27 November 1909.
109 There is a profile of Watkins in *Stratford Express*, 2 January 1909.
110 *Stratford Express*, 14 January 1911.
111 *East Ham Echo*, 24 April 1908.
112 For a profile of Little, see *Stratford Express*, 5 December 1908.
113 Tresadern was Wanstead's best player in the win over Plumstead St John's in 1910. *Stratford Express*, 5 November 1910.
114 *Victoria History of Middlesex*, pp. 5, 365.
115 Ibid., pp. 5, 370.
116 *Tottenham and Edmonton Weekly Herald*, 5 April 1901, 4 April 1902 (for Dewar finals), 3 March 1900, 21 February 1902 (for Corinthian finals).
117 Ibid., 12 April 1901. The London boys won 13–1, the highest margin of victory achieved by a LSFA team in almost 300 representative matches over the hundred year period.
118 Ibid., 29 March 1901. The match was the semi-final of the Dewar Shield for 1900/01.
119 Ibid., 13 September 1901.
120 Ibid., 13 November 1903.
121 Ibid., 19 February 1904.
122 Ibid., 3 February 1905.
123 Ibid., 10 February 1905.
124 Ibid., 14 April 1905.
125 Ibid.
126 *Football Chat*, 11 April 1905.
127 Page Green won Division One of the West Green and District League in 1909/10. *Tottenham and Edmonton Weekly Herald*, 22 April 1910.
128 Page Green finished sixth of eight in a strong League that featured Hampstead Town (winners), Walthamstow Grange and Barnet and Alston. *Tottenham and Edmonton Weekly Herald*, 9 May 1913.
129 *Tottenham and Edmonton Weekly Herald*, 12 May 1911.
130 Ibid., 29 September 1911.
131 The final League table is in *Tottenham and Edmonton Weekly Herald*, 3 May 1912. Downhills Old Boys won the League the following season. *Tottenham and Edmonton Weekly Herald*, 9 May 1913.
132 This seems to have occurred as a direct result of C. Cook moving from Page Green to Belmont.
133 *Tottenham and Edmonton Weekly Herald*, 12 May 1911.
134 Ibid., 19 June 1914.
135 Ibid., 12 March 1915.
136 Clapton beat Bishop Auckland in the final of the 1914/15 FA Amateur Cup. *Stratford Express*, 24 April 1915.
137 The Clapton team that won the FA Amateur Cup in 1906/07, for example, contained at least two ex-elementary-school players, J. Wilding and C. Rance, both of whom played for the West Ham SFA district team. Rance was in the Clapton team that won the same trophy two seasons later. Also in the team were W. Tull, discussed above, W. Attwood (ex-Page Green), E.R. Rist (ex-Park, West Ham), H.B. Duce, who had played for Islington SFA before training to be a teacher at Saltley College and J.E. Olley, whose first club was Millwall St John's, a club which, as will be explained in Chapter 7, consisted almost exclusively of boys who had attended Glengall Road in the Isle of Dogs. Five of the six

forwards in the Leytonstone team that Clapton beat in the Amateur Cup quarter-final that season are identifiable as ex-elementary-school players: S.F. Kennerley (Cann Hall, Leyton), H.J. Pearce (Park, West Ham), W. Scorey (Page Green), the Seaton brothers (Plashet Lane, East Ham) and C. Bradley (Page Green) was left back on the Leytonstone team.

7 London schoolboys and professional football

Introduction

This chapter explores the possible contribution of London SFAs in providing professional players for London clubs which had hitherto relied almost exclusively on players 'imported' from Scotland, the Midlands and the North. A commitment to the amateur ideal was evident in many of the teachers studied in Chapter 5. Wilson's association with the Corinthian FC, for example, Schumacher's role in founding the strictly amateur Isthmian League and Earle's refusal to accept payment even for playing in the Football League suggest that any contribution they might have made to the development of professional football may have been for the most part an unintentional one. At the same time, many important schoolboy games were played on professional clubs' grounds and there is evidence to show that some teachers took great pride in a past pupil making a mark in professional football.[1]

Strictly controlled professional football was accepted by the FA in 1885 and given a boost by the introduction of regular fixtures for the clubs that gained admittance to the Football League in 1888. Professional football made rapid progress in the North and Midlands. This was not the case in the South, where the attitudes of the public-school 'old boy' clubs were still influential, with their commitment to the amateur ideal. When Woolwich Arsenal, at the time playing in Plumstead, became the first club in the London area to turn professional in 1891, it was expelled from the prestigious LFA, refused entry to all competitions in the South of England and had to make do with playing friendlies with professional clubs in the Midlands and North until entry to the Football League was secured in 1893.[2] When Millwall Athletic (as it was then called) joined Arsenal in the professional ranks in 1893, less hostility to professionalism was evident, owing to some extent to Millwall's secretary playing a leading part in organising the Southern League. This new league was made up mainly of professional clubs in the South, as well as a handful of senior amateur teams.[3]

Millwall Athletic

Although the Millwall Athletic team in the 1890s contained the occasional Londoner like the Rotherhithe-born goalkeeper O. Caygill, the club's first teams normally consisted of players from Scotland, Wales and the North of England. In the 'amateur' days of the club, these players were attracted by promises of work in the docks, but with the acceptance of professionalism by the FA less oblique financial incentives could be offered. Good attendances at the club's East Ferry Road ground in the Isle of Dogs (a Southern League tie against Tottenham in 1898 attracted 14,000) enabled the club to offer contracts to promising young players like John Calvey from Middlesbrough and Arthur Millar from Melrose, both signed in 1896.[4] But evidence that Millwall Athletic was also interested in talented young players in the East End is provided by an offer to the Tower Hamlets SFA to use the club's pitch on Saturday mornings, as noted in the discussion of pitches in Chapter 3, and the permission given to Millwall St John's to use it on Saturday afternoons when the professionals were playing away from home.[5] Millwall St John's origins were similar to those of many of the elementary-school 'old boy' clubs considered in Chapter 6 in that its teams seem to have consisted mostly of players who had attended local elementary schools. While the origins of all players in the club have not been traced, the majority of those who have been identified were past pupils of Glengall Road, a school prominent in Tower Hamlets SFA competitions, having won the junior championship in 1892/93 and the senior shield three seasons later.[6] The club must have had a close association with Millwall Athletic, as Elijah Moore, the professional club's trainer, also trained the Millwall St John's team that won the Middlesex Junior Cup in 1898/99. Shortly after the end of that season, the St John's team became Millwall Athletic's reserve side. Under its new name, the team played in the London League, which it won in 1900/01.[7]

The Millwall St John's team that won the Middlesex Junior Cup final for 1898/99 contained as many as five players (J. Hunt, R. Jones, D. Maher, J. Riley and H. Squires) who had been in the Glengall Road side that won the Tower Hamlets SFA junior championship in 1892/93 and would therefore have all been aged around twenty when their team became Millwall Athletic Reserves.[8] On the way to reaching the FA Cup semi-final in 1899/1900, Millwall Athletic had to travel to Birmingham for a replay against Aston Villa at the beginning of March 1899. The Millwall Athletic directors, wishing to rest the team for the Monday game, selected several reserve team players for the Southern League fixture against Queen's Park Rangers on the Saturday before. Among them were Jones, Maher and Riley, with Jones scoring Millwall's goal in a 3–1 defeat.[9] In addition, yet another of the Glengall Road team, R. Donkin, played, as well as F. Bevan, a local player who had made his name in schoolboy football while playing with Byron Street, which, as noted in Chapter 3, was one of the more prominent schools in Tower Hamlets SFA competitions. Jones and Bevan got another first team opportunity a few weeks later but it was to be the following season (1900/01) before they were given an extended run of games in the Southern League. Both of them, along with S. Frost, another local player, were sold to Manchester City in the climate of uncertainty that surrounded Millwall Athletic's future when the club was given notice to quit its ground in East Ferry Road.

There can be no doubting the footballing talents of these East End youngsters. Jones played for Manchester City in Division One of the Football League before returning to establish himself as Millwall's inside right for many seasons. He also gained two caps for Wales, although, having been born in England of Welsh parents, he was ineligible to do so under the rules as they then stood.[10] Frost was in the Manchester City team that won the FA Cup in 1903/04 and was voted the eighth best player in England in the *Umpire* poll of 1904.[11] Bevan spent two seasons with Manchester City and, following periods with other clubs, was captain of Clapton Orient for several seasons before the First World War.[12] Riley established himself as Millwall's right back in 1901–02 and, except for a short period at Reading, rarely missed first team matches up to the end of the 1908/09 season.[13] Maher held a regular place in Millwall's first team in 1901/02 and later played for Brentford, Preston North End and Carlisle.[14]

If several schoolboys from an impoverished area like the Isle of Dogs could make a breakthrough into professional football within 8 years of leaving school, how was it that so few Londoners appeared on the books of professional clubs in London in the early years of the twentieth century?[15] When Tottenham Hotspur won the FA Cup in 1901, there was not a single Londoner in the team and very few were to appear in the north London club's sides in the years immediately following. The *Football Who's Who* for 1903/04, for example, listed fourteen Tottenham players, of whom seven were Scottish, three were from the Midlands or North of England, two were Welsh, one came from Essex and one was Irish.[16] Of the seventeen Woolwich Arsenal players listed in the same source, the majority came from the Midlands or North, with only one identifiable as a Londoner.[17] None of the players listed from Queen's Park Rangers, Fulham or West Ham United was identifiable as a Londoner, although the latter had a few players from the South, including Syd King from Chatham, who had made a few appearances at full back the previous season but by the 1903/04 season was almost exclusively engaged in the role of secretary-manager.[18] Brentford also had a few Southerners in the squad at the end of the 1902/03 season, one of whom was Maher from Millwall, but most of them were released at the end of the season when Brentford finished bottom of Division One of the Southern League. Richard Mollyneux, the new manager, had been a founder of Everton FC 25 years earlier, so it is not surprising that his early attempts to acquire a new and better side entailed a tour of the North, where he recruited players from Blackburn Rovers, Burnley, Grimsby Town and Newcastle United.[19]

Before the start of the 1904/05 season, King went through his expected team formation for West Ham United for the coming campaign in the presence of a reporter from the local paper.[20] Only one player was referred to as 'a local lad'. This was W. Bridgeman, who had begun his football career at Marner, Bromley-by-Bow, where W.A. Nugent, secretary of the Tower Hamlets SFA was a teacher.[21] The Chelsea team that John Tait Robertson formed to contest Division Two of the Football League in the 1905/06 season consisted almost entirely of players from Scotland and the North and Crystal Palace's manager, John Robson, recruited sixteen Northerners to contest the Southern League in the same season, having failed to gain entry to the Football League.[22] Clapton Orient, having gained admission to the Football League at the same time as Chelsea, 'hired a hotel room in Manchester to receive applicants interested in joining Clapton Orient for their new campaign'.[23]

A contemporary commentary on London football drew attention to the anomaly of the wealth of schoolboy talent in a city where the professional clubs drew their players from elsewhere; and given the professional clubs' system of 'importing' players, the writer did not see much hope of the young Londoners making an impact on the professional game:

> And more's the pity! I was talking to an official of an important London club about this very thing a short time ago. I ventured to observe that, considering the improved quality of school football during recent years, there ought to be plenty of young players worth taking in hand in preference to going to Scotland and all parts of the country for the purpose of bringing to town men who have no local qualification and no local interests. His reply was unexpected, but decidedly interesting. 'The trouble with the London boy,' he said, 'is that he doesn't develop after leaving school; he doesn't make bone, and, therefore, is not able to take the wear and tear of a season in important football.' I thought it over, and came to the conclusion that there was a deal of truth in what he said. Hard work in a half-stifled city is the lot of many of these youngsters after leaving school.[24]

That London boys who played football 'made bone' less readily than the youth of other cities at the time would hardly stand up to investigation. The physique of the boys in the LSFA team that beat Leeds in 1899 was not in question: the heavy defeat of the Leeds boys, their teachers claimed, was due 'to the superior size of the Londoners'.[25] When the London team met Birkenhead in the semi-final of the first English Schools' Shield competition in 1905, the Birkenhead local paper reported the match under the heading, 'Cockneys Triumph by Superior Physique'.[26] Reviewing their team's 5–1 defeat a couple of days later, the same paper congratulated the skill and tactics of the visiting Londoners, but added that 'their superior physique was a great factor in their favour, and their length of limb told in favour of their individualistic policy'.[27] Moreover, it may be noted that 'hard work in a half-stifled city' was the lot of most working-class boys leaving elementary school at the turn of the nineteenth and twentieth centuries, whether they lived in Glasgow, Leeds, London, Manchester or Sheffield. A journalist who accompanied the LSFA team to

Leeds in 1899 remarked on how much worse the surroundings were in that city than in Millwall, taking the latter, presumably, to be the nadir of London destitution.[28] It might finally be noted in this connection that in the many matches reported in the *South London Press* in the 1890s and 1900s, that featured the ex-South London schoolboys of Dulwich Hamlet FC or Wingfield House FC against teams from the outer suburbs and towns of Surrey, no mention was ever made of any lack of size, strength or commitment on the part of the London players in relation to their opponents from more prosperous areas.

A more likely explanation might be that managers of London clubs had no confidence in London players. Prominent professional footballers in the past had come from Scotland, the Midlands and North, they reasoned, so they were likely to come from those areas in the future. Given the conservative attitudes that prevail in football, then and now, and the fact that most managers themselves came from Scotland and the North, it is not surprising that these negative attitudes to London players were perpetuated and that the success of Frost or Bevan could be seen simply as the exceptions who proved the rule. In this the managers could be considered no more blameworthy than those of more recent vintage who, seeing the obvious ability of black players in schoolboy and junior football, resisted their recruitment to the professional game on the spurious grounds that the flamboyant nature of their play could not be adapted to the strenuous demands of the Football League, that they could not accept the discipline of the professional game and they would 'go missing' in matches when the weather got cold! In the 1960s, John Charles at West Ham United and Albert Johanneson at Leeds proved publicly for the doubters that black players could show the same application and commitment as white, although it was perhaps the career of Clyde Best at West Ham, if only because strikers make more headlines than defenders or midfield players, that showed what an asset to a major club a black signing could be.[29] By the 1980s the colour of a player was considered irrelevant by most top managers and today there are few major clubs that do not have several black players in their first teams.

West Ham United

Despite the enthusiasm for Scottish players in London professional clubs early in the twentieth century, it is perhaps ironic that the breakthrough for London players, when it came, was initiated by a Scottish manager who took a chance in buying the services of a young Londoner in whom an English manager was losing confidence.[30] Syd King had not considered George Hilsdon among his likely players for the 1904/05 season in the discussion with the reporter from the *East End Echo* mentioned above. Hilsdon, whose achievements with the East Ham SFA were referred to in Chapter 3, had played some good games for West Ham United during the previous season when, according to the *Echo*, he 'was by many of the finest judges described as being one of the best forwards in the South'.[31] At the end of the 1905/06 season John Tait Robertson, the Chelsea manager, went to watch a player at a reserve game between Fulham and West Ham but was so impressed with Hilsdon's performance that, forgetting about the player he had come to see, he signed Hilsdon instead. Following a short continental tour with Chelsea, Hilsdon appeared as the club's new centre forward for the first match of the 1906/07 season. He was an instant success, scoring five times in his debut for the club, establishing a record that has not been surpassed since. His goalscoring form soon brought him a place on an English League representative side, followed shortly by the first of eight full international caps.[32]

Commenting on his success, the Chelsea match programme remarked that Hilsdon was living proof that to become a first-class professional footballer 'it is not necessary to be born North of the Tweed'.[33] Hilsdon was not, of course, the first Londoner to play for England. Indeed, Vivian Woodward, whose injury enabled Hilsdon to gain his first cap in 1907, was actually born in Kennington and had been a regular in the England team since 1903. Woodward, however, was a 'gentleman amateur', refusing even to accept travel expenses, with attitudes more akin to mid-Victorian times than to the beginning of the Edwardian era, when 'the seeds of solid professionalism were being sown that have characterised the modern game'.[34] Hilsdon, rather than Woodward, was a figure with whom London elementary-school pupils could identify and whose achievements they could try to emulate. Many of them were to follow him into professional football and some of them into the national side.

While Millwall continued to recruit the occasional local player of great potential – Bill Voisey was perhaps the most outstanding – it was West Ham United that became the leader among London clubs in the discovery and development of local football talent in the years leading up to the First World War.[35] Syd King, having permitted Hilsdon to slip through his fingers to become England's centre forward within a year of his departure, must have become more attentive to the football potential of local young-sters. The presence of two active SFAs on his doorstep helped. Both East Ham SFA and West Ham SFA were prominent in London and national schoolboy competitions, the latter in particular, as noted in Chapter 4. Progress in harnessing the talent revealed in schoolboy football was slow, however, and Scottish players were as prominent at West Ham United as at any other London club, at times even more so. At a Southern League match against Swindon Town in September 1907, no fewer than six of the West Ham team were Scottish.[36] There were two 'southern' players in the West Ham side at the time, H. Stapley, who began his career at Manor Park Albion, and L. Jarvis, from Grays in Essex. A third, T. Randall, who was a past pupil of Gascoigne Road, Barking, was shortly to secure the wing half position which he was to retain up to the outbreak of the First World War. There were three other local players at the club, all of whom had been involved in local school-boy football (S. Bourne, S. Hammond and D. Woodards), and all of whom had the occasional game in the first team.[37]

In December 1907 Danny Shea from Wapping, the first of a series of outstanding East End goalscorers to serve West Ham United, made his debut for the first team. He had attended St Patrick's, Wapping, which did not take part in Tower Hamlets SFA competitions at the time and had been recruited by West Ham from Manor Park Albion. From 1909 Shea formed a very productive partnership with Poplar-born George Webb, who had learned his football at Shaftesbury Road, East Ham. Webb's rapid advance, which he attributed largely to the help he received from Shea, led to him gaining two England caps in 1911, four years before Shea himself was to receive that honour.[38] When Shea's goalscoring partnership with Webb was terminated by the latter's injuries and illness (he was to die of consumption at the early age of twenty-eight), his place at centre forward was taken by Albert Denyer, who had been in the West Ham SFA team that had won the English Schools' Shield in 1906/07 and was the first Londoner to gain an international schoolboy cap.[39]

Shea was transferred to Blackburn Rovers at the beginning of 1913 for a fee of £2,000, the highest paid for a player up to that time, and helped his new club win the Football League championship the following season.[40] Meanwhile, at West Ham United, his place at inside right was taken by another local player, Dan Bailey, who had distinguished himself as a schoolboy while playing with Napier Road, East Ham.[41] Denyer held the West Ham United centre forward position for two years and for a time had Bailey at inside right and Hilsdon, who had by this time returned from Chelsea, at inside left.[42] When Denyer was sold to Swindon Town in 1914, the all-East End strike force at West Ham was continued with the promotion to the first team of Syd Puddefoot, who had been scoring consistently for the reserves. Puddefoot had been an outstanding schoolboy player with Park and the West Ham SFA district team until he broke his arm in the 1907/08 Corinthian Shield semi-final.[43] At West Ham United he developed into one of the great goalscorers of the period, and, but for the First World War, when he was reaching his peak, might have gained many more England caps than the two he earned in the 1920s. When West Ham sold him to Falkirk in 1922, he became the first footballer to command a £5000 transfer fee.[44]

Other London professional FCs

The publication of statistical histories of London professional clubs over the last 20 years has permitted the examination of team lists for 1914/15 to see if there is any evidence of other London clubs' attempts to recruit local players in a way comparable to West Ham United. A survey of the sixteen players who played most frequently for each of six London clubs (Arsenal, Clapton Orient, Chelsea, Crystal Palace, Fulham and Queen's Park Rangers) indicates that, with one exception, little or no effort seems to have been made to harness the talent that was evident in schoolboy football in a way that was comparable to what was done at West Ham United. At Chelsea, Fulham and Queen's

Park Rangers, players from the North, Midlands and Scotland made up two-thirds of the forty-eight players who appeared most often for these three West London clubs in the 1914/15 season. There were some Southern players on each of the three teams. Five played for Fulham, including two Londoners, one from Barking and one from the Isle of Dogs.[45] There were five Southerners in Chelsea's sixteen players. Two of them, J. Harrow and R. Thompson, had come to the club from Croydon Common FC, near to their places of birth. A third, Vivian Woodward, although born in Kennington, South London, had began his football career at Ascham College, Clacton. The much-travelled Harold Halse was the only player among Chelsea's sixteen to have taken part in LSFA competitions.[46] The only identifiable London player among the Queen's Park Rangers' sixteen was H.T. Simons, from Clapton, East London, who had began his playing career in the Football League with Clapton Orient.[47] Among the forty-eight players who appeared most often for these three West London clubs (Chelsea, Fulham and Queen's Park Rangers), not a single one could be identified as having played with the West London SFA district team.

As complete team lists and places of birth of players who represented Crystal Palace in the Southern League for 1914/15 are not available, it is difficult to comment with any degree of certainty on the absence of ex-London elementary schoolboys at that club. However, a comparison of South London team lists up to 1910 where available, with the names of players at Crystal Palace in 1914/15, revealed only one possible ex-South London player to have been at the club at that time.[48] While at least two of the Page Green Old Boys' team that was examined in Chapter 6 made appearances in the Tottenham Hotspur Reserves, there was only one Londoner among that club's sixteen.[49]

Of the six London clubs examined here, the case of Arsenal alone suggests that an interest was shown in talented local players. Although the club had by this time moved from Plumstead to North London it had retained most of its players from its time south of the Thames. Five of the Arsenal sixteen came from London, four of them from the area adjoining the club when it was in Plumstead. The fifth, P. Sands, though born a few miles away in Norwood, was a teacher in Plumstead, and managed to combine a career in the classroom with one on the football field. F. Ford was born in Woolwich and 'Wally' Hardinge, an international at both football and cricket, was born in Greenwich and as a schoolboy played for Blackheath Road in Greenwich SFA competitions.[50] Two players, G. Grant and C. Lewis, were actually born in Plumstead.[51] Lewis had played with Woolwich SFA in the Corinthian Shield competition in 1899/1900 and was described as 'the best forward on the field' when West London beat Woolwich 4–1.[52]

Before passing a final verdict on those London clubs which refused to develop talent on their doorstep rather than import it from outside, it might be thought relevant to look at the relationship between schoolboy football and local professional clubs in another part of the country at the time. Sheffield, with two professional clubs in the city since the late 1880s, and a pioneer in the promotion of both adult and schoolboy football, might serve as a useful comparison.

Adult and schoolboy football in Sheffield

'Is there any city in the United Kingdom', asked the first historian of Sheffield Wednesday, writing in 1926, 'which has contributed more to the development of the national pastime than Sheffield?'[53] His claim was a strong one. Organised football, with rules similar to (but not identical with) those agreed by the FA in 1863, had been played in Sheffield from at least the decade before the FA's attempts at codification. Football as a winter pastime for cricketers was the motive behind the Sheffield Cricket Club's decision to form an FC in 1857, with Nicholas Creswick, a successful local manufacturer, as first secretary and treasurer.[54] Adrian Harvey's recent questioning of the public-school origins of the rules of the Sheffield FC, which became acceptable to other clubs in the area, has in its turn been questioned by Eric Dunning.[55] Neither the origin of these rules nor the long drawn-out disagreement over them between the Sheffield FA, founded in 1867, and the FA in London can be traced here, although it may be noted that it was a disagreement that was always conducted in the best spirit, largely through the diplomacy of C.W. Alcock, the FA Secretary and the energies of J.C. Shaw, of the Sheffield Association.[56] This is evident from the fact that even before the disagreements were resolved, London and Sheffield often played each other under the 'home' team's rules and J.C. Clegg, who was later responsible for the amalgamation of the Sheffield and Hallam clubs, was picked for the FA's England team in the international against Scotland in 1872.[57] When Sheffield eventually accepted the FA's code in 1877, many of the rules thought essential to the playing of the game by the Sheffield Association had in fact been incorporated into the FA's code. One of the rules to be included as a direct consequence of Sheffield's stand, for example, was the corner kick, one of the most exciting features of modern football.

There is evidence that association football in Sheffield might have been less exclusive than in London at the time. Speaking at the annual dinner of the Sheffield FA in 1877, Shaw, president of the club, expressed his gratification that the rules of the London and Sheffield associations had been unified 'and more particularly that the S(heffield) FA's representative's team was now composed of gentlemen, the middle class and working men'. From the evidence of the study of the players at Upton Park FC in Chapter 2, this could hardly be said of the players in the leading football teams in London at the time.

That the earlier participation of working men in Sheffield football might have been the cause of a breach in the amateur ideal in that city at an earlier date than in London is suggested by circumstances surrounding the adoption of professionalism by Sheffield Wednesday in 1887. As with the Sheffield FC, the origin of the Wednesday was in a cricket club of the same name that wanted to keep players together during the winter months. It split from the cricket club in 1883, by which time it had established a reputation as one of the leading clubs in the country, having reached the FA Cup quarter-final in 1880–81 and the semi-final in 1881/82. With the acceptance of strictly regulated professionalism by the FA in 1885, there was resistance to its introduction in Sheffield by the industrialists and professional people who ran the game, some like the solicitor J.C. Clegg, ever fearful about the image of football and what he saw as 'the moral purpose of the game'.[58]

With the increasing opportunities of earning money for playing the game and the large number of working men who were playing it in Sheffield in the late 1880s, matters came to a head in the city in 1887. There had been approaches to the better Wednesday players to play with clubs that would pay them and when a new club, Sheffield Rovers, was formed, the Wednesday players were able to use the threat that they would depart to the new club if Wednesday did not adopt professionalism. The club capitulated and, leasing the Olive Grove Ground, won the Football Alliance League as a professional team, having failed to gain admittance to the Football League.[59] The club's present ground in Owlerton was acquired in 1899, by which time Wednesday had won the FA Cup (in 1895/96) and had been in the Football League long enough to have been relegated to Division Two.

Following the excitement generated by an FA Cup semi-final played at the Bramall Lane Ground in 1889, it was proposed by one of the Ground Committee to form a second professional side in Sheffield, the new club to be based at the Bramall Ground, a venue that had long been a centre for sporting events in the city. Players were recruited and a team formed before the end of the year. Playing first in the Midland League and then the Northern League, Sheffield United, as the new club was called, gained admission to Division Two of the Football League in 1892/93, the same season as Sheffield Wednesday gained admission to Division One. Following a play-off match at the end of the season, Sheffield United were promoted and joined Sheffield Wednesday in Division One.[60]

While the Sheffield SFA was founded in the same year as Sheffield United, it seems to have been more closely associated with the older Sheffield Wednesday in its earliest years. This was probably because, in that period of inter-school friendly matches between schools which invariably preceded the formation of SFAs at the time, the Wednesday was in existence while the United was not. Wednesday's Olive Grove Ground was the venue for the first of Sheffield SFA's many representative matches when South London SFA came to play against them in 1890. W.E. Clegg, brother of J.C. Clegg mentioned above and himself an ex-Sheffield Wednesday player, refereed the match, which the South Londoners won 1–0. Writing about the match 45 years later, B. Creswick, one of the founders of the Sheffield SFA and the first chairman of the ESFA, recalled that the 'play on both sides was so keen and good that it drew forth vociferous cheers from the crowd'. Reporting on the match, the *Evening Telegraph and Star and Sheffield Daily Times* wrote that the introduction of the Clegg Shield that season for a Sheffield inter-schools championship had created 'a lively interest' in schoolboy football in Sheffield, something that would seem to have been confirmed by the large crowd who came to see the boys play South London.[61]

Statistical works published on Sheffield Wednesday in 1987 and on Sheffield United in 1999, together with lists of Football League players compiled by the Association of Football Statisticians, permit the identification of every player who played a first team match for either club.[62] Before trying to trace Sheffield schoolboy players who might have gone on to play for one of Sheffield's professional clubs, a preliminary enquiry into a sample of the birthplaces of players at these two clubs was thought to be necessary. For, if none or very few Sheffield-born players appeared for either club in the period under review, the search for Sheffield schoolboy teams to see if any boys went on to play for these clubs would almost certainly prove to be a futile one. A list was therefore compiled of the players in the most successful three teams from each of the clubs between 1895/96 and 1914/15 and the places of birth of the players identified, if known. The teams were, for Wednesday, the FA Cup winning side of 1895/96 and the League winning sides of 1902/03 and 1903/04, and for United, the FA Cup winning sides of 1898/99, 1901/02 and 1914/15. All players who played one match or more in the relevant competition were included and when a player played in more than one of the competitions, his details were counted only once.

The total number of players came to 69 – 33 from Wednesday and 36 from United. Of these, the places of birth of twelve were unknown, eight were born in Sheffield, 12 more in areas near to Sheffield, nine were born in the North East, nine in the Midlands, nine in Scotland, four in the North West and the remaining six had six different birthplaces not classifiable under the above headings (e.g. Wales and Ireland). If the 12 players whose places of birth were unknown are discounted, the proportion of Sheffield-born players formed only 14 per cent, but when those born in areas near to Sheffield were included, the percentage rose to 35. With such a high percentage of the players born in or near the city, it was therefore decided to search Sheffield schoolboy team lists with a view to seeing if any of the boys reappeared later in Wednesday or United teams.

The names of the boys in six Sheffield schoolboy teams between 1890 and 1910 teams have been traced, giving a total of sixty-six boys. This is rather less than one-third of the total number of boys who represented the city during the period. While more teams may yet be traced, the number is sufficient to offer some indication of a possible relationship between schoolboy and professional football in the city, although it will of course have to be adjusted if and when further team lists come to light.

The Sheffield SFA team that played the match against South London at the Olive Grove in 1890, to which reference has been made above, contained only one boy who might have later played in the Football League, but not with either of the Sheffield clubs.[63] The next Sheffield team traced, that which played West Ham SFA in 1894, had two boys in the team who were later to play with Sheffield United.[64] One was W.E. Parker, who was with United for seven seasons but never secured a regular first team place.[65] The other was Archibald Needham, who, after four seasons with United, went to Crystal Palace, where he played more than 100 matches.[66] The Sheffield team that played South London in 1900 did not contain any player who later played in the Football League.[67]

The Sheffield team that played the LSFA team in the first ESFA championship in Llandudno in 1905 contained two future Football League players, one of whom was the team's captain, Harry Bentley. When Sheffield qualified for the final again the following year, the *Yorkshire Telegraph and Star* carried a portrait and profile of Bentley, saying that he had attended the 1906 final to support Sheffield and that a bright future was predicted for him in football.[68] He first appeared for Sheffield Wednesday in the 1911/12 season and in a career at Hillsborough disrupted by the First World War played a total of more than forty matches. After the War he played more than sixty times for Brighton and Hove. The two wingers in the 1906 team that beat Manchester in the English Schools' Shield final both went on to play in the Football League. One of them, R.W. Firth, began his career with Sheffield United and later played League football with Luton Town in the last two seasons up to 1915, when the Football League closed down for the remaining years of the First World War. The last team traced between 1890 and 1910 was that for 1908/09, which contained two future Football League players, neither of them with Sheffield clubs.

The number of district players from the Sheffield schoolboy teams who became professionals (eight players from sixty-six) is, at just over 12 per cent, substantially higher than was found in the only other survey that has been carried out to assess the likelihood of schoolboy district players becoming professional footballers.[69] That four of the eight boys went to a Sheffield professional club might seem to suggest that the Sheffield SFA might have played a role in Sheffield that resembled that of the West Ham SFA and the East Ham SFA in relation to West Ham United. None of the four Sheffield boys who went on to Sheffield professional clubs was a major figure in the clubs, however, in the way that internationals Hilsdon, Puddefoot, Tresadern, Shea or Webb were at West Ham United. Rather than the rich harvest reaped by West Ham United from their local SFAs, the number and quality of Sheffield schoolboy players going to Sheffield professional clubs, on the present evidence, resembles more that which Woolwich Arsenal gained from the schoolboy associations of Greenwich and Woolwich. That is to say, some players went from local schools to the local professional clubs, but they were not major players.

Finally, in comparing schoolboy football in Sheffield with that in London, it may be wondered if the proportion of Sheffield-born players in Wednesday and United increased as the Sheffield SFA developed into one of the strongest SFAs in the country. While insufficient evidence is available to provide a definite answer, a look at the position of Scottish players in the two Sheffield professional clubs may suggest some possibilities.

One of Sheffield United's earliest matches after it was founded as a professional club in 1889 was against a team from Nottingham, in connection with which it was noted that whereas the Nottingham team consisted of local players, Sheffield United was made up mostly of Scottish players.[70] When Sheffield United won the FA Cup in 1898/99 and 1901/02, only one Scottish player had been identified as playing for them in either competition. When they won the trophy again in 1914/15 there were no Scottish players in the side. When Sheffield Wednesday won the FA Cup in 1895/96, there were five Scottish players in the team and only one (Tom Crawshaw) had been born in Sheffield. When Wednesday won the competition again in 1906/07 there was one Scottish player in the team and four players were Sheffield-born.

More evidence than is available at present would be needed to attribute this change, even in part, to the Sheffield SFA's progress as a national force in schoolboy football in the quarter century from its foundation until the First World War. Many of the players who replaced the strong Scottish presence in both clubs, for example, came from towns not far from Sheffield, but who would not have been eligible to play for Sheffield SFA teams. The contribution of other SFAs in the area would have to be taken into account – that of Leeds, as noted in Chapter 3, had been formed before the turn of the century, for example, and those of Barnsley and Bradford were prominent from the earliest days of the English Schools' Shield competition. In addition, many of the players that replaced those from Scotland in the two Sheffield clubs came from the North East and Midlands in particular, and account would have to be taken of the many successful schoolboy associations in these two areas. Taking all these qualifications into account, however, there are indications that a change of playing staff of the two Sheffield clubs may, to some extent, be attributable to a successful local SFA.

Conclusion

A study of professional clubs in the London area has shown that Millwall, West Ham and to a lesser extent Arsenal were able to translate the schoolboy talent of Londoners into an ability to play senior football at the highest level. That progress was slower than it might have been in turning outstanding schoolboys into accomplished professional footballers may be attributable in part to the other clubs not following the lead set by those three clubs. Of particular interest is the fact that none of the talented players in so many outstanding West London SFA teams found their way into professional teams. Given that their teams were comparable in standard, if not superior to those of the West Ham SFA throughout the period under review, it must be assumed that their players made no impact on professional football comparable to that made by their eastern competitors partly at least because the directors, managers, scouts and coaches of the professional clubs in West London did not take the same interest in local schoolboy players that was taken by West Ham United.

Comparisons with Sheffield were limited by the scarcity of team lists and by the different situation prevailing in Sheffield in that professional football, resisted initially in a manner comparable to London, was embraced earlier and with greater enthusiasm. This meant that outstanding local players were playing for Sheffield professional clubs at an earlier date and while Sheffield officials might have been as convinced as those in London of the superiority of Scottish players, they had no reason to believe that the young players of their own city and county were in any way inferior to those in any other part of England.[71] The question of the inferiority of local players did not therefore arise.

In London, elementary-school teachers had played their part, whether intentional or not, in raising elementary-school football to the level where the better players in their teams were potential professional footballers. A final verdict on those London professional clubs that did not look at the talented players thus produced in the years before the First World War might be that the loss was theirs. The officials of those clubs would no doubt have been surprised and, one hopes, embarrassed to read the following in the *Star* newspaper in 1925:

> It is doubtful whether any of Soccer's most advertised forcing grounds, even the highly productive regions around Newcastle and Sunderland, are growing more good players than the Metropolitan area. I am continually hearing about boys from the 'Big Smoke' who are shining in provincial teams.[72]

The high standard of schoolboy football in London, highlighted by the success of teams affiliated to the LSFA in the English Shield competition from 1905, suggests that the young stars were there all the time. It was simply that most of the professional clubs in London did not notice them shine.

Notes

1 As noted in Chapter 3, when George Hilsdon was picked for England, great numbers of East End football teachers claimed to have trained him as a boy. *Football Chat*, 5 March 1907.
2 Ollier, *Arsenal*, p. 8.
3 L. Francis, *Seventy Years of Southern League Football* (London: Pelham, 1969), pp. 21–2; Harrison, *Southern League Football: The First Fifty Years*, pp. 4–5.
4 Lindsay, *Millwall*, pp. 48, 75.
5 *East End News*, 19 October 1898.
6 Tower Hamlets SFA, *Programme of Entertainment*. This item contains lists of the prizewinners at the Association's 1892/93 presentation evening. Tower Hamlets Local History Collection, Poplar Box 825.
7 Lindsay, *Millwall*, p. 385.
8 *East End News*, 8 April 1899; Tower Hamlets SFA, *Programme of Entertainment*.
9 Lindsay, *Millwall*, pp. 152–3.
10 D. Sullivan, 'Dick Jones, Welsh International', *Island History Newsletter*, 10, 2 (February 1992), p. 3.

11 S.F. Kelly, *Back Page Football* (London: McDonald, 1988), p. 21. Frost returned to Millwall and had several successful seasons with the club before having to retire because of a knee injury, for which he made a successful claim for compensation against the club. He committed suicide in 1926. *East London Advertiser*, 6 March 1926.
12 Kaufman and Ravenhill, *Leyton Orient*, p. 104.
13 Lindsay, *Millwall*, p. 92.
14 There is a profile of Maher in West Ham United's match programme, 18 January 1910.
15 Entries in the log book for Glengall Road in the 1890s testify to the level of destitution in the area. Log Book Glengall Road School (Boys). LMA, EO/DIV5/GLE/LB1.
16 *Football Who's Who 1903/4*, pp. 31–85.
17 This was James Bellamy, born in Barking. Ollier, *Arsenal*, p. 38.
18 Northcutt and Shoesmith, *West Ham United*, p. 395.
19 White, *Brentford*, p. 81.
20 *East Ham Echo*, 26 August 1904.
21 Bridgeman was shortly to move to Chelsea, where he remained until 1919. Cheshire, *Chelsea*, 64. Nugent was the Tower Hamlets SFA representative at the meeting to found the LSFA in 1892. Min LSFA, 11 October 1892.
22 Cheshire, *Chelsea*, p. 10; Purkiss, *Crystal Palace*, p. 9.
23 Kaufman and Ravenhill, *Leyton Orient*, p. 16.
24 Gibson and Pickford, *Association Football*, 3, p. 54.
25 The Leeds teachers' view was quoted before the return game a few months later. *Football 'Sun'*, 10 February 1900.
26 *Birkenhead and Cheshire Advertiser*, 5 April 1905.
27 Ibid., 8 April 1905.
28 *Football 'Sun'*, 18 November 1899.
29 Hogg and McDonald, *West Ham United*, pp. 16, 43–4. While there is no evidence that it was related to their being the first black players to make a mark in modern British football, Charles and Johanneson both became alcoholics in later life, leading to a breakdown in the case of the former and suicide in the case of the latter. For Charles, see *Sun*, 19 September 1994 and for Johanneson, see *Daily Telegraph*, 30 September 1995. Best had a successful career in Dutch football after leaving West Ham and was the manager of the Bermudan national team in 1997. West Ham United v. Newcastle United match programme, 21 January 1978; *Newham Recorder*, 9 April 1997.
30 The confidence in the ability of Scottish players seemed limitless, and not only in London. When Bradford City won the FA Cup in 1911 there were eight Scottish players in the team. Jim Hossack, *Head Over Heels: A Celebration of British Football* (Edinburgh: Mainstream, 1989), p. 38.
31 *East Ham Echo*, 17 November 1905.
32 N.F. Jenson 'George Hilsdon: The man behind a small print record', Association of Football Statisticians, *Report*, 56 (September 1987), pp. 36–7; C. Kerrigan, 'Gatling Gun George', *The Footballer*, 2, 6 (1990), pp. 39–41.
33 *Chronicles of Chelsea Football Club*, 26 November 1906. The *Chronicles* were the Chelsea FC match programmes and have been republished in facsimile by Scott Cheshire, Stoke-on-Trent.
34 D. Turner, 'Ripping yarns', *The Footballer*, 1, 6 (1989), p. 4.
35 For Voisey, see Lindsay, *Millwall*, p. 101.
36 Northcutt and Shoesmith, *West Ham*, p. 20.
37 For Randall and Stapley, see Northcutt and Shoesmith, *West Ham United*, pp. 382, 387; for Jarvis, see *Football Chat*, 18 November 1908; for Woodards see *Borough of West Ham Herald & South Essex Mail*, 9 April 1909; for Bourne see *Stratford Express*, 10 February 1939; for Hammond see *East Ham Echo*, 1 December 1905.
38 For Shea, see C. Kerrigan, 'The Wapping wizard', *The Footballer*, 3, 5 (1992), pp. 4–6.
39 West Ham SFA's English Shield win is related in Chapter 4. George Webb's football career is covered in his obituary in the *East London Advertiser*, 30 March 1915.

40 Shea was reported to have received 35 per cent of the transfer fee. *East Ham Echo*, 24 January 1913.

41 For Bailey see *East Ham Echo*, 28 January 1913. Another ex-East Ham schoolboy player, Frederick Burrill, played a few games as an inside forward in 1912, but was not successful. He later played for Wolverhampton in the 1921 FA Cup final, when his team lost to Tottenham Hotspur. M. Tyler, *Cup Final Extra* (London: Hamlyn, 1981), p. 68.

42 For Hilsdon's return to West Ham see *Fulham Observer*, 7 June 1912 and *Borough of West Ham Herald and South Essex Mail*, 23 August 1912.

43 Playing without Puddefoot in the final, West Ham SFA were still good enough to beat Walthamstow SFA 4–1. *Borough of West Ham Herald and South Essex Mail*, 28 February 1908.

44 See Korr, *West Ham United*, pp. 58–60.

45 Turner and White, *Fulham*, pp. 153, 193, 256–7.

46 Cheshire, *Chelsea*, pp. 80, 86–7, 88–9, 136–7, 151–2, 214–15.

47 Macey, *Q.P.R.*, pp. 149, 252.

48 Purkiss, *Crystal Palace*, pp. 306–14.

49 This was Billy Minter. Goodwin, *Spurs Alphabet*, p. 263.

50 Hardinge later expressed gratitude that he had attended a school where football was encouraged. H.T.W. Harding, 'How football stands today' in *The Boy's Own Annual*, 37 (1914/5), p. 202.

51 Ollier, *Arsenal*, pp. 55, 58, 60, 71, 91.

52 *Football 'Sun'*, 3 March 1900.

53 R.A. Sparling, *The Romance of the Wednesday* (Westcliffe-on-Sea: Desert Island Books, 1997), p. 13.

54 Sparling noted that the first minute book of the Sheffield Club went back to 1855. Sparling, *The Wednesday*, p. 13. See also P.M. Young, *Football in Sheffield* (London: Stanley Paul, 1962), pp. 16–17. A footnote addresses the suggestion that the club may have originated two years earlier.

55 Harvey, 'An epoch in the annals of national sport', p. 60; Dunning, 'Some Comments', pp. 90–1. Further episodes in the same debate are in Harvey, 'The curate's egg put back together' and in Gunning and Curry, 'The curate's egg scrambled again'.

56 For Shaw see John Steele, 'John Charles Shaw' in Association of Sports Historians, *Newsletter*, July 1996, pp. 3–8.

57 Nicholas Fishwick, *From Clegg to Clegg House* (Sheffield: Sheffield and Hallamshire County FA, 1986), p. 5.

58 Fishwick, *From Clegg to Clegg House*, p. 10.

59 J. Dickinson, *One Hundred Years of Hillsborough: 2 September 1889–1999* (Sheffield: Hallamshire Press, 1999), p. 10.

60 Young, *Football in Sheffield*, pp. 64–5.

61 *Evening Telegraph and Star and Sheffield Daily News*, 5 May 1890. The Clegg trophy 'was presented by the Clegg family'. John Wilkinson, 'From little acorns, major oak trees grow', *Football in Schools*, 15 (1990), p. 12.

62 K. Farnsworth, *Sheffield Wednesday: A Complete Record 1867–1987* (Derby: Breedon, 1987); D. Clarebrough and A. Kirkham, *A Complete Record of Sheffield United Football Club 1889–1999* (Sheffield: Sheffield United FC, 1999).

63 The probable future FL player was Oxspring (Barnsley).

64 The match, which the Sheffield boys won 2–0, was reported in (Sheffield) *Evening Telegraph and Star*, 28 March 1894.

65 Clarebrough, *Sheffield United*, pp. 90–104.

66 Ibid., pp. 98–100; Purkiss, *Crystal Palace*, p. 311.

67 The teams are listed in *The Sportsman*, 7 April 1900.

68 *Yorkshire Telegraph and Star*, 12 May 1906.

69 Les Jolly and the present writer have examined the team lists for 21 seasons of Hackney SFA, at a time when it was a prominent force in schoolboy football, to ascertain what

percentage of the boys later played for professional clubs and found this was as low as 3.3, or, approximately one boy from every two district squads. L. Jolly and C. Kerrigan, 'Predicting success: Hackney schoolboy teams 1919–1939' in the Association of Football Statisticians, *Report*, 86 (November 1994), pp. 23–5.

70 Young, *Football in Sheffield*, p. 62.

71 Around 1890, the secretary of the Sheffield and Hallamshire FA was quoted as saying 'Oh, we don't want locals, let's have some Scotchmen. I never knew a Scot yet but he was a good footballer'. Young, *Football in Sheffield*, p. 62.

72 *Star*, 9 February 1925.

8   Conclusions

Introduction

At an early stage of investigating the history and influence of the LSFA and the SFAs affiliated to it, it was found that there was a need for a preliminary study of the other agencies that had been engaged in promoting football among working-class boys and youths in the period immediately before the formation of SFAs. This entailed an examination of the sporting dimensions of rescue work in Central London from the 1860s, a study of a football club with mainly ex-public-schoolboys as players but with a pitch located in a working-class area, and an exploration of the way the public-school mission and university settlement movements had an impact on the football played by boys and young men in working-class areas in London in the late nineteenth century.

The findings of this study and their contribution to historical knowledge will be considered as they relate in turn to the work of the public-school agencies in working-class areas, to policy towards outdoor games in elementary schools, to elementary-school pupils, to elementary-school teachers and, finally, to amateur and professional football.

Public-school football in working-class areas

There is no evidence of a football dimension to the rescue work of the distinguished Old Etonian footballer Quintin Hogg among destitute boys in Central London in the 1860s, but when the success of his work permitted a concentration on youths in more favourable social circumstances in the Hanover Institute and the Regent Street Polytechnic, such a dimension was soon apparent. Assisted by helpers, several of whom had established a reputation in public-school football and other sports, Hanover United FC and the Polytechnic's many teams gained a reputation for a high standard of sportsmanship in their matches which were played throughout the London area.

The study of Upton Park FC revealed that a great number of the more prominent players at the club had attended public schools and that many of those players who could not be traced to particular public schools had the kind of occupations that suggested they might have attended public schools for which lists of past pupils have not been compiled. It also indicated that few of them had any association with the East London area other than their membership of the club. Although no records of the club have survived, it may be inferred from newspaper accounts of their activities and in particular the absence of any evidence of an appeal for players from the population of the area surrounding their pitch, that the club was an exclusive one, with membership restricted to ex-public-schoolboys and professional gentlemen.

The incidental influence that the club might have had on the development of football in the surrounding area was likely to have been threefold. In the first place, with several club members involved in the early discussions on what the rules of the then newly formed FA should be, the club was in the forefront of those initiatives, revisions and alterations of rules that characterised the early years of association football. At a time when disagreement about rules of play was widespread, those in force at Upton Park FC's roped-off ground in West Ham Park were likely to have been the rules most recently sanctioned by the FA. Second, the local population which came to watch Upton Park FC's matches would have seen the game played in accordance with the highest sporting standards, resembling those that guided the Hanover and Polytechnic teams noted above. Finally, by virtue of the high standard of football in which it participated, Upton Park FC offered opportunities for East Londoners to witness the game at the highest level and to appreciate the skills of some of the national football heroes of the day. How much this may have contributed to the football players and teams in the area that later gained a reputation for skilful play in schoolboy, amateur and professional football competitions, with a reliance on technique and speed over strength and endurance, can never be known. A causal connection can only remain a possibility, as it must also remain in connection with 'spectatorism'. For it is impossible to prove that East Londoners' appreciation of a high standard of football, played skilfully and fairly, as indicated later, for example, by the support given to West Ham United FC's professionals, Clapton FC's amateurs and West Ham SFA's schoolboys, had its origin in the high standards of play and sportsmanship pioneered in the area by the ex-public-schoolboys of Upton Park FC.

Many of the clubs founded by the university settlement movement in East London for boys who had recently left school had football teams and the account of a German visitor to Toynbee Hall, the first such settlement, was emphatic on the value of football both in promoting a club spirit and as a training in discipline. Some of these teams, like that of Fairbairn House connected with the Mansfield College Settlement in Canning Town, trained players to a high level of football, not only winning youth competitions but providing players with opportunities to continue to improve in the period between leaving elementary school and entering senior amateur or, in some cases, professional football.

Motivated by a concern to spread the gospel among the urban poor, most of the public-school missions became involved in youth work at an early stage and found that football was a point of contact between public-school educated missioner and elementary-school educated boy. Many of the missioners had been prominent in their football teams while in their public schools and others, once a boys' club team was established at the mission, invited 'old boys' who were prominent at football to help with the mission teams. A London-wide competition for the boys' clubs associated with university settlements and public-school missions was established, where the sporting attitudes thought valuable by the missioners and settlers were given prominence in the conduct of matches. Many of those who were later to campaign for improved playing facilities for young people in cities had been associated with Hogg's rescue work or the university settlement and public-school mission movements, most particularly those involved in the work of the London Playing Fields Society.

A detailed study of the Eton Mission to Hackney Wick identified the way that public-school football made an impact on the traditional street football played by local youths. Emphatic that the way the boys were shown how to play the game by the missioners and their friends was the proper way, the Etonians at Hackney Wick were able to prove their point by the success of the Mission's teams against opponents, while at the same time placing an emphasis on fair play and sportsmanship. Pitches, previously let by the local park in an arbitrary manner which permitted matches to encroach on each other, were measured out by the missioners and a rational system of pitch bookings introduced. The Mission played a leading part in the campaign that led to the acquisition of Hackney Marshes as an open space for football and cricket. From being a rather disorderly and dishevelled spectacle, boys' football became a rule-bound game played on a correctly measured and marked pitch, free from encroachments, by boys who were suitably, if not expensively, attired for outdoor exercise.

In general, in transmitting public-school attitudes towards games to working-class boys in youth clubs, the university settlements and public-school missions seem to have had considerable success in transforming for the better the football culture that the boys and youths had been engaged in before the arrival of the settlers and missioners. And while the study of these agencies was preparatory to rather than central to the main concerns of this study, there is evidence here to suggest that more detailed research on the sporting dimensions of a greater number of university settlements and public-school missions would throw considerable light on two questions that have not been adequately addressed in the histories of football reviewed in Chapter 1, namely, why did the game spread so quickly from the 1870s onwards and how much were former public-schoolboys responsible for this?

Policy towards outdoor games in elementary schools

It was noted in Chapter 1 that while reference was often made to football in elementary schools in the late nineteenth century both in studies of the history of physical education in schools and in histories of football, no substantial study of its origins and development has been published. With the exception of a recent article exploring the adapted form of athleticism that was transmitted from the public schools to the elementary schools, and which saw elementary-school football in South London as one of its expressions, this is still the case.[1] In Chapters 3 and 4 of this book the origin and development of SFAs in London in the late nineteenth and early twentieth centuries has been traced in detail, with particular attention given to the voluntary work undertaken by the teachers who promoted it and the difficulties they encountered. How much did the work of these teachers and the SFAs they founded change attitudes towards games in elementary schools, both as extra-curricular activities and as part of the school curriculum?

In a discussion of Neil Wigglesworth's idea about the exclusive nature of much public-school sport in Chapter 1, it was argued that while the 'social prejudice' he saw as guiding this exclusiveness was evident in some of the early attempts to retain football as the preserve of the public-school educated elite, some ex-public-schoolboys like Lord Kinnaird and C.W. Alcock were in fact conciliatory figures when the dispute about paid players came to a head. Given the preponderance of ex-public-schoolboys among the influential officials and inspectors at the Board of Education and, to a lesser extent, among the elected members of the SBL, it might be thought that their failure to show any substantial support for the early SFAs was a reflection of the same prejudice. The small number who did express support for the value of games, like the Old Etonian managers of Windsor Road in Hackney, could, on this view, like Lord Kinnaird and C.W. Alcock in relation to professionalism, be seen as the exceptions who proved the rule. Games were all very well for the public-school elite, but they had no place in the elementary schools for working-class and lower middle-class children.

There is substantial evidence in this thesis to question this view. In the first place, while support was indeed lacking for the work of the South London SFA in its early days, this was not the case in the first years of the SFAs in the East End, where a regular feature of presentation evenings was fulsome praise for the unpaid efforts of teachers in promoting games in elementary schools and a homily, often delivered by a politician with a public-school background, on the moral and physical value of football.

In addition, there were some HMIs, like Rankine in West Ham in 1893, who were sufficiently impressed with the usefulness of cricket and football clubs in schools to recommend that they be encouraged, while some HMI reports on annual inspections of individual elementary schools, carefully copied into school log books, testify to the value of these clubs to the education of children in the schools.[2] It needs to be added, however, that there is no evidence of the

Education Department or HMI communicating this approval to the officers of the schoolboy cricket and FAs, whose voluntary efforts both stimulated the formation of so many of these clubs and arranged the inter-school competitions that provided them with the motivation to continue.

While the response of the SBL to the work of the LSFA and the SFAs affiliated to it may in general be categorised as one of silence, at the same time, no examples have been found of elected members or officials of the Board expressing opposition to the work of promoting schoolboy football. From this it might be inferred that the Board, while approving of the voluntary efforts of teachers who organised football for board school children, did not wish to be associated publicly with the movement because of the financial implications of such approval. For, once such approval was given, the Board might be expected to provide facilities for outdoor games for *all* children in London's elementary schools, even in those areas where open space suitable for playing football was non-existent. Fears of incurring additional expenditure by a body already regularly arraigned for profligacy with public money might have silenced those members who feared that the good they were doing in promoting an acceptance of elementary education for all London schoolchildren would be compromised by any further increase in the rate needed to underwrite outdoor games. Whether they were right or not in their perception of the likely response if they were to promote outdoor games is open to question, they were certainly correct in assessing that it would be expensive. For despite the efforts of bodies like the LPFS and the generally good response of public parks to the requests for pitches from the SFAs, the provision of playing surfaces for outdoor games in the London area remained poor throughout the period covered here.

Further evidence on these points comes from two assessments of the SBL's achievements, both published in its final year. The first, an independent study, drew attention to the usefulness of football in the Board's elementary schools, especially in reaching the more difficult boys, while the official *Final Report of the School Board for London* noted no more than that the Board 'encourage their teachers, as far as possible, to make arrangements for outdoor games outside school hours'.[3]

Alan Penn's recent book has recorded how military drill gave way to physical exercises of a non-military character and how the Education Department, in revisions to the Code communicated to HMIs in 1896, acknowledged that the best form that these physical exercises might take would be that of 'healthy games', although conditions in urban areas made provision for the latter impossible. Commenting on this, Penn remarks that HMIs and teachers must have been surprised that 'the Education Department had turned from its advocacy of military drill to support of physical exercises and, where circumstances permitted, to "healthy games"'.[4]

The work of SFAs outlined in this book, and which must have been known to HMIs and teachers at the time with an interest in outdoor games, would suggest that no such surprise would have been likely. Inter-school football competitions had been organised for 10 years in South London by that date and for shorter periods in at least ten other districts in London, as well as in cities like Birmingham, Leeds, Liverpool, Manchester, Nottingham and Sheffield. There was visible evidence of its existence in public parks throughout London on Saturday mornings, and some local newspapers carried accounts of matches, presentation evenings and annual reports of SFAs, as noted in Chapter 3.

There can be little doubt that this pioneering work of the SFAs in the ten years between 1886 and 1896 played a part in the change in the Education Department's policy on the value of 'healthy games'. For the work of these associations had been demonstrating that, even in the most difficult urban schools with the worst playing facilities, it was possible to arrange football matches between schools when there was a willingness on the part of teachers to organise them. The influence of schoolboy football associations was even more evident when, in 1905, the Board of Education gave its formal approval to sports teams in elementary schools in a set of suggestions for those involved in the work of such schools. First focusing on the value of games in their contribution to the development of character, it was held that 'the scholars may learn, under the guidance of their teachers, to obey rules, to avoid rough play and to exercise self-restraint'. In a chapter devoted to physical training, the suggestions paid particular attention to the value of organised games in schools containing the less fortunate children. In these and in other schools, it was held that in addition to the individual contribution to the development of character, games could foster the communal values of *esprit de corps* and the subordination of scholars' individual powers and wishes to a common end. It went on to make the further assertion that 'schools which can raise football and cricket teams, swimming clubs and cadet corps, are wont to exhibit such excellent work inside the walls of schools'.[5] Although no evidence is cited in support of this, it corresponds to several responses to George Sharples' survey that appeared in the Education Department's *Special Reports* of 1898.[6]

Evidence is lacking to link directly the successful work of SFAs with the Board of Education's acknowledgement of games as an alternative to Swedish drill and physical exercises in instructions issued to HMIs in 1900 and in the Board's outright advocacy of games in 1905. But the origin, development and flourishing of schoolboy football in the London area over the two decades from 1885, as outlined here in Chapters 3 and 4, suggests that it must have provided a crucial and consistent example to the Education Department, and later the Board of Education, that organised games were not only beneficial to elementary-school children but a practical proposition even for difficult schools in uninspiring environments. The Education Department's invitation to George Sharples, founder of the Manchester SFA, to write the 1898 report on elementary-school games out of school hours, is an indication that officials found this voluntary work of teachers to be of some educational value. That HMIs were aware of the development of outdoor games in London elementary schools is confirmed in Graves' account of the experiments in Eltringham Street, as related in Chapter 4. A key element in his argument for the physical improvements in the boys was their improved performances in South London elementary-school competitions.

Pupils in elementary schools

The first and most obvious contribution of the early SFAs to pupils in elementary schools was that they proved not only that the games played in public and preparatory schools by the children of the upper and middle classes could be played with equal enthusiasm by, and benefit to, the children of the working and lower middle classes, but that they could be played by schools located in the most unfavourable environments as regards open space. While it was schools located nearest to public parks that were most prominent in the competitions organised by some SFAs, boys more removed from suitable playing space also benefited. By its block bookings of Victoria Park on Saturday mornings in the 1890s, for example, co-ordinated with its fixture list, the Tower Hamlets SFA was able to provide the opportunity of playing competitive football to schools in the overcrowded riverside parishes of the East End that, in the absence of a local SFA, would have been unlikely to have found the space to play regularly, or even at all.

SFAs also enabled schools 'to stimulate friendly rivalry amongst the boys', as the treasurer of the Hackney SFA put it in 1892. As there is ample evidence in school log books of inter-school rivalry taking the form of stone-throwing and worse, the introduction of organised inter-school football can only have been of benefit in the correct harnessing of the spirit of rivalry that existed between elementary schools, or at least those that were in immediate proximity to each other. In addition to meeting boys from neighbouring schools in local competitions, the LSFA's programme of London-wide competitions, for district teams from 1893/94 and for individual schools from 1898/99, gave boys the opportunity of meeting other schoolboys from all parts of the Metropolis and, from 1899, when the first LSFA representative team played, boys from different parts of England.[7] At an individual level, a boy with ability at football could have his successful mastery of the game acknowledged within the context of his education at an elementary school, rather like Siegfried Sassoon's talent at cricket was allowed to express itself in his preparatory school team.[8]

Football practices after school and at dinner time, like those recorded for Ruckholt Road School in Leyton in 1898, became a feature of elementary-school life, and, along with regular matches on Saturday mornings in the autumn and winter months, gave a new dimension to elementary-school education. For, while what we would now call extra-curricular events like school concerts and drill displays had preceded the introduction of football, and training for them may have taken place in part at least outside school hours, their public aspect was normally confined to one or two performances a year, while school football teams would have played up to thirty matches per season.

In the absence of any evidence that the boys felt compelled to train and play, the fact that so many of them in numerous elementary schools attended these practices and matches in their own time suggests that they enjoyed them.[9] The happiness of the boys in Victoria Park reported by the *Football 'Sun'*, that was noted in Chapter 3, reinforces the impression that they thoroughly enjoyed football, as does the fact that the boys from the Isle of Dogs were prepared to walk up to three miles each way on Saturday mornings to take part in school matches. The account of Len Usher's sacrifice of his right football boot so that his team captain could be at least half-suitably attired for a school match suggests that the game evoked the *esprit de corps* and the spirit of self-sacrifice that the Board of Education's *Suggestions* of 1905 were confident it would.[10]

Evidence that this *esprit de corps* had implications beyond the football pitch was suggested by an entry in the log book of Berkshire Road in Hackney to the effect that good staff–pupil relationships were exemplified by success at football and other games. The fact that school FCs were organised by the boys themselves (although teams for inter-school matches were selected by teachers) offered opportunities for the exercise of some element of discretion within an education system that was highly regulated and directed from above. Some benefits to boys' self-esteem might be expected from this, as from the boys seeing themselves, and being seen by others, as representing the school or district in matches, especially when these were reported in the local press. Some, like that in the *Tottenham and Edmonton Weekly Herald*, which compared the Tottenham boys' footballing achievements with those of Tottenham Hotspur, the local professional club, helped to identify the elementary school as a significant part of the local community. That the boys, for their part, were pleased to be identified with their elementary school's sporting achievements is evident from the pride they took in the symbols of success, as when the Oban Street boys wore their football medals around their necks and the Hackney player cherished his Sun Shield medal until the day he died.[11]

The influence of schoolboy football in establishing the identity of an elementary school as a part of the local community was given further impetus by the formation of elementary-school 'old boy' teams, explored in Chapter 6. Such teams helped to forge links between the school and the community and between present and past pupils, and in so doing, promoted a closer connection between the world of school and the world of work. By the end of the period under review, there is evidence that the elementary school was a recognised and esteemed part of the local community and that schoolboy football may have been partly responsible for this.

A regular feature of reports of fatalities, woundings or awards for outstanding bravery in the *Stratford Express* from the first weeks of the First World War was the identification of the young servicemen by the elementary schools they had attended. Sometimes the contribution to the War of a particular elementary school was highlighted, as when two former pupils of St Anthony's, Forest Gate, were awarded military medals for bravery in the same week.[12] News of individual servicemen was sometimes accompanied by an appraisal of their character by their 'old' headmasters or by reference to their achievements while at school. When Private H.S. Woodruffe was wounded by a shell near La Basse at the end of 1915, for example, it was noted that he had been a pupil at Godwin Road, Forest Gate and that 'he (had) played football under Mr Harry Earle, for the school, afterwards joining the Clapton Football Club'.[13] When 21-year-old Thomas Claydon was killed in action the following year, the same newspaper not only recorded that he had attended Newport Road, Leyton, as a boy but that while there he had been good enough a footballer to gain selection for the LSFA representative team that played Glasgow.[14]

There is evidence also that school sport was a subject that formed a significant link for many servicemen between life at the front and their former lives in peacetime. A letter from a Private Johnstone serving at the front in 1915, published in the *South London Press*, thanked the headmaster of Rolls Road, 'for finding a Steve Bloomer and a W.G. Grace' to help his twenty-second Battalion (Bermondsey) win matches.[15] When the future Clapton Orient and England player, John Townrow, was selected for the England schoolboy team to play Wales in 1915, he received a letter from a past pupil of his school, Pelly Memorial, West Ham. The writer was serving in France, and having congratulated Townrow on the honour he had brought to the school he concluded his letter as follows: 'In the trenches out here I often think of West Ham schoolboy football, and wish I was back seeing a match between Pelly and Creedon. Remember me kindly to Mr Mann.'[16]

Pride in the achievements of the school football team extended far and wide. For example, Central Park Road had been successful in many East Ham SFA and LSFA competitions both before and during the First World War. In a newspaper article in 1917, the headmaster said that many of the 123 letters he had received from past pupils on active service 'were inspired by a wish to congratulate the school on the maintenance of its sporting traditions. After winning the Dewar Shield last year, letters of congratulation came in from young soldiers wherever the British army are to be found.'[17]

How much schoolboy football and other elementary-school games may have contributed to the War effort is impossible to determine, but it was certainly believed by its advocates to have been significant. The ESFA justified the continuation of its programme throughout the War on the grounds that

> the mental, moral and physical development of the schoolboy was of great and vital importance to the well-being of the country. Also, hospital statistics have incontestably proved that the soldier who has played an out-door game and taken part in field athletics, makes a quicker and better recovery from wounds received in battle than one who has not so played.[18]

The efforts of teachers towards the elementary schools' contribution to the war was acknowledged by the Right Hon. Dr Macnamara, Minister for War, who had himself been an elementary-school teacher.[19] Speaking at a function to commemorate the memory of John Cornwall, the boy-hero of the Battle of Jutland, Macnamara said that the teachers at Walton Road, East Ham, 'had taught the young Cornwall to learn the British lesson and to be filled with the British spirit'.[20] The president of the East Ham branch of the NUT, referring to General French's praise for the men under his command, emphasised that the men concerned were products of the elementary-school system.[21] Neither the minister nor the teacher made any reference to games. The *South London Press*, always forthcoming in its support for schoolboy games, was less cautious about suggesting a connection between the field of play and the field of battle. When S.B. Peart, ex-captain of the football and cricket teams at Bellenden Road, a school long prominent in South London inter-school competitions, was killed by machine gun fire in France at the age of twenty-three, it concluded its tribute as follows: 'A man and a "sport" to the end, he died a man's death.'[22]

How much the training of teams led to the boys becoming better players depended to a great extent on the abilities of the teachers who did the training. A reading of the sports pages of the *Stratford Express* over the whole of the period under review confirms beyond doubt that it was thought such training was of crucial importance to boys' football development. Over and over again, when a player made a breakthrough into a higher level of football or when a profile of a successful player appeared in its pages, the *Express* referred to the player's elementary-school football career where he learnt the game 'under the able tuition of' a named teacher.[23] Now that the football education of the most talented schoolboy players has been placed exclusively in the hands of the Football Academies and Schools of Excellence attached to professional clubs, it might perhaps be appropriate to be reminded of the time when such training was undertaken almost exclusively by teachers and, in the context of the time, was thought to have been accomplished successfully. With a more professional and scientific approach to the development of the talents of gifted players in recent years, the move towards the professional clubs taking a more central role was inevitable. At the same time, the contribution of SFAs to the development of young players, including the most talented, the origins of which have been examined in this book, should not be overlooked. It should remind us also that further discoveries about the way children learn football skills and dispositions in the future may lead to revisions of the latest regulations, however suitable they may seem to present circumstances.

Elementary-school teachers

The teachers who introduced inter-school football to elementary-school pupils in London in the 1880s took an initiative that demanded considerable courage. For despite some approval by politicians and others committed to the value of games, those pioneering teachers received no official support for their voluntary work with pupils outside school hours. Their initiative is all the more worthy of commendation in that it took place during a period when the relationship between elementary teachers and the Education Department and school boards was poor owing to the lack of agreement about the harmful consequences of the Revised Code, which reached a head in the 1880s.[24] On the disputed issue of classification of pupils by ability rather than age, the Department resisted the Union's representations for selection by ability.[25]

Less committed teachers might have agreed to put their enthusiasm for games for their pupils on hold until a more appropriate time in order not to raise another potentially contentious issue between the Education Department and the NUET, the union to which almost all the teachers engaged in promoting elementary-school football belonged. In the event, no open conflict arose on the issue of games, but it is perhaps significant that the period immediately following the introduction of Kekewich's new code in 1890, which met with the approval of the Union as a constructive step towards the abolition of the hated system of 'payment by results', saw the foundation of SFAs in a great number of areas that were later to feature prominently in schoolboy football in London.[26]

The three main sources employed in trying to identify the motivation of teachers engaged in schoolboy football in the period under review were newspaper reports of speeches made by politicians at presentation evenings, school log books and the recorded actions of teachers when dealing with a number of incidents pertaining to schoolboy matches. Taken together, these sources indicate a discernible link between the public-school attitude to games brought to working-class areas by the university settlements and public-school missions and the attitude of the teachers promoting games in elementary schools. Speeches by politicians and by men associated with the university settlement and public-school missions clearly represented the promotion of football in elementary schools as having the same purpose as games in public schools. Football was to help in the formation of character, as it developed the pluck, endurance, skill, co-operation and competitiveness that prepared the boys for the struggles of life.

Newspaper reports on the conduct of games and evidence from the details of a small number of contentious issues that found their way into the minutes of the South London SFA suggests that teachers emphasised fair play and sportsmanship and saw games as valuable in the formation of character. This, and the fact that a great number of the teachers promoting football had attended training colleges where attitudes to games resembled those of the public schools, would suggest a case for a commitment to some form of athleticism, appropriately adapted to the elementary school, as suggested by Mangan and Hickey. A search through the log books of more than forty schools that were prominent in schoolboy football at the time found little evidence to confirm this. For while most made some mention of the existence of a football team in the school, if only to record that the team had won a competition, few gave it any more than passing attention and none contained anything that could be considered a substantial case for games that related to their value in the development of character. As noted in Chapter 5, there may have been several reasons why this was so, but it does suggest that the reasons why teachers trained teams and organised matches for their pupils were more complex.

The biographical studies of teachers in Chapter 5, for example, indicated that many of the teachers prominent in promoting football had themselves been good at the game and were known as referees or other officials in adult football. The wish to promote among their pupils a game from which the teachers themselves had obviously gained great satisfaction might be considered a reasonable form of motivation, as might also be the pride taken by many teachers in the success of their teams in competition. The commitment to the value of fresh air, emphasised in the extract from the log book of Marner Street quoted on page 13, was also a probable motivating factor. This would seem particularly likely at a time when, as shown in Chapter 4, there was a great emphasis on the value of fresh air for children from the kind of environments inhabited by many of the children who contested football competitions promoted by the LSFA and the associations affiliated to it.

Teachers were in the front line in the battle against the harsh effects of the poverty that characterised the environments of so many elementary schools in late Victorian and early Edwardian London. In 1881 Lord Brabazon (later Lord Meath) observed that in some schools the teachers paid for meals for their impoverished pupils out of their own pockets.[27] A recent study has confirmed the prominent role played by teachers in late nineteenth-century schemes 'to feed hungry children to make it possible for them to learn'.[28] Later, not only were teachers engaged in promoting cleanliness and nutrition among the pupils they taught, but many of them were associated with campaigns committed to providing a range of welfare facilities in schools.[29] The lack of fresh air and healthy exercise endured by their pupils was seen by some teachers as a form of impoverishment and the promotion of outdoor games after school hours was their contribution towards addressing it.

While the motivation of some teachers may have been to exercise greater control over their pupils' free time, there is no evidence to support this in the minutes or handbooks of SFAs or in the log books of schools that were prominent in competitions. Insofar as declared intentions are ascertainable, they indicate that teachers wished, through the medium of association football, to provide healthy outdoor exercise for children, gain prestige for the school, the boys and on occasions the teachers themselves, offer opportunities for competitive games in an atmosphere of fairness and help towards improved relationships between teachers and scholars.

The biographical studies of teachers in Chapter 5 revealed the enormous amount of time many teachers spent in promoting schoolboy football. Given that one of the results of these efforts was an increasingly positive acceptance of the value of organised outdoor games by the Education Department and the Board of Education which succeeded it, leading eventually to the official approval of outdoor games, first outside school hours and later as part of the elementary-school curriculum, it is surprising that historians of teachers and teaching have not shown any interest in their achievements. They do not feature in the standard histories of education in Victorian England and even Tropp's specialised book makes no mention of this valuable work by men who were nearly all members of the NUT, the union that featured in a central position in his study of the positive aspects of the growth of the teaching profession.[30] The extent and influence of the work of such teachers, as set out and evaluated in this book, will make a contribution to raising the profile of elementary-school teachers in their role in the vanguard of the struggle to confront in a humane and positive manner the enormous difficulties with which they were presented, especially in urban schools. In addition, the detailed account here of their remarkable achievements will both make up for an omission in previous histories of elementary-school education and ensure that such an omission could not be repeated in the future. If teachers' willingness to accept without question the immutability of the curriculum of the Victorian elementary school is one of the 'stereotyped caricatures' that, according to Wendy Robinson, needs to be contested by historians of education, the role of teachers in bringing about change in the official policy towards outdoor games, as outlined in this book, may be seen as undermining one such caricature.[31]

Amateur and professional football

In their commitment to the amateur ideal, fair play and the value of football as healthy exercise rather than a performance for paying spectators, the teachers who were the pioneers of schoolboy football in London were following closely in the footsteps of the university settlements and public-school missions, whose attitudes were noted in Chapter 2. An examination in Chapter 4 of the post-elementary-school football careers of four players who had been prominent in LSFA competitions in the early twentieth century suggested that, besides a lifelong love of football, each had carried with them from their schoolboy days attitudes of integrity, dignity and gentlemanly conduct in all matters relating to football.

By the 1890s great numbers of boys were leaving London elementary schools with experience of having played organised football for their school teams. At the same time, local amateur leagues were being established to give the amateur player the regular fixtures that had proved so successful for professional players in Football League teams. To prove a connection between the availability of boys experienced in schoolboy football and the introduction of these amateur leagues would be impossible because so few lists of players in these early schoolboy or amateur leagues have survived. But the possibility of such a connection is suggested by the fact that the amateur leagues began in the South London area where the local schoolboy association, with its large number of affiliated schools, had been giving boys experience of organised football for some years before the leagues were established.

A preliminary study of elementary-school 'old boy' FCs in Chapter 6 located a considerable number of them in all parts of London and a more detailed account of four of the more prominent identified how they attained a position at the top level of senior amateur football in London at the time. This, and the fact that a great number of outstanding ex-elementary-school players also played for most of the leading amateur clubs other than the elementary-school 'old boy' clubs, revealed the great contribution made by ex-elementary-school scholars to top-class amateur football in London. It also offered further evidence of the significant role of elementary-school teachers in establishing football as the national game.

'English football is fully as good (i.e. as Scottish), and English footballers would be fully as successful if only local talent were fostered', wrote John Goodall, the English international player who was born in England of Scottish parents.[32] Just as English players in general were thought inferior to Scottish, and neglected accordingly by some professional clubs, so also many London professional clubs believed that young London players were inferior not only to young players from Scotland but to young players from other parts of England.

The success by London association teams that competed with such distinction in the English Schools' Shield, as noted in Chapter 4, would suggest that the standard of schoolboy footballers in London was equal to, if not superior to, that of the leading schoolboy footballers in the country. Nevertheless, London professional clubs continued to recruit players almost exclusively from Scotland and the North and Midlands. An examination of the recruitment patterns of London professional clubs at the time revealed that those clubs that showed an interest in the schoolboy football talent that surrounded them were successful in recruiting players good enough to play at the top level of the professional game, with many of them going on to play for England. Those London clubs that showed no confidence in local players and continued to seek recruits in the traditional heartlands of professional football may simply have been lacking in any spirit of adventure. They may also have been guilty of the same kind of prejudice as their successors in professional clubs held towards black players.

It is also possible, of course, that many London schoolboy, while being sufficiently talented to make a mark on professional football, had no wish to do so. This could have been because of their attachment to the amateur game which was so dominant in the South, or to a particular amateur club to which they might have belonged since leaving school. Or it could have been, as in the case of Tommie Fitchie whose career was examined in Chapter 6, that the prospect of a career as a professional footballer held less appeal than one in business. Social conditions and employment patterns and opportunities were clearly relevant. G.L. Crandon, who had been manager of the ESFA's national

side for many years, in reflecting on how so few England schoolboy internationals became professional players, identified the precariousness of professional football as a living to have been a significant deterrent. He continued:

> In the North, when conditions of industry were neither stable nor remu-
> nerative, professional football was a very attractive proposition and many
> boys graduated from school football and became stars later, so that the
> North-East became quite a famous nursery for professional football.[33]

Whatever the influence that these social and economic factors might have
had in limiting the number of London players in London professional clubs,
the breakthrough, when it came, must be largely attributed to the work of
those who founded and ran the pioneering SFAs, which, if the extent of their
efforts on behalf of players in London elementary schools is anything to go by,
had unlimited confidence in the abilities of their elementary-school footballers.

The precise conditions that prevailed in London with regard to the development of amateur and professional football in the period between the 1880s
and the First World War were not replicated in any of the cities where SFAs
were founded at a comparable date to those in London. Nevertheless, an
investigation in Chapter 7 of Sheffield schoolboy players who went on to
professional FCs suggests that research on the growth of schoolboy football in
areas outside London would offer fruitful insights into the elusive relationship between the schoolboy and adult game. In particular, such research
might go far towards confirming on a national scale what has been shown
throughout the period under review in connection with London, namely, that
the work of elementary-school teachers was a major factor in the growth and
development of football as the national game. This in turn should lead to a
more substantial acknowledgement of the work of elementary-school teachers
and the SFAs they founded in future histories of the game.

Notes

1 Mangan and Hickey, 'Elementary education revisited'.
2 In W.J. Wilson's Oldridge Road in Balham, for example, the HMI's report for 1888, copied
   into the log book on 15 March 1889, included the following: 'Cricket, Football and Swimming
   Clubs exist in connection with the school, to the obvious benefit of the boys.' LMA, EO/DIV9/
   OLD/LB/1.
3 Philpott, *London at School*, p. 127; *Final Report of the School Board for London*, p. 115.
4 Penn, *Targeting Schools*, pp. 38–9.
5 Board of Education, *Suggestions for the Consideration of Teachers and Others Concerned in the Work
   of Public Elementary Schools*. P.P. 1905 (Cd 2838) LX, p. 76.
6 See, for example, the report from Leicester, where it was claimed that boys in teams try
   harder at their school work. Sharples, 'Organisation of games outside school', p. 165.
7 In the case of South London, playing against teams from outside London dated from 1890,
   when South London SFA first went to play Sheffield SFA.
8 J.M. Wilson, *Siegfried Sassoon: The Making of a War Poet; A Biography 1886–1918* (London:
   Duckworth, 1999), p. 87.

9 That boys in any age and of any age need no inducements to train for and play in football matches is something that is confirmed in my own experience of schoolboy football.

10 Information on Len Usher is in a letter from his daughter, Jaqui Ball, 4 November 2000.

11 For Oban Street see Chapter 3. Information on the Hackney player Arthur Watts is in a letter from his son, Owen Watts, 2 November 2000.

12 *Stratford Express*, 25 March 1915. The article also notes that as many as 300 past pupils of St Anthony's were serving with the naval or military forces at the time.

13 Ibid., 22 January 1916.

14 Ibid., 4 November 1916.

15 *South London Press*, 3 September 1915.

16 *Stratford Express*, 1 May 1915. Creedon was another West Ham school and Mann trained Pelly Memorial and West Ham district teams.

17 C.W. Cook, the headmaster, was interviewed in the *West Ham Herald and South Essex Mail*, 11 May 1917.

18 ESFA, *Handbook 1917/8*. The words cited were from the Annual Report for the 1916–17 season.

19 R. Betts, *Dr Macnamara 1861–1931* (Liverpool: Liverpool University Press, 1999), pp. 14–20.

20 *Stratford Express*, 16 September 1916.

21 Ibid., 30 January 1915.

22 *South London Press*, 2 July 1915.

23 C. Beal of Park, West Ham, was the teacher of H.J. Pearce, in this instance. *Stratford Express*, 4 September 1909.

24 Tropp, *The School Teachers*, pp. 126–9.

25 Phillips, 'The NUET', p. 185. The NUET was more successful in persuading the Education Department to abolish the annual endorsements of certificates for those teachers who had attained first-class certificates with ten years' satisfactory service in the classroom. Phillips, 'The NUET', p. 186. Conflict between union and government remained, and was carried into the new century. In 1907, when West Ham Council was trying to reduce the amount that teachers could charge for their services, as noted in Chapter 4, the Board of Education was content to permit the local council to break the Board's own regulations in pursuit of the aim of breaking the power of the NUT. Lawn, *Servants of the State*, p. 33. An issue more directly comparable to the promotion of games, in that it was concerned with voluntary efforts to promote a subject which eventually became part of the curriculum and that it entailed no open conflict between teachers and the education authorities, was that of the folk dance movement. In a recent article, Anne Bloomfield has shown that by popularising this art form and providing the support system that ensured its survival, the pioneering English folk-dance movement succeeded in having folk-dance become a valued part of school life. A. Bloomfield, 'The quickening of the national spirit: Cecil Sharp and the pioneers of the folk-dance revival in English state schools (1900–26)', *History of Education*, 30, 1 (January 2001), p. 75.

26 SFAs were founded in West Ham in 1890 and in West London and Hackney in 1891.

27 Lord Brabazon, 'Health and physique of our city populations', *The Nineteenth Century*, 10 (July 1881), p. 87.

28 A.S. Williams, P. Ivin and C. Morse, *The Children of London: Attendance and Welfare at School 1870–1990* (London: Institute of Education, 2001), p. 40.

29 Lawn, *Servants of the State*, p. 9.

30 Tropp, *The School Teachers*, passim.

31 W. Robinson, 'Finding our professional niche: Reinventing ourselves as twenty-first century historians of education' in D. Crook and R. Aldrich (eds), *History of Education for the Twenty-First Century* (London: Institute of Education, 2000), p. 61.

32 J. Goodall, *Association Football* (Edinburgh: Blackwood, 1898), p. 33.

33 ESFA, *Golden Jubilee Centenary Brochure* (The Association, 1954), p. 26.

Bibliography

Primary sources

1   Manuscript and other collections in archives, museums and libraries

(a)   **Birmingham City Archives**
Minute Book of the Birmingham Athletic Institute 1898–1917.

(b)   **Brentwood School Archives**
Records relating to football teams 1866–75.

(c)   **British and Foreign School Society Archives Centre, Brunel University**
Records relating to teachers trained at Borough Road College, to sports teams, College discipline and the College curriculum.

(d)   **College of St Mark and St John, Plymouth**
Records relating to teachers trained at St Mark's, Chelsea and St John's Battersea, including admission registers, College and 'Old Boy' teams and the College curriculum.
Year Book of the Battersea Club, 1901–25
Year Book of St Mark and St John's Clubs, 1926–39.

(e)   **Croydon Central Library Archives**
Log Book for all Saints School.

(f)   **English Schools' Football Association Archives, Stafford**
Minutes of the ESFA (Council and Annual General Meetings), 1904–1925
ESFA handbooks 1907–08 to 1924–25.

(g)   **Essex Record Office, Chelmsford**
Log Book for Ilford Higher Elementary School.

(h)   **Felsted School Archives**
Records relating to football at the school 1875–80
Old Felstedian, 1875–1890.

(i)   **Football Association, Soho Square**
Minutes of Council Meetings 1904–06
FA handbooks 1871–1915.

(j) **Forest School, Snaresbrook**
Records relating to school football teams 1866–80
Forest School Magazine, 1866–72.

(k) **Hackney Archives Centre**
Eton Mission minute books 1880–1915 (on microfilm)
Eton Mission Handbooks from 1896–1913 (on microfilm)
Manuscript history of the Eton Mission
Chinwag (magazine of Eton Manor Clubs), 1913–21.

(l) **Imperial War Museum**
First World War Papers of Captain W.P. Newell.

(m) **John Harvey Library, Southwark**
Nunhead Football and Sports Club Minute Book, 1920–25.

(n) **London Borough of Newham Archives, Stratford**
Records relating to Mansfield House Settlement and the Settlement's Fairbairn
House (Youths and Boys) football teams.
Log Books for the Boys' Departments of the following schools:
   Canning Town
   Custom House
   Hallsville, Canning Town
   Hermit Road, Canning Town
   Plashet Lane, East Ham
   St Paul's, Stratford
   Sandringham Road, East Ham
   Shaftesbury Road, East Ham
   Shrewsbury Road, East Ham
   South Halsville, Canning Town
   West Silvertown.

(o) **London Borough of Tower Hamlets Archives, Mile End**
Minutes of Broad Street and Highway Clubs
Manuscript history of the Broad Street Clubs
Log Book for Guardian Angels RC School.
Oxford House Magazine, 1894–1905
Annual Reports Toynbee Hall University Settlement
Toynbee Record, 1886–92.

(p) **London Football Association, Catford**
Minutes of London FA Council Meetings 1893–1902
London FA handbooks 1882–3 to 1905–06.

(q) **London Metropolitan Archives, Farringdon**
Minutes of School Board for London 1880–95
Final Report of the School Board for London
Minutes of the London County Council (Education Committee) 1907–09
Log Books for the following schools, all of which are for Boys' Departments or
Mixed Departments unless otherwise stated:
   Atley Road, Bow
   Battersea Park

    Bellenden Road, Peckham
    Bellenden Road, Peckham (Girls)
    Daubeney Road (Girls)
    Deodar (later Brandlehow) Road, Putney
    Glengall Road, Isle of Dogs
    Goodrich Road, Camberwell
    Hazelrigge Road, Wandsworth
    Lewisham Bridge (Girls)
    London Fields, Hackney
    Mitcham Lane, Streatham
    Monteith Road, Bow
    Munster Road, Fulham
    Oban Street, Poplar
    Oldridge Road, Balham
    Priory Road, Merton
    Sidney Road, Homerton
    Swaffield Road, Wandsworth
    Windsor (later Berkshire) Road, Hackney Wick
Photographs of schoolboy football teams
Photograph of Borough Road College team, 1884.

(r) **London Playing Fields Society, Boston Manor**
Minutes of Council Meetings 1890–95
Annual Reports 1890–99.

(s) **Public Record Office, Kew**
Application Form for Organised Games (LCC, 1916).

(t) **Valance House Archives, Dagenham**
Log Books for the Boys' Department of the following schools:
    Gascoigne Road, Barking
    Westbury Road, Barking.

(u) **Vestry House Museum, Walthamstow**
Photographs of drill and football at Harrow Green School, Leyton, 1894–6.
Log Books for the Boys' Departments of the following schools:
    Capworth Road, Leytonstone
    Church Road, Leytonstone
    Harrow Green, Leyton
    Ruckholt Road, Leyton.

(v) **Villiers Park, Bicester**
Records relating to Eton Manor Boys' Clubs.

2   *Manuscript and other collections in private possession*

(a) **London Schools' Football Association** (in possession of Hon. Secretary when consulted, but now in the London Metropolitan Archives)
Minutes LSFA 1892–1919 (with gaps)
LSFA handbooks 1905–06 to 1914–15.

(b) **South London Schools' Football Association** (in possession of the Hon. Secretary)
Minutes 1885–1919 (with gaps)
South London SFA handbooks 1905–6 to 1914–15.

(c) **Log Books consulted at the schools**
Dulwich Hamlet
Godwin Road, Forest Gate
Marner, Bromley-by-Bow
Napier (now Ranalagh) Road, West Ham
Park, West Ham.

3   *Printed records*

(a) **Parliamentary papers**
Final Report of the Commissioners appointed to inquire into the Elementary Education Acts (XXXV 1888)
Special Reports on Educational Subjects (Sadler Reports) (XXIV 1898)
Minute of the Board of Education . . . Establishing Higher Elementary Schools (LXIV 1900)
Report of the Inter-Departmental Committee on Physical Deterioration (XXXVI 1904)
Suggestions for the Consideration of Teachers and Others Concerned in the Work of Public Elementary Schools (LX 1905)
Code of Regulations for Public Elementary Schools (LXXXV 1906).

(b) **Newspapers (British Library, Colindale)**
Athletic News 1885–1915
Barking Advertiser 1896–1910
Birkenhead and Cheshire Advertiser 1905
Borough of West Ham Herald 1910–12, 1917
Burnley Express 1923–24
Croydon Advertiser 1930–31
East End News 1883–1905
East London Advertiser 1883–1905
Evening Telegraph and Star 1890–1894
Football Chat 1907
Football 'Sun' 1898–1904 (some issues missing)
Kent Messenger 1960
Non-League Paper 2001–4
Northampton Mercury 1925–26
Schoolmaster 1885–1890
South London Press, 1885–1919
Star 1925
Stratford Express 1866–1925
Tottenham and Edmonton Weekly Herald 1895–1921
West London Press 1909–1914.
West London Observer 1913
Western Independent 1946.

(c)   **Short histories of Schoolboy Football Associations, published by the associations for private circulation**
Edmonton and District SFA, *Jubilee Handbook 1902–1952* (1952)
Essex County SFA, *Golden Jubilee Handbook 1922–1972* (1972)
South London SFA, *The Half Century: A Souvenir* (1935)
Walthamstow Schools Cricket and FA, *Diamond Jubilee Handbook 1898–1958* (1960)
West Ham SFA, *Diamond Jubilee Handbook* (1950).

4   *Interviews and correspondence*

(a) Account of the early life of Jack Tresadern told to his daughter Poppy, written shortly before her death in 1996 and forwarded to me, with additional information, by her husband Alan Ronson.
(b) Interviews dated 25 May, 20 June 1997, 26 January, 2 May 1998, 9 March, 4 April, 22 June, 3 August 2000, with Horace Panting, who died in 2004, on the work of Bert Stock and other teachers promoting schoolboy football from before the First World War, some of whom he had known personally in the 1930s.
(c) Interviews with the late Fred Newton, 7 June, 23 August 1992, relating to his memories of early officers of the South London SFA, some of whom were still active when he began his own work for schoolboy football in 1923.
(d) Correspondence arising out of a request for information on named games' teachers from the period under review in the *Cockney Ancestor* (88, Autumn 2000), the magazine of the East of London Family History Society. The written responses included biographical information on Hackney SFA secretary J. Hollick (from Frank Graham, 8 November 2000 and Owen Watts, 2, 21 November 2000), information and photographs of W. Chapman, first secretary of Barking SFA (from his grandnephew Andrew Beeching, 12 November 2000, 23 January 2001) as well as memories of several people who had either themselves been in the classes of one of the named teachers or was a son or daughter of someone who had.
(e) Letters from Les Jolly (21 February, 23 April 1994, 9 March, 18 September 1995, 25 February, 4 July, 27 September 1998, 28 January 2000, 16 March, 16 August 2001) relating to the later careers of boys who played schoolboy football in the period under review, with particular reference to boys who played with Hackney SFA.
(f) Letters Fred Wright (3 December 1990, 19 July 1992, 17 December 1993, 3 May, 2 June 1994, 10 September 1995, 9 September 1996) with particular regard to his father's involvement in the Broad Street Clubs and to biographical information on his relative, Jack Tresadern.
(g) Accounts of football career of Charlie Warren in letters from his son Brian Warren dated 17 April, 10 May 1996, 4 May, 6 December 1999, 3 March 2000.

Secondary sources

Books

Anon. *The Lancing Register* (Cambridge: Cambridge University Press, 1933).
Anon. *Nunhead Football Club 1888 to 1938* (London: The Club, 1938).
Anon. *The Oxford House in Bethnal Green 1884–1948* (London: Oxford House, 1948).
Anon. *Centenary Record of St Mary's College* (Twickenham: The College, 1950).

Anon. *The History of Dulwich Hamlet Football Club* (London: The Club, 1968).

Anon. *'They Made the Day': A History of the First Hundred Years of the Polytechnic Sports Clubs and Societies* (London: The Polytechnic, *c.* 1976).

Adams, P.C. *From Little Acorns: A Centennial Review of the Foresters Football Club* (privately printed, 1976).

Adams, R. *Protests by Pupils: Empowerment, Schooling and the State* (Basingstoke: Falmer Press, 1991).

Adkins, T. *The History of St John's Battersea: The Story of a Notable Experiment* (London: National Society, 1906).

Alcock, C.W. *The Football Annual* (London: FA, 1879).

——. *Association Football* (London: George Bell and Sons, 1906).

Alden, M. *Child Life and Labour* (London: Headley, 1908).

Aldrich, R. *An Introduction to the History of Education* (London: Hodder and Stoughton, 1982).

Aldrich, R. and Gordon, P. *Dictionary of British Educationists* (London: Woburn Press, 1989).

Association of Football Statisticians, *Who's Who of the Football League 1888–1915* (Basildon: The Association, n.d.).

——, *Who's Who of the Football League 1919–1939* (Basildon: The Association, n.d.).

Bailey, P. *Leisure and Class in Victorian England: Rational Recreation and the Contest for Control* (London: Routledge & Kegan Paul, 1978).

Ballard, P.B. *Things I Cannot Forget* (London: University of London Press, 1937).

Barnett, Canon S.A. and Mrs S.A. *Practicable Socialism* (London: Longman, Green and Co., 1915).

Bartle, G.F. *A History of Borough Road College* (Isleworth, the College, 1976).

Barton, B. *History of the F.A. Amateur Cup* (privately printed, *c.* 1974).

Beevor, E., Evans, R.J. and Savory, T.H. *The History and Register of Aldenham School* (Aldenham: The School, 1948).

Beevor, R.J., Garrard, S.M. and Windsor, F.D. *Alumni Felstedienses* (Felsted: The School, 1948).

Betts, R. *Dr Macnamara 1861–1931* (Liverpool: Liverpool University Press, 1999).

Bingham, J.H. *Education Under the Local Authority in Sheffield: The Period of the Sheffield School Board, 1870–1903* (Sheffield: J.W. Northend, 1949).

Birchenough, C. *History of Education in England and Wales from 1800 to the Present Day* (London: University Tutorial Press, 1938).

Birley, D. *Land of Sport and Glory: Sport and British Society 1887–1910* (Manchester: Manchester University Press, 1995).

Blakeman, M. *Nunhead Football Club 1888–1949* (Harefield: Yore, 2000).

Booth, C. *Life and Labour of the People in London* (London: Hutchinson, 1968 edn; originally published in 1889).

Booth, K. *The Father of Modern Sport: The Life and Times of Charles W. Alcock* (Manchester: Parrs Wood Press, 2002).

Booth, W. *Darkest England and the Way Out* (London: Salvation Army, 1890).

Bosanquet, H. *Social Work in London 1869 to 1912: A History of the Charity Organisation Society* (London: John Murray, 1914).

Bousfield, W. (ed.) *Prize Essays in Feeding School Children* (London: Joseph Causton, 1890).

Bowen, W.E. *Edward Bowen: A Memoir* (London: Longman, Green and Co., 1902).

Briggs, A. and Macartney, A. *Toynbee Hall: The First Hundred Years* (London: Routledge & Kegan Paul, 1984).

Brown, T. *The Ultimate FA Statistics Book* (Basildon: Association of Football Statisticians, 1994).

Buchan, C. *Association Football* (London: Hutchinson, 1928).

——. *A Lifetime in Football* (London: Phoenix House, 1955).

Buckley, M.E. *The Feeding of School Children* (London: Bell and Sons, 1914).

Butler, B. *The Official History of the Football Association* (London: Queen Anne Press, 1991).

Cameron, C. *The Valiant 500: Biographies of Charlton Athletic Players, Past and Present* (privately printed, 1991).

Card, T. *Eton Renewed: A History of Eton from 1860 to the Present Day* (London: John Murray, 1994).

Carrington, C. *Rudyard Kipling: His Life and Work* (London: Macmillan, 1978 edn).

Catton, J.A.H. *Wickets and Goals: Stories of Play* (London: Chapman & Hall, 1926).

Chapman, D.I. *Dubbed Boots and Shin Pads: A History of Leyton Football Club* (privately printed, 1999).

Chapman, M. *St Mary of Eton with St Augustine, Hackney Wick: A History 1880–1980* (London: The Church, 1980).

Cheshire, S. *Chelsea FC Playetrs Who's Who* (privately printed, 1987).

Chesterton, T. *The Theory of Physical Education in Elementary Schools* (London: Gale and Polden, 1895).

Christian, G.A. *English Education From Within* (London: Wallace Gandy, 1922).

Clarebrough, D. and Kirkham, A. *A Complete Record of Sheffield United Football Club 1889–1999* (Sheffield: The Club, 1999).

Clutton-Brock, A. *Eton* (London: George Bell and Sons, 1900).

Corbett, B.O. *Annals of the Corinthian Football Club* (London: Longman, Green and Co., 1906).

Coulton, G.G. *Fourscore Years: An Autobiography* (Cambridge: Cambridge University Press, 1944).

Cox, R.W. *Theses and Dissertations on the History of Sport, Recreation and Dance* (Liverpool: University of Liverpool, 1981).

Craze, M. *A History of Felsted School 1547–1947* (Ipswich: Cowell, 1955).

Creek, F.N.S. *The History of the Corinthian Football Club* (London: Longman, Green and Co., 1933).

Daglish, N. *Education Policy-Making in England and Wales: The Crucible Years, 1895–1911* (London: Woburn Press, 1996).

Darch, O.W. and Tween, A.S. *Chigwell Registers, Together with a Historical Account of the School by the Rev Canon Swallow* (Chigwell: The School, 1907).

Davin, A. *Growing Up Poor: Home, School and Street in London 1870–1914* (London: Rivers Oram Press, 1996).

Dawes, F. *A Cry From the Streets: The Boys' Club Movement in Britain from the 1850s to the Present Day* (Hove: Wayland, 1975).

Dickinson, J. *One Hundred Years of Hillsborough: 2nd September 1899–1999* (Sheffield: Hallamshire Press, 1999).

Dimmock, J. *Association Football* (London: C. Arthur Pearson, 1927).

Douglas-Smith, A.E. *The City of London School* (Oxford: Basil Blackwell, 1965).

Dunning, E. and Sheard, K. *Barbarians and Players: A Sociological Study of the Development of Rugby Football* (Oxford: Martin Robertson, 1979).

Dunning, E., Maguire, J.A. and Pearson, R.E. (eds) *The Sports Process: A Comparative and Developmental Approach* (Leeds: Human Kinetics Publishing, Leeds, 1993).

Eager, W. McG. *Making Men: The History of Boys' Clubs and Related Movements in Great Britain* (London: University of London Press, 1953).

Eaglesham, E. *From School Board to Local Authority* (London: Routledge & Kegan Paul, 1956).

Elias, N. and Dunning, E. *Quest for Excitement: Sport and Leisure in the Civilizing Process* (Oxford: Blackwell, 1982).

Ellis, C. *The Life of Charles Burgess Fry* (London: Dent, 1984).

Ereault, E.J. *Richmond Football Club: From 1861 to 1925* (London: Howlett and Sons, 1925).

Fabian, A.H. and Green, G. (eds) *Association Football* (London: Caxton, 1961).

Farnsworth, K. *Sheffield Wednesday: A Complete Record 1867–1987* (Derby: Breedon Books, 1997).

Fishwick, N. *From Clegg to Clegg House* (Sheffield: The Sheffield and Hallamshire County FA, 1986).

Fishwick, N. *English Football and Society, 1910–1950* (Manchester: Manchester University Press, 1989).

Fletcher, S. *Women First: The Female Tradition in English Physical Education* (London: Athlone Press, 1984).

Francombe, D.C.R. and Coult, D.E. (eds) *Bancroft's School 1737–1937* (privately printed, 1937).

Fry, K. *A History of the Parishes of East and West Ham* (privately printed, 1888).

Gardiner, R.B. *The Admission Registers of St Paul's School from 1748 to 1884* (London: George Bell and Sons, 1884).

Gautry, T. *"Lux Mihi Laus": School Board Memories* (London: Link House Publications, 1937).

Gibson, A. and P1ckford, W. *Association Football and the Men Who Made It* (London: Caxton Publishing Co., 1905–06), 4 vols.

Goodall, J. *Association Football* (Edinburgh: Blackwood, 1898).

Goodwin, B. *The Spurs Alphabet: A Complete Who's Who of Tottenham Hotspur FC* (Leicester: ACL & Polar, 1992).

Gordon, P. and Lawton, D. *Curriculum Change in the Nineteenth and Twentieth Centuries* (London: Hodder and Stoughton, 1978).

Gordon, P., Aldrich, R. and Dean, D. *Education and Policy in England in the Twentieth Century* (London: Woburn Press, London, 1991).

Gorst, J.E. *Children of the Nation: How their Health and Vigour should be Improved* (London: Methuen, London, 1906).

Gosden, P.H.J.H. *The Evolution of a Profession: A Study of the Contribution of Teachers' Associations to the Development of School Teaching as a Professional Occupation* (Oxford: Basil Blackwell, 1972).

Goulstone, J. *Football's Secret History* (Upminster: 3–2 Books, 2001).

Graves, A. *To Return to All That: An Autobiography* (London: Jonathan Cape, 1930).

Grayson, E. *Corinthians and Cricketers, and Towards a New Sporting Era* (Harefield: Yore, 1996 edn; originally published in 1955).

Green, G. *The History of the Football Association* (London: Naldrett Press, 1953).

Greenland, W.E. *The History of the Amateur Football Alliance* (Harwich: Standard, 1965).

Hamilton, A.L.D. *Kynaston Studd* (London: The Polytechnic, 1953).

Hargreaves, J. *Sport, Power and Culture* (Oxford: Polity Press, 1995 edn; originally published in 1986).

Harris, J. *Arsenal's Who's Who* (London: Independent Sports Publications, n.d.).

Harrison, P. *Seventy Years of the Southern League: The First Thirty Years* (privately printed, 1989).

(Harrow School) *The Harrow Calender* (Harrow-on-the-Hill: Crowley and Clark, 1871).

Heasman, K. *Evangelicals in Action: An Appraisal of their Social Work in the Victorian Era* (London: Geoffrey Bles, 1962).

Hendrick, H. *Images of Youth: Age, Class and the Male Youth Problem 1800–1920* (Oxford: Clarendon Press, 1990).

———. *Children, Childhood and English Society 1880–1990* (Cambridge: Cambridge University Press, 1997).

Hill, F.W.N. *A History of the Manchester Schools' Football Association 1889–1989* (Manchester: The Association, 1989).

Hogg, E.M. *Quintin Hogg: A Biography* (London: Constable, 1904).

Hogg, Q. *The Story of Peter from Bethsaida to Babylon* (London: Horace Marshall, 1900).

Hogg, T. and McDonald, T. *Who's Who of West Ham United* (London: Independent Sports Publications, 1994).

Hollingshed, J. *Ragged London in 1861* (London: Dent, 1986 edn).

Holmes, E. *What is and What Might be: A Study of Education in General and Elementary Education in Particular* (London: Constable, 1911).

Holt, R., Mangan, J.A. and Lanfranchi, P. (eds) *European Heroes: Myth, Identity, Sport* (London: Frank Cass, 1996).

Honey, J.R. de S. *Tom Brown's Universe: The Development of the Victorian Public School* (London: Millington, 1977).

Hossack, J. *Head Over Heels: A Celebration of British Football* (Edinburgh: Mainstream, 1989).

Howarth, E.G. and Wilson, M. *West Ham: A Study in Social and Industrial Problems, being the Report of the Outer London Inquiry Committee* (London: Dent, 1907).

Hughes, T. *Tom Brown's Schooldays* (Oxford: Oxford University Press, 1989 edn; originally published in 1857).

Humphries, S. *Hooligans or Rebels: An Oral History of Working-Class Childhood* (Oxford: Basil Blackwell, 1981).

Hurt, J.S. *Elementary Schooling and the Working Classes* (London: Routledge & Kegan Paul, 1979).

Hutton, J. *Dedication to the Public of Hackney Marshes* (London: LCC, 1894).

Jackson, N.L. *Association Football* (London: George Newens, 1900).

———. *Sporting Days and Sporting Ways* (London: Hurst and Blackett, 1932).

Jameson, E.M., Porter, F.S., Radcliffe, A.F., Rice, C.C., Stokes, J.L. and Tod, A.H. (eds) *Charterhouse School* (Guildford: Charterhouse School, 1932).

Jarman, T.L. *Landmarks in the History of Education: English Education as part of the European Tradition* (London: Cresset Press, 1951).

Jobson, R. *Highgate Primary: The Story of a School* (London: Highgate School Association, 1977).

Joy, B. *Forward Arsenal* (London: Sportsman, 1954 edn).

Kane, J.E. (ed.) *Curriculum Development in Physical Education* (London: Crosby, Lockwood, Staples, 1976).

Kaufman, N. and Ravenhill, A. *Leyton Orient: A Complete Record 1881–1990* (Derby: Breedon, 1990).

Kekewich, G.W. *The Education Department and After* (London: Constable, 1920).

Kelly, S.F. *Back Page Football* (London: Macdonald, 1988).

Kerrigan, C. *A History of the English Schools' Football Association 1904–2004* (Stafford: The Association, 2004).

King, G.G.S. *A Popular History of Association Football* (London: Findon, 1959).

Kingsley, C. *Westward Ho!* (Oxford: Oxford University Press, 1922 edn; originally published in 1855).

Kipling, R. *Stalky & Co* in *Selected Works* (New York: Gramercy, 1982 edn; originally published in 1899).

Kirk, D. *Physical Education and Curriculum Study: A Critical Introduction* (London: Croom Helm, 1988).

——. *Defining Physical Education: The Social Construction of School Subjects in Postwar Britain* (London: Falmer Press, 1992).

——. *The Body, Schooling and Culture* (Victoria: Deakin University Press, 1993).

——. *Schooling Bodies: School Practice and Public Discourse 1880–1950* (Leicester: Leicester University Press, 1998).

Korr, C. *West Ham United: The Making of a Football Club* (London: Duckworth, 1986).

Laborde, E.D. *Harrow School Yesterday and Today* (London: Winchester Publications, 1948).

Lamming, D. *An English Football Internationalists' Who's Who* (Beverley: Hutton Press, 1990).

Lawn, M. *Servants of the State: The Contested Control of Teaching 1900–1930* (Lewes: Falmer Press, 1987).

Lawson, J. and Silver, H. *A Social History of Education in England* (London: Methuen, 1973).

Lewis, R.R. *A History of Brentwood School* (Brentwood: Brentwood School, 1981).

Leinster-Mackay, D. *The Educational World of Edward Thring: A Centenary Study* (London: Falmer Press, 1987).

Lindsay, R. *Millwall: A Complete Record 1885–1991* (Derby: Breedon, 1991).

Lowerson, J. and Myerscough, J. *Time to Spare in Victorian England* (Brighton: Harvester Press, 1977).

Macey, G. *Queen's Park Rangers: A Complete Record* (Derby: Breedon, 1993).

Mack, E.C. *Public Schools and British Public Opinion since 1800: The relationship between Contemporary Ideas and the Evolution of an English Institution* (New York: Columbia University Press, 1941).

Maclure, S. *A History of Education in London 1870–1990* (London: Allen Lane, 1990).

McDougall, D. *Fifty Years a Borough 1886–1936: The Story of West Ham* (London: Curwen Press, 1936).

McIlroy, J. *The Story of a Season: Dulwich Hamlet 1919–20* (London: The Club, n.d.).

McIntosh, P. *Physical Education in England since 1800* (London: Bell and Hyman, 1979 edn; originally published in 1952).

McIntosh, P. *Sport in Society* (London: West London Press, 1987 edn; originally published in 1963).

McIntosh, P. *Fair Play: Ethics and Sport in Education* (London: Heinemann, 1979).

McIntosh, P.C. and others *Landmarks in the History of Physical Education* (London: Routledge & Kegan Paul, 1981 edn; originally published in 1957).

Malcolmson, Robert W. *Popular Recreations in English Society 1700–1850* (Cambridge: Cambridge University Press, 1973).

Mangan, J.A. *Physical Education and Sport: Sociological and Cultural Perspectives* (Oxford: Blackwell, 1973).

——. *Athleticism in the Victorian and Edwardian Public School: The Emergence and Consolidation of an Educational Ideology* (Cambridge: Cambridge University Press, 1981).

——. *The Games Ethic and Imperialism: Aspects of the Diffusion of an Idea* (London: Harmsworth, 1986).

March, W.C. *History of the Polytechnic Football Club* (London: The Club, n.d.).

Marples, M. *A History of Football* (London: Secker and Warburg, 1954).

Marwick, A. *The Deluge: British Society and the First World War* (London: Macmillan, 1991).

Mason, T. *Association Football and English Society 1863–1915* (Brighton: Harvester Press, 1981).

Meacham, S. *Toynbee Hall and Social Reform 1880–1900: The Search for Community* (New Haven: Yale University Press, 1987).

Messiter, M. (ed.) *Repton School Register 1557–1910* (Repton: Old Reptonian Society, 1910).

Milliken, E.K. (compiler) *Brighton College Register 1847–1922* (Brighton: Brighton College, 1922).

Minchin, J.G. *Our Public Schools: Their Influence on English History* (London: Swan Sonnenschein, 1901).

Miracle, A.W. and Rees, C.R. *Lessons of the Locker Room: The Myth of School Sports* (New York: Prometheus, 1994).

Money, T. *Manly and Muscular Diversions: Public Schools and the Nineteenth Century Sporting Revival* (London: Duckworth, 1997).

Montague, C.J. *Sixty Years of Waifdom or, The Ragged School Movement in English Society* (London: Woburn Press 1969 edn; originally published in 1904).

More, C. *The Training of Teachers, 1847–1947: A History of the Church Colleges at Cheltenham* (London: Hambledon, 1992).

Murray, B. *Football: A History of the World Game* (Aldershot: Scolar Press, 1994).

Neuman, B. *The Boys' Club in Theory and Practice: A Manual of Suggestions for Workers* (London: David Nutt, 1900).

Newman, G. *The Health of the State* (London: Headley, 1907).

Newsome, D. *Godliness and Good Learning: Four Studies on a Victorian Ideal* (London: John Murray, 1961).

Northcutt, J. and Shoesmith, R. *West Ham United: A Complete Record 1900–1987* (Derby: Breedon, 1987).

Norwood, C. *The English Tradition of Education* (London: John Murray, 1929).

Ollard, R. *An English Education: A Perspective of Eton* (London: Collins, 1982).

Ollier, F. *Arsenal: A Complete Record 1886–1992* (Derby: Breedon, 1992).

Opie, I. and P. *The Lore and Language of Schoolchildren* (Oxford: Oxford University Press, Oxford, 1967 edn).

Osborne, J. (ed.) *Saltley College Centenary 1850–1950* (Birmingham: Saltley College, 1950).

Pagenstecher, Dr *The Story of West Ham Park* (London: Wilson and Whitworth, 1908).

Parker, P. *The Old Lie: The Great War and the Public School Ethos* (London: Constable, 1987).

Penn, A. *Targeting Schools: Drill, Militarism and Imperialism* (London: Woburn Press, 1999).

Peters, H.W. de B. *The London Playing Fields Society: Centenary History 1890 to 1990* (London: The Society, 1990).

Philpott, H.B. *London at School: The Story of the School Board 1870–1904* (London: T. Fisher Unwin, 1904).

Picht, W. *Toynbee Hall and the English Settlement Movement* (London: Bell and Sons, 1914).

Pilkington, E.M.S. *An Eton Playing Field: A Reminiscence of Happy Days Spent at the Eton Mission* (London: Edward Arnold, 1896).

Pimlott, J.A.R. *Toynbee Hall: Fifty Years of Social Progress* (London: Dent, 1935).

(Post Office) *Post Office Directory of Essex, Herts, Middlesex, Kent, Surrey and Sussex* (1879).

(Post Office) *Post Office London Directory* (1879).

Powell, W.R. (ed.) *West Ham 1886–1986* (London: Borough of Newham, 1986).

Purkiss, M. with Sands, Rev. N. *Crystal Palace: A Complete Record 1905–1989* (Derby: Breedon, 1989).

Quick, A. *Charterhouse: A History of the School* (London: James and James, 1990).

Reason, W. (ed.) *University and Social Settlements* (London: Methuen, 1898).

Reed, J.R. *Old School Ties: The Public Schools in British Literature* (New York: Syracuse University Press, 1964).

Reeves, J. *Recollections of a School Attendance Officer* (London: Arthur Stockwell, n.d.).

Reid, T.W. *Life of Rt. Hon. W.E. Forster* (New York: Kelly, 1888).

Rosenthal, M. *The Character Factory: Baden-Powell and the Origins of the Boy Scout Movement* (London: Collins, 1986).

Rous, S. *Football Worlds: A Lifetime in Sport* (London: Readers Union, 1979 edn; originally published in 1978).

Rubinstein, D. *School Attendance in London 1870–1904* (Hull: University of Hull Publications, 1969).

Runciman, J. *Schools and Scholars* (London: Chatto and Windus, 1887).

Russell, D. *Football and the English: A Social History of Association Football* (Preston: Carnegie Publishing, 1997).

Sands, Rev. N. *Crystal Palace F.C.: The A to Z* (London: Sporting and Leisure Press, 1990).

Seaman, L.C.B. *The Quintin School 1886–1956: A Brief History* (London: The School, 1957).

Seddon, P.J. *A Compendium of Football: A Comprehensive Guide to the Literature of Association Football* (London: British Library, 1995).

Sexby, J.J. *The Municipal Parks, Gardens, and Open Spaces of London: Their History and Associations* (London: Elliot Stock, 1905).

Sharpe, I. *40 Years in Football* (London: Sportsmans, 1954).

Shearman, M. *Athletics and Football* (London: Longman, Green and Co., 1889).

Silver, P. and H. *The Education of the Poor: The History of a National School 1824–1974* (London: Routledge & Kegan Paul, 1974).

Simon, B. *Education and the Labour Movement 1870–1920* (London: Lawrence and Wishart, 1965).

Simon, B. and Bradley, I. (eds) *The Victorian Public School: Studies in the Development of an Educational Institution* (Dublin: Gill And Macmillan, 1975).

Sims, George R. *How the Poor Live* (London: Chatto and Windus, 1883).

Smith, D.W. *Stretching their Bodies: The History of Physical Education* (Newton Abbott: David and Charles, 1974).

Smith, F. *A History of English Elementary Education 1760–1902* (London: University of London Press, 1931).

Smyth, A.W. *Physical Deterioration: Its Causes and the Cure* (London: Murray, 1904).

Soar, P. *Tottenham Hotspur: The Official Illustrated History 1882–1995* (London: Hamlyn, 1995).

Spalding, T. *The Work of the London School Board* (London: King and Son, 1900).

Sparling, R.A. *The Romance of the Wednesday 1857–1926* (Southend: Desert Island Books, 1997 edn; originally published in 1926).

Spencer, F.H. *An Inspector's Testament* (London: English University Press, 1938).

Spencer, H. *Education: Intellectual, Moral and Physical* (London: Watts, 1929 edn; originally published in 1861).

Springhall, J. *Youth, Empire and Society: British Youth Movements 1883–1940* (London: Croom Helm, 1977).

Springhall, J., Frazer, B. and Hoare, M. *Sure and Steadfast: A History of the Boys' Brigade 1883–1983* (Glasgow: Collins, 1983).

Stanley, A.P. *The Life and Correspondence of Thomas Arnold, D.D.* (London: B. Fellows, 1882 edn; originally published in 1844).

Stott, G. *A History of Chigwell School* (Ipswich: W.S. Cowell, 1960).

Sturt, M. *The Education of the People: A History of Primary Education in England and Wales in the Nineteenth Century* (London: Routledge & Kegan Paul, 1967).

Tod, A.H., *Charterhouse* (London: George Bell and Sons, 1900).

Tonkin, W.S. *All About Argyle 1903–1963: The Plymouth Argyle Diamond Jubilee Book* (Plymouth: The Club, 1963).

Tozer, M. *Physical Education at Thring's Uppingham* (Uppingham: The School, 1976).

Tropp, A. *The School Teachers: The Growth of the Teaching Profession in England and Wales from 1800 to the Present Day* (London: Heinemann, 1959 edn; originally published in 1957).

Turner, D. and White, A. *Fulham: A Complete Record 1879–1987* (Derby: Breedon, 1987).

———. *The Breedon Book of Football Managers* (Derby: Breedon, 1993).

Twydell, D. *Gone But Not Forgotten* (Harefield: Yore, 1984).

Tyler, M. *The Story of Football* (London: Cavendish, 1976).

Tyler, M. *Cup Final Extra!* (London: Hamlyn, 1981).

Vasili, P. *Colouring Over the White Line: The History of Black Footballers in Britain* (Edinburgh: Mainstream, 2000).

Vlaeminke, M. *The English Higher Grade Schools: A Lost Opportunity* (London: Woburn Press, 2000).

Wall, Sir F. *Fifty Years of Football* (London: Cassell, 1935).

Walvin, J. *The People's Game: The Social History of British Football* (Newton Abbott: Allen Lane, 1975).

———. *A Child's World: A Social History of English Childhood 1850–1914* (Harmansworth: Penguin, 1984 edn; originally published in 1982).

Waugh, A. *The Lipton Story: A Centennial Biography* (London: Lipton International, 1952).

Webb, S. *London Education* (London: Longman, Green and Co., 1904).

Weir, C. *The History of Oxford University Amateur Football Club* (Harefield: Yore, 1998).

Welldon, Rev. J.E.C. *Sermons Preached to Harrow Boys in the Years 1885 and 1886* (London: Rivington, 1887).

———. *Recollections and Reflections* (London: Cassell, 1915).

White, E. *100 Years of Brentford* (Brentford: The Club, 1991).

White, W. *History, Gazetteer and Directory of the County of Essex* (London: Simpkin, Marshall and Co., 1863).

Wigglesworth, N. *The Evolution of English Sport* (London: Frank Cass, 1996).

Wilkinson, H. *Football Education for Young Players: 'A Charter for Quality'* (London: FA, 1997).

Wilkinson, R. *The Prefects: British Leadership and the Public School Tradition* (Oxford: Oxford University Press, 1964).

Williams, A.S., Ivin, P. and Morse, C. *The Children of London: Attendance and Welfare at School 1870–1990* (London: Institute of Education, 2001).

Williams, G. *The Code War* (Harefield: Yore, 1994).

Wilson, J.M. *Siegfried Sasoon: The Making of a War Poet: A Biography 1866–1914* (London: Duckworth, 1999).

Winterbottom, W. *Soccer Coaching* (London: Naldrett Press, 1952).

Wood, E.M. *The Polytechnic and its Founder, Quintin Hogg* (London: Nisbet and Co., 1932).

——. *Robert Mitchell: A Life of Service* (London: Frederick Muller, 1934).

——. *A History of the Polytechnic* (London: Macdonald, 1965).

Wright, F. *A Book of Wrights and Buckleys* (privately printed, 1994).

Yeo, E. and S. *Popular Culture and Class Conflict 1590–1914: Explorations in the History of Labour and Leisure* (Brighton: Harvester, 1981).

Young, P.M. *The Wolves: The First Eighty Years* (London: Stanley Paul, 1959).

——. *Football in Sheffield* (London: Stanley Paul, 1962).

——. *A History of British Football* (London: Arrow, 1973).

Articles and chapters

Anon. 'A short sketch of the rise and progress of the Institutes', *Polytechnic Magazine*, 20 May 1896, pp. 247–9.

Ackland, N. 'The Amateur Football Alliance', in Fabian and Green (eds) *Association Football* (1961), 1, pp. 365–72.

Bamford, T.W. 'Thomas Arnold and the Victorian idea of a public school', in Simon and Bradley (eds) *The Victorian Public School* (1975), pp. 58–71.

Barnett, H.A. 'Recreation in town and country', in Barnett and Barnett (eds), *Practicable Socialism* (1915), pp. 89–95.

Barnett, S.A. 'University settlements', in Reason (ed.) *University Settlements* (1898), pp. 11–26.

——. 'The recreation of the people', in Barnett and Barnett (eds) *Practicable Socialism* (1915), pp. 53–69.

Bilsborough, P. 'School sport for boys in Glasgow', *Physical Education Review*, 11, 2 (1988), pp. 97–105.

Bloomfield, A. 'Muscular Christian or mystic? Charles Kingsley reappraised', *International Journal of the History of Sport*, 11, 2 (1994), pp. 172–90.

——. 'The quickening of the national spirit: Cecil Sharp and the pioneers of the folk-dance revival in English state schools (1900–26)', *History of Education*, 30, 1 (2001), pp. 59–75.

Brabazon, L. 'Health and physique in our City populations', *Nineteenth Century*, 10 (1881), pp. 80–9.

Chance, J. 'A hundred years of teacher training: Centenary celebrations at Saltley College', *Educational Review*, 2, 3 (1949–50), pp. 192–7.

Chandler, T.J.L. 'Emergent athleticism: Games in two English public schools', *International Journal of the History of Sport*, 5, 2 (1988), pp. 312–30.

Colquhound, D. and Kirk, D. 'Investigating the problematic relationship between health and Physical Education: An Australian study', *Physical Education Review*, 10, 2 (1987), pp. 100–9.

Cooper, A.B. 'Public school missions'. This was a series in *Boys' Own Annual*, 38 (1915–16) and 39 (1916–17), passim.

Dunning, E. 'The origins of modern football and the public school ethos', in Simon and Bradley (eds) *The Victorian Public School* (1975), pp. 168–76.

———. 'Something of a curate's egg: Comments on Adrian Harvey's "An epoch in the annals of modern sport"', *International Journal of the History of Sport*, 18, 4 (2001), pp. 88–94.

Dunning, E. and Curry, G. 'The curate's egg scrambled again: Comments on "The curate's egg put back together"', *International Journal of the History of Sport*, 19, 4 (2002), pp. 200–4.

Elias, N. 'The Genesis of sport as a sociological problem', in Elias and Dunning (eds) *Quest for Excitement* (1982), pp. 126–49.

Elias, N. and Dunning, E. 'The quest for excitement in leisure', in Elias and Dunning (eds) *Quest for Excitement* (1982), pp. 63–90.

Evans, T. 'The university settlements, class relations and the city', in G. Grace (ed.) *Education and the City: Theory, History and Contemporary Practice* (London: Routledge & Kegan Paul, 1984), pp. 139–58.

Evans, J. and Davies, B. 'Sociology, schooling and Physical Education', in J. Evans (ed.) *Physical Education, Sport and Schooling: Studies in the Sociology of Physical Education* (Lewes: Falmer Press, 1986), pp. 11–37.

Fletcher, S. 'The making and breaking of a female tradition: Women's physical education in England 1880–1980', *British Journal of Sports History*, 2, 1 (1980), pp. 29–39.

Fox, K.R. 'Physical Education and the development of self-esteem in children', in N. Armstrong (ed.) *New Directions in Physical Education* (Leeds: Human Kinetics Publishers, 1992), 2, pp. 33–54.

Fry, C.B. 'Association football', in A. Budd and others (eds) *Football* (London: Lawrence and Bullen, 1897), pp. 40–63.

Gearing, B. 'More than a game: The experience of being a professional footballer in Britain', *Oral History*, 25, 1 (1997), pp. 63–70.

Gordon, P. 'Commitments and developments in the elementary school curriculum', *History of Education*, 6, 1 (1977), pp. 43–52.

Gouldstone, J. 'The working-class origin of modern football', *International Journal of the History of Sport*, 17, 1 (2000), pp. 135–43.

Graves, A.P. 'Physical Education in primary schools', *Contemporary Review*, 85 (1904), pp. 888–98.

Gruneau, R. 'The critique of sport in modernity: Theorising power, culture and the politics of the body', in Dunning, Maguire and Pearson (eds) *The Sports Process* (1993), pp. 85–109.

Hardinge, H.T.W. 'How football stands to-day', *Boys' Own Annual*, 37 (1914–15), pp. 202–4.

Harnett, G.H. 'Rugby football: An asset of empire', *Boys' Own Annual*, 39 (1916–17), pp. 175–7.

Harvey, A. 'Football's missing link: The real story of the evolution of modern football', *European Sports History Review*, 1 (1999), pp. 92–116.

——. '"An epoch in the annals of national sport": Football in Sheffield and the creation of modern soccer and rugby', *International Journal of the History of Sport*, 18, 4 (2001), pp. 53–87.

——. 'The curate's egg put back together: Comments on Eric Dunning's response to "An epoch in the annals of national sport"', *International Journal of the History of Sport*, 19, 4 (2002), pp. 192–9.

Hogg, Q. 'Polytechnics', *Journal of the Society of Arts*, 45 (1897), pp. 857–63.

Horn, P. 'English elementary education and the growth of the imperial ideal: 1880–1940', in J.A. Mangan (ed.) *Benefits Bestowed: Education and British Imperialism* (Manchester: Manchester University Press, 1988), pp. 39–52.

——. 'Changing attitudes to welfare in elementary schoolchildren in the 1880s', in R. Aldrich (ed.) *In History and in Education: Essays Presented to Peter Gordon* (London: Woburn Press, 1996), pp. 36–57.

Humble, N.J. 'Leaving London: A study of two public schools and athleticism 1870–1914', *History of Education*, 17, 2 (1988), pp. 149–61.

Hunt, K.R.G. 'Some football memories', *Boys' Own Annual*, 39 (1916–17), pp. 12–13.

Hurt, J.S. 'Drill, discipline and the elementary school ethos', in P. McCann (ed.) *Popular Education and Socialization in the Nineteenth Century* (London: Methuen, 1977), pp. 167–91.

Jenson, N.F. 'George Hilsdon: The man behind a small print record' in Association of Football Statisticians, *Report*, 56 (1987), pp. 36–8.

Jolly, L. and Kerrigan, C. 'Predicting success: Hackney schoolboy teams 1919–1939' in Association of Football Statisticians, *Report*, 86 (1994), pp. 23–5.

Jones, D. 'The genealogy of the urban schoolteacher', in S.J. Ball (ed.) *Foucault and Education: Discipline and Knowledge* (London: Routledge, 1990), pp. 57–77.

Kerrigan, C. 'Gatling Gun George', *The Footballer*, 2, 6 (1990), pp. 39–41.

——. 'The Wapping wizard', *The Footballer*, 3, 5 (1992), pp. 4–6.

——. 'London schoolboys and professional football, 1899–1915', *International Journal of the History of Sport*, 11, 2 (1994), pp. 287–97.

——. 'Upton Park FC 1866–1887: Gentleman footballers in West Ham Park', *Rising East: The Journal of East London Studies*, 3, 1 (1999), pp. 48–63.

——. 'Football missionaries at Hackney Wick 1880–1913', *Hackney History*, 6 (2000), pp. 39–49.

——. '"Thoroughly good football": Teachers and the origins of elementary school football', *History of Education*, 30, 6 (2000), pp. 517–41.

——. 'Boys at play: Football in elementary schools', *Educate*, 1, 2 (2002), pp. 36–45.

Kirk, D. 'Foucault and the limits of corporeal regulation: The emergence, consolidation and decline of school inspection and physical training in Australia, 1909–30', *International Journal of the History of Sport*, 13, 2 (1996), pp. 114–31.

Lammer, M. 'The concept of play and the legacy of Ancient Greece', in G. Bonnhomme and others (eds) *La Place du jeu dans l'education: Historie et Pedagogie* (Paris: Federation Francaise d'education Physique et de Gymnastique Volontaire, 1989), pp. 75–81.

Lawn, M. 'Teachers in dispute: The Portsmouth and West Ham strikes', *History of Education*, 14, 1 (1985), pp. 35–47.

Lowe, R. 'The early twentieth century open-air movement: Origins and implications', in N. Parry and D. McNair (eds) *The Fitness of the Nation: Physical and Health Education in the Nineteenth and Twentieth Centuries* (Leicester: History of Education Society, 1983), pp. 86–99.

McCrone, K. 'Class, gender, and English women's sport, c. 1890–1914', *Journal of Sport History*, 18, 1 (1991), pp. 159–81.

McIntosh, P.C. 'The curriculum of Physical Education: An historical perspective', in Kane (ed.) *Curriculum Development* (1976), pp. 13–45.

Maguire, J. 'Images of manliness and competing ways of living in late Victorian and Edwardian Britain', in *International Journal of the History of Sport*, 3, 3 (1986), pp. 265–87.

Mangan, J.A. 'Physical Education as a ritual process', in Mangan (ed.) *Physical Education and Sport* (1973), pp. 87–102.

——. 'Imitating their betters and disassociating from their inferiors: Grammar schools and the games ethic in the late nineteenth and early twentieth centuries', in Parry and McNair (eds) *The Fitness of the Nation* (1983), pp. 1–45.

——. ' "Muscular, militaristic and manly": The British middle-class hero as messenger', *International Journal of the History of Sport*, 13, 1 (1996), pp. 28–47.

Mangan, J.A. and Hickey, C. 'English elementary education revisited and revised: Drill and athleticism in tandem', *European Sports History Review*, 1 (1999), pp. 63–91.

——. 'Athleticism in the service of the proletariat: Preparation for the English elementary school and the extension of middle-class manliness', *European Sports History Review*, 2 (2000), pp. 112–39.

Mangan, J.A. and Ndee, H.S. 'Military drill – rather more than "brief and basic": English elementary schools and English militarism', in *European Sports History Review*, 5 (2003), pp 65–96.

Nurse, B. 'Planning a London suburban estate: Dulwich 1882–1920', *London Journal* 19, 1 (1994), pp. 54–70.

Offord, H.J.W. 'Schoolboy football', in *The Book of Football* (Westcliffe-on-Sea: Desert Island Books, 1997 edn; originally published in 1905), pp. 151–2.

Onslow, G.M. 'The necessity of physical culture and recreation', in William Bousfield (ed.) *Elementary Schools: How to increase their Utility* (London: Percival and Co., 1890), pp. 49–80.

Rabble, B.A. 'The educational thought of Charles Kingsley (1819–1875)', in *Historical Studies in Education/Revue d'historie de l'education* 9, 1 (1997), pp. 46–64.

Reason, W. 'Settlements and education', in Reason (ed.) *Settlements* (1898), pp. 45–62.

Reason, W. 'Settlements and recreation', in Reason (ed.) *Settlements* (1898), pp. 71–88.

Reeder, D.A. 'Predicaments of city children: Late Victorian and Edwardian perspectives on education and urban society', in D.A. Reeder (ed.) *Urban Education in the Nineteenth Century* (New York: St Martin's Press, 1978), pp. 75–94.

Rees, C.R. 'Still building American character: Sport and the Physical Education curriculum', *Curriculum Journal*, 8, 2 (1997), pp. 199–212.

Robinson, W. 'In search of a "plain tale": Rediscovering the champions of the pupil-teacher centres 1900–1910', *History of Education*, 28, 1 (1999), pp. 53–71.

——. 'Finding our professional niche: Reinventing ourselves as twenty-first century historians of education', in D. Crook and R. Aldrich (eds) *History of Education for the Twenty-First Century* (London: Institute of Education, 2000), pp. 50–62.

Rubinstein, D. 'Socialization and the London School Board 1870–1904: Aims, methods and public opinion', in P. McCann (ed.) *Popular Education and Socialization in the Nineteenth Century* (1977), pp. 231–64.

——. 'Sport and the Sociologist 1890–1914', *British Journal of Sports History*, 1, 1 (1984), pp. 14–23.

Scott, P. 'The school and the novel: *Tom Brown's Schooldays*', in Simon and Bradley (eds) *Victorian Public School* (1975), pp. 34–57.

Siegal, H. 'Education and cultural transmission/transformation: Philosophical reflections on the historian's task', *Pedagogia Historica*, Series 2 (1996), pp. 25–46.

Springhall, J. 'Building character in the British boy: The attempt to spread Christian manliness to working-class adolescents 1880–1914', in J.A. Mangan and J. Walvin (eds) *Manliness and Morality: Middle-Class Masculinity in Britain and America 1800–1940* (Manchester: Manchester University Press, 1987), pp. 52–74.

Steele, J. 'John Charles Shaw', in Association of Sports Historians, *Newsletter*, July 1996, pp. 3–8.

Strachey, L. 'Dr Arnold', in *Eminent Victorians* (London: Chatto and Windus, 1938 edn; originally published in 1918), pp. 177–208.

Sullivan, D. 'Dick Jones, Welsh International', *Island History Newsletter*, 10, 2 (1992), p. 3.

Tawney, R.H. 'The problem with public schools', *The Political Quarterly*, 14, 2 (1943), pp. 117–49.

Tooley, S. 'The polytechnic movement: An interview with Mr Quintin Hogg', *The Young Man: A Monthly Journal and Review*, 1 (1895), pp. 146–50.

Tozer, M. 'The joy and strength of movement: A centennial appreciation of Edward Thring', *Physical Education Review*, 10, 1 (1987), pp. 58–63.

——. '"The readiest hand and the most open heart": Uppingham's first mission to the poor', *History of Education*, 18, 4 (1989), pp. 323–32.

Tranter, N. 'The first football club', *International Journal of the History of Sport*, 10, 1 (1993), pp. 104–8.

Treadwell, P. 'The games mania: The cult of athleticism in the late Victorian public school', *History of Education Bulletin*, 32 (1983), pp. 24–31.

Turner, D. 'Ripping yarns', *The Footballer*, 3, 5 (1989), pp. 4–5.

Vance, N. 'The ideal of manliness', in Simon and Bradley (eds) *Victorian Public School* (1975), pp. 115–28.

Wright, F. 'F.C. Mills and the Broad Street Clubs', *East London Record*, 13 (1990), pp. 18–22.

Dissertations and theses

Britton, J.A. 'The Origin and Subsequent Development of St Mary's College (Hammersmith) 1847–1899', MA, London, 1964.

Davin, A. 'Work and School for the Children of London's Labouring Poor in the Late Nineteenth and Early Twentieth Centuries', PhD, London, 1992.

Hargreaves, J.E.R. 'Hegemony and Social Class: An Assessment of the Significance of Sport in the Culture and Political Consciousness of the British Working Class', PhD, London, 1984.

Humble, N.J. 'Games Philosophy and the Girls' Public Schools 1870–1950', PhD, London, 1987.

May, J. 'Curriculum Development Under the School Board for London: Physical Education', PhD, Leicester, 1971.

Molyneux, D.D. 'The Development of Physical Recreation in the Birmingham District from 1871–1892', MA, Birmingham, 1957.

Moran, M.P. 'Central Schools and the Reorganisation of Elementary Education, 1902–1939, with Special Reference to the London County Council and the City of Manchester', MPhil, London, 1995.

Phillips, T.R. 'The National Union of Elementary Teachers 1870–1882', MPhil, London, 1991.

Taylor, G.D. 'A Study of the Pressures Influencing the Elementary School Curriculum 1833–1902', MPhil, London, 1973.

Weiner, D.E.B. 'The Institution of Popular Educatiom: Architectural Form and Social Policy in the School Board for London, 1870–1904', PhD, Princeton, 1984.

Waterman, M.I. 'The History of the Birmingham Athletic Club – Birmingham Athletic Institute 1866–1918', Special Study for Dip Adult Ed, Nottingham, 1969.

Williams, R.A. 'The Development of Professional Status among the Elementary School Teachers under the London School Board 1870–1904', PhD, London, 1953.

Index